Changing Conceptions in Jewish Education

IN TWO BOOKS

BY

EMANUEL GAMORAN, Ph.D.

EDUCATIONAL DIRECTOR, DEPARTMENT OF SYNAGOG AND SCHOOL EXTENSION,
CINCINNATI, FORMERLY SUPERVISOR OF EXTENSION EDUCATION FOR
CHILDREN, BUREAU OF JEWISH EDUCATION, NEW YORK CITY

New York
THE MACMILLAN COMPANY
1925

THE MACMILLAN COMPANY
NEW YORK · BOSTON · CHICAGO · DALLAS
ATLANTA · SAN FRANCISCO

MACMILLAN & CO., Limited
LONDON · BOMBAY · CALCUTTA
MELBOURNE

THE MACMILLAN CO. OF CANADA, Ltd.
TORONTO

BOOK ONE

JEWISH EDUCATION
IN RUSSIA AND POLAND

Printed in the United States of America by
J. J. LITTLE AND IVES COMPANY. NEW YORK

TO

THE MEMORY OF MY FATHER

INTRODUCTION

JEWISH education in Russia and Poland presents one of the most fascinating aspects of the history of Jewish education in general. In this volume the writer aims to give a historical, descriptive account of Jewish education in these countries based on a study of primary sources in Hebrew, Yiddish, German, Russian, and English. Besides the historical value that this study may have, a knowledge of Jewish education in Russia and Poland has significant practical implications for the adjustment of the Jew to America.

The problem of immigrant groups in America is not one of self-effacement but one of adjustment. The peoples who come to this country from all parts of the world bring with them traditions, habits, ideas, and ideals. It is a mistake to expect that the process of adjustment will be easy. The American must regard the immigrant with sympathy and must realize that many of the immigrant groups bring with them a rich past, many elements of which are worth preserving both for their intrinsic value and for their enrichment of American life.

The cultural ideal of the Jew in Eastern Europe resulted in an intensive intellectual activity, suitable to the conditions of life in Eastern Europe. It will necessarily have to undergo modification in order to be in harmony with the conditions of American life.

This study of Jewish education in Russia and Poland is the first of a series of studies on the educational adjustment of the immigrant Jew. If this volume makes clear the close relationship that existed between the Jewish curriculum and the environment of the Jew in Russia and Poland, it may perhaps prepare the way for the adjustment of this curriculum to the new conditions in America.

E. G.

ACKNOWLEDGMENTS

THESE studies on *Jewish Education in Russia and Poland* and the *Principles of the Jewish Curriculum in America* have been accepted in partial fulfillment of the requirements for the degree of Doctor of Philosophy, in the faculty of Philosophy, Columbia University. The approval of the University authorities, while indicating satisfaction as to the quality of the work, does not of necessity imply an endorsement of the point of view presented, for which the author assumes full responsibility.

My sincere thanks are due to those who helped in the preparation of this book: to my teachers at Teachers College, Columbia University, Professor William H. Kilpatrick, Professor Frederick G. Bonser, and Professor Isaac L. Kandel for their critical and friendly guidance; to Professor John Dewey for his clear and constructive criticism of the criteria of Jewish values in Chapter IV, Book Two; to my friends and associates in the field of Jewish education, Dr. Isaac B. Berkson, Mr. Israel S. Chipkin, Mr. Jacob S. Golub, Mr. Leo L. Honor, and Dr. Judah Kaufman for many suggestions and criticisms; to Dr. Samuel Margoshes for a critical reading of the text and for placing at my disposal his valuable manuscript and notes on the curriculum of the Jewish schools in Germany from the middle of the 17th to the middle of the 19th century;

to Rabbi George Zepin, Director of the Department of Synagog and School Extension, for many helpful comments; to the late Mr. A. S. Freidus, Chief of the Jewish Division of the New York Public Library, and to Mr. Israel Shapira, Cataloguer of the Library of the Jewish Theological Seminary, for valuable assistance in the preparation of the bibliography; to Miss Elsa Weihl for revision of the manuscript; and to Mr. Joseph Schonthal of Columbus, Ohio, for his generous help in the publication of the book.

I wish to acknowledge with thanks the kind permission of the following authors and publishers to quote from their books: Dr. David Philipson and Mr. P. M. Raskin; The Jewish Forum, The Jewish Publication Society, Longman's, Green and Company, The Macmillan Company, G. P. Putnam's Sons of New York and London, Teachers College, Columbia University, and The University of Chicago Press.

I am deeply grateful to Dr. Samson Benderly, Director of the Bureau of Jewish Education of New York City, who is responsible for the stimulation of scientific studies on Jewish education in America. Finally, I wish to thank my wife, Mamie G. Gamoran, for assistance in the preparation of the manuscript and for the sincerity and devotion with which she helped in its revision.

CONTENTS

PART I

HISTORICAL BACKGROUND

PART II

JEWISH EDUCATION BEFORE THE HASKALAH

PART III

JEWISH EDUCATION UNDER THE INFLUENCE OF HASKALAH AND JEWISH NATIONALISM

PART I
HISTORICAL BACKGROUND

JEWISH EDUCATION IN RUSSIA AND POLAND

CHAPTER I

THE CHANGING JEWISH CURRICULUM

THE history of Jewish education, like the history of the Jewish people, is a story of continuity through change. In its struggle for self-preservation, the Jewish people found the ability to adjust as necessary as the power to conserve. In fact adjustment was often the means by which the end, group preservation, was attained.

A brief survey of the history of Jewish education will show how the curriculum of the Jewish school changed whenever Jewry came in free contact with another culture. The lofty conception which the Jewish people had of education is reflected in the fact that as early as 64 C.E. universal elementary education was introduced. Without the actual use of compulsion the provisions made by Joshua ben Gamala made education practically compulsory for children of the ages of six or seven. The manner in which this fact is recorded in the Talmud illustrates the appreciation of the value of education. "Therefore is that man to be remembered for good, Joshua ben Gamala is his name, for if not for him Torah would have been forgotten in Israel. At first he who had a father was taught by his

1

father but he who had no father did not study the
Torah . . . till Joshua ben Gamala came and arranged
that teachers for elementary schools be on duty in
every province and in every city and that the children
enter at the age of six and seven." [1]

The fact that universal elementary education was
introduced at an early period when the power of tradition held sway would naturally lead to great constancy
in the curriculum. It should not, however, be imagined
that the curriculum of the Jewish school did not undergo any change. Far from it. Even a cursory glance
at the history of the Jewish curriculum from ancient
to modern times will reveal some significant changes.
Jewish adaptability had shown itself in its responsiveness to surrounding conditions. The curriculum of the
Jewish school, accordingly, changed not only as the
traditions of the people increased and the literature of
the people developed, but also as the people came in
contact with new environments.[2]

A.   THE CURRICULUM DURING THE NATIVE PERIOD

In early times Jewish education was given in the
home. The parents were the teachers, and they instructed the child in the duties of daily life. Customs
and ceremonies significant in the life of the tribes were
transmitted from father to son, particularly to the
oldest son who was expected to have a more intimate
knowledge of the customs and institutions of the tribe.
The social and economic environment of the group

[1] *Talmud*—Tractate Baba Batra, p. 21.
[2] Kandel, I. L., and Grossman, L., "Jewish Education," in
Cyclopedia of Education, edited by Paul Monroe.

regulated the studies and activities of the young. In the days of nomadism the needs of a shepherd people had to be considered, hence the children were prepared to be herdsmen. The frequency of war made necessary a knowledge of the use of the sling, bow, arrow, sword, shield, and spear.[1] After the conquest of Canaan, when the people became agriculturists, education had to provide the industrial training necessary to a new type of life, hence, "agriculture, cattle raising, grazing, fishing, mining, building, carpentry, woodworking, metal work, spinning, weaving, dyeing, tent making, pottery making, and tools," [2] were the important subjects of training. Athletics, sports, and dancing also found their place in the early curriculum of the Hebrews.[3]

As the years passed, teachers arose who performed the specific function of training the people for their life duties. The Prophets were the teachers of a lofty conception of God and of ideals of social justice and peace. The Priests and Levites were the teachers of the people in connection with the Temple services.[4] With the coming of the Scribes in the days of Ezra, the Law became a definite subject for study. The synagogue served as a school where the Law was read

[1] Swift, Fletcher H., *Education in Ancient Israel.*
[2] *Ibid.,* p. 23.
[3] It is interesting to note that during the native period physical education was taught, but that it was neglected after the exile. Two reasons may account for this change. On the one hand, the struggle with Hellenism led to its being associated with paganism and idolatry. On the other hand, the sacred literature was made the subject of study, and little time was left for anything else.
[4] *Ibid.,* pp. 32-34.

and interpreted by the teachers, the Scribes.[1] The
entire life of the people was steeped in a religious
atmosphere. The Temple, the ceremonial observances,
the explanations of the priests which accompanied
them, the inspired words of the Prophets were all of
educational value. During the period of the Scribes
especially, religious observances, prayers, and festival
celebrations in the home were so identified with life as
to make religion interwoven with the daily activities
of the people. Religion and ethics were inseparable
from life.

The introduction of universal education by Joshua
ben Gamala organized the education previously given
and improved upon it. The three R's, the literature of
the people, the prayers, and the actual life activities
all served to give the child a well-rounded education.[2]
In the schools of the Scribes, advanced literature,
written and oral, was taught and discussed. In this
way the education of the Jewish child was the normal
education given by a people living on its own soil and
conscious of the need of transmitting to its young all
those essentials of the race heritage which enabled them
to develop in accordance with the possibilities of the
environment in which they lived.

B. Contact with Greek Culture

The first serious adjustment that had to be made in
the Jewish curriculum resulted from contact with the
influence of Hellenism. The conquests of Alexander
the Great united the East and the West and brought

[1] Swift, Fletcher H., *Op. cit.*, pp. 80-84.
[2] *Ibid.*, p. 96.

Greek influence into Judea. The pseudo-Hellenism, which was brought into Palestine and which attracted some Jews, was resisted by the Hasidic party and was finally overcome in the Maccabean struggle. A much purer form of Greek culture and literature was brought to the Jewish community in Alexandria. In this way during the days of Philo (about 20 B.C.E. to about 50 C.E.), before the destruction of the second Temple, when Palestine was still a center of Jewry, Hellenism exerted tremendous influence upon the Jews in Alexandria. The need for a Greek translation of the Bible, which resulted in the Septuagint, is an indication that the masses spoke Greek and that Greek was taught in the schools. The Bible was read in Greek in the synagogues and to a considerable extent services were held in Greek. The Jews of Alexandria engaged in polemics with some non-Jewish literary men of the time. There was free interaction between Jews and their neighbors. Of some it was probably true that "within 100 years of their settlement (in Alexandria) Hebrew or Aramaic had become a strange language and they spoke and thought in Greek," but it is also true that Alexandrian Judaism, particularly through Philo, was working to harmonize Plato with Judaism, while Palestine was busy developing the oral Law as a basis for Jewish ritual and as a means for regulating Jewish life.

C. The Expansion of the Curriculum

Up to the destruction of the Temple, Jewish education had been a means of transmitting the social heritage of the Jewish people to the Jewish children in

Palestine. After the destruction of the Temple, Jewish education became the sole means of maintaining the unity of the people in the *Diaspora*. The seemingly modest request of R. Yohanan ben Zakkai to be permitted to establish an academy at Yabneh at the time when Rome was at the gates of Judea, maintained Jewry for thousands of years after Rome had disappeared. The academy at Yabneh was the first of many similar academies established in Palestine and in Babylonia. From time to time, assemblies known as the "Kallah" were the occasions for multitudes of students to come together to Babylonia to listen to the discussions of the Oral Law and to bring new decisions to the people at home. These gatherings were so well attended that Rabbah was accused of preventing 12,000 Jews from paying government taxes two months in the year, during which they were away from their homes listening to his learned discourses.[1] These vast meetings which supplied extension education to many were very democratic in their nature. "The Patriarch and president of the academy at Yabneh, R. Gamaliel the second, undoubtedly the most aristocratic Jew of his time, shared the dignity of his office with the poor smith, R. Joshua, who held the post of Ab Beth Din." [2] And the dictum, "Take heed of the children of the poor, for from them shall go forth the Law," is well known to the Talmud student.

With the closing of the Mishnah by R. Judah Hanasi in the second century, and the sealing of the Talmud,

[1] *Talmud*—Tractate Baba Mezia, p. 86.
[2] Ginzberg, L., *The Talmud Student,* pp. 22-23: Ab Beth Din, Vice-President.

the Oral Law, by R. Ashi in the sixth century, the Mishnah and the Gemara were added to the curriculum of the Jewish school as distinct subjects of study. The study of the Talmud involved a considerable amount of information along general lines. Agriculture, nature study, logic, astronomy, and mathematics arose out of the study of the text itself, and to these we may add the teaching of a trade and of swimming, both mentioned in the Talmud among the responsibilities of a father in teaching his children.

Although it is true that the study of the Talmud involved many fields of knowledge, such as astronomy, natural phenomena, biology, zoölogy, and medicine, the center of gravity was in the Halakah or the legal discussion. The Jewish curriculum in the Diaspora, therefore, became limited in scope. The child began the study of the Bible at the age of five, Mishnah at the age of ten, Gemara at the age of fifteen, and these three subjects constituted the bulk of the Jewish curriculum throughout the Middle Ages and up to modern times until the days of Mendelssohn.

D. The Curriculum during the Middle Ages

An idea of the general uniformity of the curriculum during the Middle Ages will enable us to appreciate the contrast presented by the Spanish-Jewish curriculum and the one that prevailed in most places in Europe. Primary instruction was generally so arranged as to give the child a knowledge of the Hebrew text of the Bible and the prayers, with the translation into the vernacular. The boy first learned Hebrew reading. Beginning with the letters of the alphabet, he pro-

ceeded to study the vowel signs, then their combination.
At first the boy merely read a portion of the week's
lesson in Hebrew; later he learned to translate it into
the vernacular. Still later he studied the Aramaic
version of the Pentateuch and translated it into the
vernacular. The Prophets and the Hagiographa then
followed. At ten the pupil began the study of Mishnah,
and at thirteen the study of the Talmud. Professional
students continued the study of the Talmud for seven
additional years.[1]

In addition to the elementary schools, the Yeshibahs,
the schools of higher learning, that were spread all
over Europe, attracted many wandering students who
were welcomed everywhere and who pursued the study
of the Talmud, with the commentary of Rashi. On
the whole they were better prepared than the university
student of the Middle Ages, who "presented his petition
to the rector (of the university of Paris) without resort-
ing to French words" [2] (using Latin only). Nevertheless "their knowledge was confined within the
boundaries of the Talmud and the literature growing
out of it." [3] A concrete idea of the curriculum during
the Middle Ages can be obtained from the following
course of study placed by Güdemann about the 13th
century: [4]

[1] For a discussion of the curriculum in the Middle Ages see
Güdemann, M., *Geschichte des Erziehungswesens und der Cultur der Juden in Frankreich und Deutschland*, v. 1, pp. 50-58;
also Abrahams, I., *Jewish Life in the Middle Ages*, pp. 350-353.

[2] Ginzberg, L., *The Rabbinical Student*, pp. 13-15.

[3] *Ibid.*, p. 35.

[4] The exact date being unknown.

"It is the duty of the father when his son reaches the age of five to bring him to a teacher who will instruct him in the Holy Scriptures. This is to be done at the beginning of the month of Nisan which time is favorable for every sort of enterprise. The father is to give the teacher a definite course of study and tell him: 'Know that you are to teach my son the alphabet during this month, the vowels during the second month and the syllables the third month.' From that time on let the clean one busy himself with the clean, that is, with the third book of Moses [1] . . . 'From month to month increase the portion of the Law you take up with my son. If during this month my son studies half a portion of the week, let him study the entire portion of the week the next month. From Tammuz to Tishri let him study the entire portion of the week, in Hebrew, and from Tishri to Nisan, in the vernacular!' The boy is then six years old. In the second year of his schooling, that is, in the child's seventh year, let him study the Targum with the text, and let him translate the Targum into the vernacular, as he does with the Hebrew text of the Bible. In the eighth and ninth years let him study the Prophets and the Hagiographa. Furthermore our sages have said, 'At the age of ten to the Mishnah.' Then introduce the boy to the Talmud, specifically to the tractates of Berakot, and the similar tractates that belong to the order of Mo'ed.[2] Three years are to be devoted to this. In the fourth year he is holy to the Law, since he is now thirteen years of age. . . . Then let the father

[1] I.e., the laws of the sacrifices.
[2] Mo'ed is one of the six parts of the Mishnah.

take his son who had been devoted to study, win him over with good words and say to him, 'Happy art thou who hast been found worthy to take part in the holy work,' and then let the father take him into the house of those devoted to study. The duty, however, of separation for study does not devolve upon the boy before he is sixteen years old. It is then that he is to be brought before the Rosh-Yeshibah who puts his hands upon his head, saying, 'This one is holy to the Lord.' He is also to say to the boy: 'I bid you eat at my table for behold I have set you aside for the study of the Law.' Thereupon, the boy is to remain there for seven years to study the great Tractates. The heads of the Yeshibah are to pursue a definite plan in their instruction. Two years are to be devoted to the order of Mo'ed; two years to Nashim; two years to Nezikin; two years to Kadashim. All this to be taken from the Talmud (not only from the Mishnah). Either the method of literal translation or that of the study of 'Tosafot' may be followed." [1]

E.   Contact with Arabic Culture in Spain and Italy

The second great adjustment which the Jewish curriculum had to undergo, after Hellenism came in conflict with Judaism, took place in Arabic Spain. Political, social, and economic conditions of Jewry were sufficiently favorable to enable the people to interact with their neighbors on a plane of equality. Contact

[1] *Huke Hatorah:* Güdemann, M., *Geschichte des Erziehungswesens und der Cultur der Juden in Frankreich und Deutschland von X bis zum XIV Jahrhundert,* pp. 92-106.

between Jewish and Arabic culture, therefore, resulted in a very broad curriculum. During the 12th century the curriculum in Spain covered a wide range of knowledge. It contained, "Bible, Hebrew poetry, Talmud, the relation of philosophy and revelation, the logic of Aristotle, the elements of Euclid, arithmetic, the mathematical works of Nicomachus, Theodosius, Menelaus, Archimedes, and others; optics, astronomy, music, mechanics, medicine, natural science and finally metaphysics. . . . In the middle of the 13th century, Jehuda ben Samuel Ibn Abbas includes in the school curriculum, reading, translation of the Pentateuch, the historical books of the Old Testament, Hebrew grammar, Talmud with Rashi and Tosafot, the study of moral works such as Ibn Aknin's 'Cure of the Soul' and Honein's 'Ethics of Philosophers,' . . . The rabbi, the financier, the man of letters, was also poet, philosopher and often physician." [1] Joseph Ibn Aknin in his "Will" lays down an elaborate series of qualifications for teachers, as well as the characteristics of a good pupil, together with a curriculum of studies. This curriculum includes reading, writing, Bible, Mishnah, Hebrew grammar, Talmud, philosophy of religion, philosophy, logic, mathematics, arithmetic, optics, astronomy, music, mechanics, nature study, medicine, and metaphysics.[2]

Italy, which was influenced by Spain, as well as by the classical Renascence, shows a similar breadth in the construction of its curriculum. The Jewish curriculum

[1] Abrahams, I., *Jewish Life in the Middle Ages,* pp. 365-367.

[2] Güdemann, M., *Das Jüddische Unterrichtswesen während der spanisch arabischen Periode,* pp. 54-116.

in Italy of the 16th century includes Bible, Talmud with commentaries, Hebrew grammar, Jewish philosophy, composition, calligraphy, Latin and Italian, philosophy, logic, medicine, mathematics, cosmography, and astrology.[1]

The culture of the Jews in Italy, and particularly in Spain, cause the attainments of the Jews in other lands during the Middle Ages to shrink into insignificance. It is important to note, therefore, that the Jewish curriculum changed not only by the addition of the Mishnah and the Gemara to the Bible in the course of study, but also by coming in contact with other cultures that were sufficiently developed to influence Jewry. The contact with Hellenism, the contact with Arabic culture, and contact with the classical literatures led to important adjustments in the curriculum.

The contact of Judaism with modern culture, particularly in a democracy where interaction between groups takes place freely, must also bring about an adjustment of the Jewish curriculum which should result not only in additions and subtractions but also in a reinterpretation of Jewish values. The rest of this study will show how the traditional curriculum was adjusted to the changed environment in the countries of Russia and Poland. The curriculum ought to undergo some more changes in order to meet the conditions of modern Jewish life in a democracy.[2]

[1] See Margoshes, S., *A History of the Curriculum of the Jewish Schools in Germany from the Middle of the 17th to the Middle of the 19th Century*, Int., pp. 11-17, MS.

[2] See Book Two: *Principles of the Jewish Curriculum in America.*

CHAPTER II

THE ENVIRONMENT OF THE JEW IN RUSSIA AND POLAND [1]

A. POLITICAL AND ECONOMIC CONDITIONS IN POLAND

A KNOWLEDGE of the political, social, and economic conditions of the environment of the Jews in Russia and Poland is necessary for a proper understanding of the Jewish educational conditions in those countries. This chapter, accordingly, treats of the environment of the Jews in Russia and Poland. The chapters following will attempt to trace the origin and development of the educational institutions [2] of the Jews in these countries

[1] It should be remembered that the history of the Jews in Russia and Poland is really the history of a people living in the same geographical area at two different periods and under two different governments; first under the Poles up to about 1795, then under the Russians from 1795 to recent times. (The historical portions of this account of the Jews in Russia and Poland are based primarily though not altogether on Dubnow, S. M., *History of the Jews in Russia and Poland,* 3 v., and Friedlaender, I., *The Jews in Russia and Poland.*)

[2] While the description of the educational institutions given in the following pages applies throughout Eastern Europe and some of the illustrations are taken from other countries than Russia and Poland, emphasis has been placed on Russia and Poland both as a means of limiting the problem as well as for the reason that 70% of the Jewish immigrants that came to the United States from 1881-1910, came from these countries.

and to see to what extent they were conditioned by the environment. What were the educational institutions that the Jews originally brought with them to Eastern Europe? What new institutions did they develop as a result of changing conditions? To what extent were these institutions primary educational forces and to what extent were they supplemented by other forces equally or more important? These and similar questions have to be answered if we are to trace the relationship between the environment and the education of the Jews in Eastern Europe.

The position of the Jews in Poland can be understood best through a knowledge of the social composition of the Polish population. Poland consisted primarily of two classes, the Polish nobility or Shlakhta and the peasants who were held in subjection by the former. Polish nobility first turned the peasants into serfs and then organized itself into Sayms [1] for the purpose of obtaining control of the state.

In the 13th century the Polish kings encouraged immigration from Germany into Poland. [2] Their own poverty and the conditions of the country demanded a middle class. The tradesmen and handicraftsmen who

Samuel Joseph, in his study of Jewish immigration to the United States between 1881-1910, points out that 1,562,800 came to the U. S. during these years. Of these 71.6% came from Russia, 17.9% came from Austria Hungary, and 4.3% came from Roumania, constituting 93.8% of the total immigration. From this it is clear that the great majority of the Jews brought with them an Eastern European curriculum from Russia and Poland into the Jewish schools of this country.

[1] Parliaments.

[2] Vishnitzer, M., *Istorya evreiskavo Naroda,* Introduction.

came in from Germany filled this need. The Magdeburg law [1] guaranteed these immigrants autonomy in the cities in which they lived, where they organized themselves into municipalities, merchant guilds, and trade unions. But while this newly-imported middle class controlled the municipalities in which they lived, the Shlakhta managed to hold the general legislative power through the Saym. In 1495 they decreed that no burgher could hold land outside the towns. This meant that burghers were excluded from noble rank and from participation in the Saym, since membership in the Saym depended on land ownership. In this way Polish nobility first set up a machinery for state control and then proceeded to exclude all other estates from participation in the government, with the result that all the privileges were enjoyed by them alone, while the burdens of the state were in large measure thrown upon the burghers.

A third factor in the complex relationship of Polish classes to one another was the Church. The Polish king was converted to Christianity in 966 and Poland became Roman Catholic. The Church in time became very powerful and could compete with burghers, kings, and Shlakhta.

To the estates already mentioned the Jews in Poland were added as a separate estate. The origin of the Jews in Poland is uncertain. It is known, however, that the early Jews in Poland were absorbed by a large migration of Jews from Western Europe, particularly

[1] A collection of laws composed in the 13th century, which provided for the administrative and judicial independence of the municipalities.

from Germany.[1] This movement started in the 12th
century as a result of the Crusades, and continued
during the 14th and 15th centuries due to the persecutions accompanying the Black Death. At the beginning
of the 16th century another huge wave of Jewish immigration poured into Poland from various European
countries, especially from Bohemia. The Thirty Years'
War then brought still more German Jews into
Poland.

The Polish kings, who were interested in the welfare
of Poland, not only welcomed these German Jews but
even invited their settlement. The Polish Shlakhta
was indolent, extravagant, and desirous of an easy life,
and a new active, enterprising middle class was needed.
The Jews brought capital with them, became the
financiers and bankers of Poland, and through their
industrial ability, energy, and thrift supplied the
virtues which the Polish nobility sadly lacked. The
kings, who were poor, received money from the Jews
who paid for the privileges which were extended to
them. The most famous document in this respect is
the charter of privileges granted by Boleslav (1264
C.E.). This charter contains economic measures as
well as measures providing for the personal and
religious safety of the Jews. Economic rights, including freedom of transit and freedom of trade, are guaranteed. The Jews living in a municipality are declared

[1] Friedlaender, I., *Op. cit.,* pp. 28-29. It should be noted that
amongst these Jews may have been some settlers from the
Khazars or from Crimea and the Orient, but that these early
settlers were absorbed by large Jewish migrations from Western
Europe. Dubnow, S. M., *Op. cit.,* v. 1, pp. 1-43.

under the patronage of the king and the jurisdiction
of his personal representatives. In this way they were
safeguarded against the attacks of the burghers, who,
engaged in similar occupations, naturally considered
the Jews their competitors. Charges of ritual murder,
which had been brought against the Jews from time to
time, were forbidden, and a specially-appointed official,
known as the Jewish Judge, was to dispose of Jewish
litigation. The decisions of this judge had to be
approved by the Jewish elders and certain cases
might even be tried by them without the Jewish
Judge.

It is important to note the attitude of each of these
estates towards the Jews. In general it may be said
that they were all hostile. The ability of the Jews
made them formidable rivals to the burghers. As
merchants, as shopkeepers, as traders in domestic and
foreign commerce, the Jews came in conflict with them.
Their opposition displayed itself at times in violence,
at other times in severe restrictions upon the rights
of the Jews. In spite of the royal protection extended
to them, the right to reside in cities was restricted by
the burghers. In this way, although there was no legal
ghetto, a ghetto existed in fact. At times commercial
disabilities were imposed upon the Jews with the permission of the kings, who were forced against their
will to give their consent. The Jews were gradually
driven from retail trade, and their wholesale trade was
also restricted. Thus, even under the protection of
royalty, the Jews were often compelled to negotiate
with the burghers directly, a proceeding which naturally resulted to their own disadvantage.

While the burghers were fighting the middle class Jews in the cities, the Shlakhta fought the rich Jews. These rich Jews acted as farmers who leased all kinds of public revenue, who opened the natural resources of the land, and who formed a sort of Jewish nobility in Poland. The Polish nobles who needed these Jewish entrepreneurs badly, resented, nevertheless, the position of control and prominence which they held. They hated them as "men of low birth, as members of a detested race, and as professors of an accursed religion." [1] When, therefore, the Polish nobility succeeded in bringing the burghers into political subjection, they were willing to satisfy the burghers by restricting the economic rights of the Jews whose profits they envied.

But worse than the hatred of the burghers or the Shlakhta was the attitude of the Church. Even in the very early days of the prosperity of the Polish Jews no provision was made for intercourse with the rest of the population and actual efforts were made by the Church to segregate them. Its hostility expressed itself in the Synod of 1542 as follows: "Whereas the Church tolerates the Jews for the sole purpose of reminding us of the torments of the Saviour, their number must not increase under any circumstances." [2] As early as 1266 the Synod at Breslau proposed the segregation of Jews in ghettos and the wearing of separate headgear to distinguish Jews from non-Jews. That the charter of Boleslav had to forbid prosecution for ritual murder is only an indication of the prevalence of this false

[1] Friedlaender, I., *Op. cit.*, p. 50.
[2] *Ibid.*, p. 38.

accusation.[1] The Church regarded Judaism as its enemy and tried to suppress it in every conceivable way. Special statutes were promulgated spreading the seeds of religious hatred. Specific commands were given to segregate the Jews so that their Christian neighbors might not be contaminated by their presence.[2] Christians were forbidden to "invite Jews to a meal, to eat or drink or make merry with them."[3] Subsequently and almost regularly the Church used its influence with both kings and nobility to undermine the safety of the Jews in the land.

Against the attitude of these hostile classes, the Jews were protected only by a kind royalty, and the charter of Boleslav is rightly described as "a sort of safe-conduct through an enemy's land."[4]

Since the condition of Jewry was so dependent upon royal authority, one can readily conceive what the decline of royal authority meant to the Jews. Even in the early days, when the kings were powerful, the special royal privileges of the Jews were suspended or periodically annulled under pressure brought to bear upon the kings either by the burghers or by the Church. In 1572 Polish nobility succeeded in introducing elective royalty, and royal authority now meant even less than before. The Church proceeded freely against the

[1] For an account of a ritual murder accusation see Maimon, S., *Autobiography,* pp. 16-17.

[2] J. M. Zunz says that in the 16th century Jewish children in Poland used to visit some Christian schools for study of secular subjects and in 1542 the Catholic fathers opposed it. See Zunz, J. M., *Ir Ha-zedek,* p. 11.

[3] Dubnow, S. M., *Op. cit.,* v. 1, p. 48.

[4] Friedlaender, I., *Op. cit.,* p. 35.

Jews.   Thirty alleged ritual murder cases took place during the 17th century alone.[1]

To the religious antagonism of the Church were added the attacks of the municipalities where the burghers ruled, and where in the end they compelled the Jews to submit to the jurisdiction of their courts. They segregated them in quarters and restricted their freedom of trade.   The Shlakhta, who assumed political control in the Saym, approved the economic restrictions of the burghers and increased the taxation of the Jews. These trade restrictions caused the Jews to enter the handicrafts where they organized themselves into separate trade unions.   They were shoemakers, tailors, furriers, goldsmiths, carpenters, stone cutters.   They became the bulk of the artisans of the land.   But even in these fields of labor, they met with opposition.

Worse, however, than the restrictions passed by the nobles was their personal attitude towards the Jews. This was one of contempt, which displayed itself in attempts to humiliate them in every conceivable way.[2]

As if the suffering of the Jews at the hands of three hostile classes were not sufficient, the persecutions of the Cossacks under their leader Khmelnitzki in 1648 were directed against the Jews.   All the exploitation of the peasants, which enriched the nobility, was laid at the door of the Jewish stewards who managed the estates of the Polish nobles.   They became the victims of mob fury.   Hundreds of thousands of Jews were

[1] Friedlaender, I., *Op. cit.,* p. 58.

[2] For a description of the attitude of Polish nobility to the Jews see Maimon, S., *Op. cit.,* pp. 8-10, and pp. 82, 88.   See also Kotik, E., *Meine Zikronot,* v. 1, pp. 1-14.

slain and hundreds of their communities demolished. Under these circumstances the position of Polish Jewry steadily grew worse. In 1775 the Jews were expelled from Warsaw; in 1790 a pogrom took place in that city. In 1795 came the third partition of Poland, and the Jews came under a new political power—the Russians.

B. THE INNER LIFE OF POLISH JEWRY

I. ORGANIZATION

The fact that in Poland all classes formed separate estates made the organization of Jewry into a separate estate a natural result of the conditions of the environment. Had it not been for the remarkable ability for organization and control which Polish Jewry displayed in the ordering of its inner life, it would not have been able to withstand the hostile economic attitude of its neighbors, or to effect the autonomous organization which regulated its life for several hundred years. Segregated by the government as a distinct estate, the Jews formed their Kahal or community organization. The kings of Poland found it to their advantage, in connection with the payment of royal taxes, to deal with an organization rather than with the masses. For these reasons the Jews in Poland were not only nationally and culturally distinct but also had their own Kahal for the regulation of all their relations, civil as well as religious. The people elected elders and were subject to their authority. The kings would at times intervene to maintain Kahal authority. The rabbis and the Kahal elders were given the right to conduct and to supervise all the religious and social life of the Jews.

Every city or town had its Kahal Board, which was elected annually. This Board collected the State taxes, took charge of the synagogues, educational establishments, and all communal institutions, "executed title deeds on real estate, regulated the instruction of the young, organized the affairs appertaining to charity and to commerce and handicrafts and with the help of the Dayanim [1] and the Rabbi settled disputes between members of the community." [2]   Kahals of small communities were subjected to the jurisdiction of Kahals of larger centers and such "Kahal Boroughs" were at times subjects of dispute between large Kahal centers. The centralization of authority was attained by means of the Wa'ad Arba Ha-Arazoth, the Council of Four Lands, made up of the rabbis and elders of Kahals of the four provinces, Great Poland, Little Poland, Red Russia, and Volhynia. [3]   This council which numbered about thirty was the representative of the Jews before the government of Poland and guarded all their interests.

The Council of Four Lands at times used economic measures to enforce obedience on the part of a disobedient community.   Thus in the 17th century, the head of the Wa'ad wrote to the Kahal of Grodna as

[1] Assistants to the Rabbi who performed similar functions in the larger communities where the Rabbi alone was too busy to take care of the community himself.

[2] See Dubnow, S. M., *Op. cit.*, v. 1, p. 107; also for methods of election.

[3] This council was probably organized in the 16th century.

follows: "If you will pay no attention to the words of the Gaonim and will not heed our decisions, know ye that of a surety we shall come forth against you armed with a copper bow (i.e. with compulsion), and we will refuse to accept your wares in Lublin . . . if you have any complaints or arguments, the fair is at hand where all the elders will gather and whoever has any difficulty may come and peace will follow." [1] The Wa'ad in this particular case sustained the community of Tekotin in its dispute with that of Grodna concerning hegemony over certain neighboring districts. Provincial assemblies for each of the four lands composing the Council were held periodically and these were intermediate between the individual Kahals and the Council. In the latter part of the 17th century the activity of the Wa'ad was particularly intensified, as great efforts had to be made to overcome the evil results of the massacres of 1648.

In 1764 the Polish Diet decided to impose a uniform tax of two gulden on every registered soul of either sex. A general registration of the Jewish population was ordered which made it unnecessary to use the Kahal as a means of collecting taxes for the Polish government. In this way the Kahal lost some of its important functions such as the organization of communities and the allotment of taxes. The government soon began to disregard the Kahal autonomy and to look upon it with suspicion, regarding it as dangerous. The same Diet

[1] *Sefer Ha-yobel Le-Kebod Nahum Sokolow.* Warsaw, 1904, p. 255. Art. on the "Council of Four Lands" by S. M. Dubnow, in *Jewish Encyclopedia.*

forbade the holding of conventions of district elders.[1]
In this way the Kahal, originally encouraged and supported by the government at a time when collection of
taxes depended upon it, was later declared to be a
source of danger to the welfare of Poland.

II. THE EFFECT OF RABBINISM

The life of the Polish Jew, regulated to a considerable
extent by Kahal autonomy, was influenced by two
ideals, the ideal of Abodah, or religious practice, and
the ideal of Torah, or learning.[2] Religious practice
meant the regulation of the whole of life by Talmudic
Law. The rigorous observance of ceremonies, though
regarded as a burden by outsiders, was a natural outgrowth of an environment in which all of life was regulated by the learned Rabbi or layman.

The love of Torah resulted in a wide dissemination
of learning amongst the Jews of Poland. The study of
Talmud especially was carried on with great intensity.
The hero in Poland was the Lamddan, the man of
learning, and to him all paid homage. Polish Jewry
during the 16th century developed a remarkable
literary activity in the field of rabbinic learning.
Rabbi Jacob Pollak (1541) established a Yeshibah in
Lublin. Simon Shalom Shakhna (1500-1558) and his
disciples, Rabbi Solomon Luria (1510-1573) and Rabbi
Moses Isserles (1520-1572), continued to carry the
torch of learning. Rabbi Isserles, not considering the
Shulhan Aruk, the code regulating the daily life of the

[1] Dubnow, S. M., *Op. cit.,* v. 1, p. 198.
[2] *Ibid.,* v. 1, chap. 4; v. 2, pp. 111-116. Also Friedlaender, I.,
Op. cit., pp. 158-161.

Jew, sufficiently inclusive, prepared his *Mappah*[1] which also incorporated some of the customs of Polish Jewry. Along similar lines many other scholars continued their literary activity during this period. Polish Talmudism became famous throughout Europe, and Jews in Western Europe, Germany, and Bohemia submitted questions of Jewish law for the decision of Polish Rabbis.

But the Massacre of 1648,[2] which destroyed hundreds of Jewish communities, also destroyed some of the centers of Jewish learning. General depression followed. Jewish autonomy broke down as a result of these disturbing conditions and also as a result of the new method of tax collecting. Talmudic learning, which hitherto had been the possession of many, became the possession of the few. The intensive activities of men like Isserles and Luria, which were closely related to the Jewish life about them, ceased. Talmudism, no longer as applicable to the environment as it had been, became here mere casuistry. Hairsplitting arguments were carried on that were of no practical application to life. Jewish mentality developed, but it was exercised in useless discussion. This resulted in an intellectualism which was snobbish as it was impractical and lacking in the warmth of religious fervor. Book lore, dry formalism in ceremonial observance, severe punishment against deviations from accepted custom, and, at times, asceticism made conditions ripe for a reaction against such a narrow and casuistic intellectualism. The attempt on the part of

[1] *Mappah*, literally "Tablecloth," the title of his book.
[2] See page 20.

Rabbi Elijah Wilna (1720-1797) to introduce the method of textual criticism into the study of the Talmud and to try to restore Jewish learning to its original vigor, could not stem the tide of a powerful new current that came into Jewish life—Hasidism.

III. HASIDISM [1] AND RABBINISM

As a reaction against the intellectual casuistry of Rabbinism, came the Hasidic movement founded by Israel Baal Shem Tob (1700). Baal Shem Tob was a man of simple faith, sincere, pious, and emotional, and therefore particularly fit to exemplify in his personal life the revolt of Hasidism. In contrast with the Gaon of Vilna, to whom is ascribed profound knowledge of the Talmud at a very tender age, the Baal Shem Tob is described as spending a good part of his early days with little children singing hymns in the woods. His very nature represented the ideal of simple piety in opposition to the ideal of Talmudic learning. Instead of an emphasis on intellectual attainments or ceremonialism and ritualistic details, he taught the importance of simple faith as a means of bringing man nearer to God. This idea was naturally very appealing to the masses, especially the less learned who felt removed from their God due to the emphasis given to Talmudic learning as a means to communion with the Divine.

[1] See Schechter, S., *Studies in Judaism*, v. 1, pp. 1-45. Hurwitz, Saul-Israel, *Me-ayin le-ayin*, essay entitled "Ha-hasidut Weha-haskalah." Dubnow, S. M., "Hasidism," in *Jewish Encyclopedia*. Dubnow, S. M., *History of the Jews in Russia and Poland*, v. 1, pp. 220-241, 377-389; v. 2, pp. 116-125.

In accordance with Baal Shem Tob, God is everywhere. This pantheism, which is an important characteristic of Hasidism, resulted in emphasis on the worth of even ordinary acts of life provided they are done in a spirit of service to God. A Jew might have communion with God in the simple activities of his daily life. Hence all the asceticism which was associated with some of the rigorists amongst the followers of Rabbinism, was violently opposed by this Hasidic leader. On the contrary, "Serve the Lord with joy," was one of the fundamental ideas of the Hasidim. In this way they brought some rays of happiness into Jewish life in the ghetto and made up in a measure for the political and economic persecution which the Jews had to suffer at the hands of hostile neighbors. The value of sincere and fervent prayer was emphasized as against the study of the Law. What counted most was the attitude of the person. The aim of Hasidism "was to change not the belief but the believer." The believer was to strive always for communion with the divine. Hence arose the "Zaddik," the pious man, who by his faith succeeded most in having communion with God. The Hasidim followed these pious men and believed in their special ability as intermediaries between the divine and the human. Although in later years this faith degenerated into a cult which endowed some unworthy people with miraculous power and proved to them a fruitful source of revenue, at the beginning this faith in the Zaddik supplied a felt need of the masses. It brought a bit of poetry and joy into their lives in the troublous days during the partitions of Poland. By bringing faith and ecstasy into Jewish life, the Hasidim succeeded in winning over nearly one half of the Jewish masses.

Into Lithuania, the stronghold of Rabbinism, Hasidism could not readily penetrate. But even there the formulation of Hasidism as a system, giving it intellectual justification, resulted in increasing the numbers of Hasidim. This was done by Rabbi Zalman of Ladi (1747-1812) who organized the Habad and in his work entitled *Tanya* pointed out the importance of the new movement and emphasized intelligent, instead of blind, faith in the Zaddik as a religious teacher. The movement was violently opposed by the Mithnaggedim [1] who continued to hold the traditions of Rabbinism. The Mithnaggedim were forbidden to intermarry or to have any intercourse with Hasidim. Especially in Lithuania, where the Gaon of Vilna was the spiritual leader of the Mithnaggedim, was the struggle intense. He thought that Hasidism with its spirit of freedom from rigorous ceremonialism resulted in moral laxity and that its "Zaddikism" fed on the superstitions of the masses. With his approval the rabbinical Kahal arrested the leaders of the Hasidim in Vilna. Rabbi Zalman, too, was arrested as a political suspect due to the intrigues of his opponents. He was, however, soon released and the number of Hasidim increased as a result of these persecutions. Hasidism reached its high water mark during the first half of the 19th century.

Both Rabbinism and Hasidism closed the doors to enlightenment which was knocking at the ghetto walls. Rabbinism resulted in too much scholasticism and

---

[1] Mithnaggedim—the opposers, so named because they were the party that opposed the Hasidim.

Hasidism depended too much upon the cultivation of the imagination for a new cultural movement to reach them. As a result those who sought to come in contact with other cultures had to leave Eastern Europe and go to Germany where under the influence of Mendelssohn the era of enlightenment had begun.[1]

Polish culture did not possess the attractive elements of Arabic culture in Spain and Italy.[2] It should also be pointed out that this fact combined with the policy of compulsory separatism made it difficult for rays of light to enter and to widen the horizon of Jewry in Eastern Europe. Nevertheless, the influence of the new enlightenment was beginning to be felt at the doors of Poland. While Rabbinism and Hasidism were struggling with each other, a new force came to threaten the underlying structure of both—Haskalah. Before this movement reached the Jews in Poland, the partition of Poland took place and the Jews came under a new régime, that of the Russians. It is, therefore, important to examine the political and economic conditions of the Jews in Russia.

C. POLITICAL AND ECONOMIC CONDITIONS OF THE JEWS UNDER THE RUSSIANS

Though the conditions of the Jews under the Poles differed in some respects from what they became under the Russians, the results were similar in matters of education. In Poland the sufferings of the Jews were the result of complex relationships of various classes of society. They were the outcome of the class struggle.

[1] See Maimon, S., Op. cit.
[2] See page 10.

In the midst of suffering, however, the Jews managed to maintain the Kahal, which was not only the product of Jewish life but also the product of the Polish environment in which all classes were divided into estates. The organization of the Kahal in its way mitigated some of the evils which Polish Jewry had to suffer at the hands of economic competitors, of a tyrannical nobility, and of a hostile, medieval church policy.

In Russia, however, the oppression of the Jews was the result, not so much of class struggle, as of the attitude of the czars.   While in Poland the kings were the protectors of the Jews, shielding them from the injustice of the masses, in Russia the czars were the sources of attack upon Jewry, very often instigating the masses to pogroms.

In contrast with Jewish autonomy in Poland, the aim of Russian officialdom from the very beginning was to destroy Jewish cultural distinctness.   Every vestige of Jewish autonomy was regarded with suspicion.   This attitude was aggravated by the fact that Russia was not ready to substitute a new culture for the old which it sought to destroy.   Jewish culture was not to be fostered, but neither were Jewish children to be admitted to the general educational institutions to attain Russian culture.   The condition of the Jews in Russia may well be summarized by the statement that, "The history of the Jews in Russia is the history of the Jews under the czars.   It is not the history of the Jews under the Russian nation or amidst the Russian nation." [1]

The idea expressed in this quotation is the key to the entire situation of the Jews in Russia and

[1] Friedlaender, I., *Op. cit.*, p. 156.

an examination of the attitude of the czars toward them reveals the condition of Jewry. The Russian government early established a hostile policy. Jews who had lived in the land for centuries were treated as aliens requiring special laws to regulate their life.

As early as 1794 the pale of settlement, one of the cruelest inventions of the Russian government, was sanctioned by law. This restriction was maintained throughout the history of the Jews in Russia up to the March Revolution. The Jews, who, because of class struggles in Poland, had been driven by the burghers from the towns into the villages, were now driven from the villages into the towns. By restrictions of residence which were increased from time to time, and by specific economic restrictions, the life of the Jews in Russia was undermined. The Jews who engaged in commerce and handicrafts were constantly persecuted by the non-Jewish middle class who controlled the giving of licenses for these pursuits. This drove them into the liquor traffic. The Russian government then accused the Jews of exploiting the poor peasants through the sale of liquor—a statement denied by the commission of 1812 which emphatically pointed out that the rural Jew was poor and barely existed from the sale of liquor.[1]

The occupations of the Jews were constantly restricted and new occupations were artificially and ineffectively promoted. The result was economic ruin. No wonder, then, that the opening of the educational institutions to the Jews at the beginning of the 19th cen-

[1] Dubnow, S. M., *Op. cit.*, v. 1, pp. 359 ff.

tury [1] did not attract large numbers, since their economic activities were suppressed, the pale of settlement was maintained, and thousands of them were driven from their homes. Over 20,000 Jews were expelled from the villages in 1823. This was the reward given by a liberal régime to the patriotism of the Jews in the War of 1812, which the czar himself publicly praised.

Under Nicholas I (1825-1855) new devices of Russian autocracy were invented. Restrictions upon the Jews were increased. An attempt at introducing secular culture was made simultaneously with the increase of Jewish disabilities. The Jews continued to be driven from the villages into the towns, and when they came to the towns their economic activities were restricted.

The climax of Jewish suffering was reached by the new device of conversion through militarism which Nicholas introduced. [2] Not satisfied with the regular term of military service which lasted twenty-five years and which began with the age of eighteen, a period of six years' preparatory training was added for Jews only. Jews were therefore subject to thirty-one years of military service. The government proceeded to tear away children of eleven and twelve from their families and to use all kinds of torture to break the bonds that tied these children to their dear ones and to their people. Each community was made responsible for a given

[1] In the days of Alexander I (1801-1825).

[2] For a description of military service under Nicholas I, see Kotik, E., Op. cit., v. 1, chap. IX. See also Steinberg, J., Bayamim Hahem.

number of recruits which the "conscription elders" were in duty bound to supply to the government under all circumstances, and when hundreds of children hid themselves in the woods and forests to escape the "Chapers," [1] the elders of the Jewish community had to pay the penalty. When caught, the children were taken by force, torn away from their mothers, and amidst wailing and lamentation driven into far-off places. Many of them died of suffering and torture and those that succeeded in completing the enormously long period of military service were rewarded at the end of it by being driven back into the pale of settlement, since, as Jews, they were not permitted to live in those very places where they had served their country.

Jewish autonomy was abolished, the only officials remaining being the "conscription elders" and the tax collectors, both of whom had to exist in order to fulfill the "good wishes" of the government. The temporary rules concerning the "assortment of the Jews" were sanctioned by the czar,[2] and in accordance with them the Jews were divided into five classes of which the "unsettled burghers" [3] were tried like criminals. This was done in spite of the fact that restrictive measures of the government excluded many Jews from the possibility of entering definite occupations.

And yet an attempt was made at enlightenment, compulsory enlightenment, aiming at the transforma-

---

[1] Catchers.

[2] In 1851.

[3] Those Jews in Russia at the time who could not be included amidst the merchants, agriculturists, artisans, and settled burghers (those engaged in petty trade).

tion of the Jewish people. Reforms were introduced
presumably intended to open up elementary and secondary schools where Jewish children might be taught
Russian, secular sciences, Hebrew, and religion. The
real aim of the government was, however, conversion.
Uvarov, who in 1840 became minister of public instruction, called upon Max Lilienthal, a German Jew who
had recently arrived in Russia, to assist in this task of
bringing enlightenment to the Jews. Lilienthal succeeded in establishing a modern Jewish school in Riga
and though little acquainted with the situation in
Russia undertook to do propaganda for the government
schools. He believed that this was a real attempt to
assist the Russian Jews, and toured the country trying
wherever he went to convince the orthodox masses
of the honest intentions of the government. He later
learned the truth, suddenly resigned, and came to the
United States.[1]

Even Alexander II (1855-1881), the liberator of the
serfs, maintained the pale of settlement. He lessened
the military evils of his predecessor, but even during
his reign the Jewish soldier could only rise to the rank
of sergeant; for any higher rank conversion was the
stepping stone. During his "liberal" reign a pogrom
took place in Odessa in 1871. Bearing in mind the
disabilities to which the Jews continued to be subjected, it was but natural that Alexander's hopes for
the assimilation of the Jews should fail.

In 1855 he decreed that only such Jewish rabbis and

---

[1] For a more detailed account of the Crown Schools and the
work of Lilienthal, see chap. 6, p. 159. See also Wegeneroff,
P., *Memoiren einer Grossmutter*, pp. 123-131.

teachers be appointed to office as had received training
in the official rabbinical seminaries.[1] In 1856 government supervision was introduced over the Hadarim
and the Melammedim. But since all these educational
efforts were made in the face of innumerable Jewish
disabilities, the response to them was not enthusiastic.
During the highest period of reform only merchants
of the first guild, mechanics affiliated with guilds, and
university graduates were permitted to enter Russian
territory. The greatest part of Russian territory was
closed to the great majority of the Jews, a fact which
left them in a state of economic misery. Nevertheless,
the freedom that had been granted to certain classes
of Jews to enter the Russian interior filled the people
with hope. Many Jewish students rushed to the gymnasia which were thrown open to them and some
attended the government schools.

As the years passed, however, the conditions of the
Jews in Russia grew worse. Alexander III (1881-1894)
was responsible for the triumph of autocracy. Statutes
were enacted sending to Siberia people whose crime was
no greater than that they were politically suspected.[2]
A series of pogroms followed, beginning with the 80's,
in which mob violence was permitted to reign without
government interference. There are incontrovertible
proofs [3] that the Russian authorities were at times
responsible not only for failure to suppress riots, but

[1] See chap. 7, p. 176.

[2] For a description of conditions of the Jews in Russia at the
beginning of the 80's see Katzovich, I., *Sechzig Jahr Leben*,
pp. 205-206, 209-210.

[3] See *Die Judenpogrome in Russland.*

for actually inciting them. The government aggravated the situation by adding new repressive measures. Military service was made more difficult for the Jews than for the rest of the population in spite of the fact that Jewish soldiers were limited to the rank of privates. Even the reactionary Pahlen Commission [1] stated in its memoirs that "no less than 650 restrictive laws directed against the Jews may be enumerated in the Russian code, and the discriminations and disabilities implied in these laws are such that they have naturally resulted in making until now the life of an enormous majority of the Jews in Russia exceedingly onerous. . . . *The repressive policy taken by itself, has been and will always be the first and main source of the clannishness of the Jews and their aloofness from Russian life.* . . . The very history of Russian legislation . . . teaches us that there is only one way and one solution—to emancipate and unite the Jews with the rest of the population under the protection of the same laws. . . . The system of repressive and discriminating measures must give way to a graduated system of emancipatory and equalizing laws." [2] This advice, coming from a source which should have commended itself to the attention of the Russian government, was secretly disposed of at some conference and Russian autocracy continued along its well-beaten path. In 1891 the Jews were expelled from Moscow [3]

[1] See Dubnow, S. M., *Op. cit.*, v. 2, pp. 336-337.

[2] Quoted from General Memoir of Phalen Commission in Dubnow, S. M., *Op. cit.*, v. 2, pp. 363-369.

[3] For a description of an "Oblava" (night raid) see Kotik, E., *Op. cit.*, v. 2, p. 229.

with the result that people who had lived there since the early days of the reforms of Alexander II were driven from their homes.

The assimilationist Russian Jewish intelligenzia, who during the days of the reforms began to hope for emancipation and to believe that they could live side by side and in peace with the Russian population and be assimilated by them, could not but look with disillusionment at the tragic state of Russian Jewry. The indifference of such men as Tolstoi and Turgenev in the face of injustice and cruel oppression intensified their sufferings and led many to give up their former ideas and to turn their eyes to the East. More and more they came to realize that the only solution to the problem lay in the return of the Jews to Palestine and in the establishment of a Jewish national home.

This feeling grew more determined as the conditions of Russian Jewry grew worse during the reign of Nicholas II. Revolutionary activity in Russia, which was the natural reaction to unparalleled autocracy, was laid at the door of the Jewish people. The pogroms in the early 20th century followed. The Massacre of Kishinev, the Massacre of Homel, and a whole series of pogroms [1] throughout the south were perpetrated upon the Jews. The inactivity of the government was marked. When the Kishinev Massacre came before the bar of Russian justice, Karabchevski, a Christian lawyer who withdrew from the court proceedings because Russian justice refused to investigate the case too deeply, declared that,"The whole of Kishinev was

[1] Kotik, E., *Op. cit.,* v. 2. pp, 311-327.

converted during the excesses into an immense circus
of antiquity, where, before the eyes of curious spec-
tators from among the administration and the army,
before a festively attired crowd, a terrible drama
was enacted in the depths of the arena. From the
one side defenseless victims were driven upon the
arena, and from the other maddened beasts were
set at them, until the signal to stop was given,
and the frightful spectacle was ended at once." [1]
Seeing that the government failed to protect their
lives, the Jews began to organize self-defense organizations, thus taking into their own hands a function which really should have been fulfilled by the
government. [2]

The Russo-Japanese War followed close upon these
pogroms and the Jews were forced to enter the service
to make "Manchuria part of Siberia in which they
were forbidden to reside." [3] The Revolution of 1905
was followed by massacres, the organized work of coun-
ter-revolutionaries. The first and second Duma, the
Russian parliaments, that were then instituted and
whose power was limited, were dissolved without helping Jewry in its struggle against autocracy. The third
"Black Duma," [4] reactionary and anti-Semitic, was
assisted in its restrictions by the government. The

[1] Dubnow, S. M., *Op. cit.,* v. 3, p. 91.

[2] The writer has the personal recollection of the organization
of such a self-defense group which patrolled the streets of the
Russian city of Beltz, Bessarabia, during the days following the
Massacre of Kishinev.

[3] Dubnow, S. M., *Op. cit.,* v. 3, p. 94.

[4] Convened in November, 1907.

story of the latest ritual murder trial, the Beilis case [1]
(1911), is too recent to be unknown to the reader.

Russian Jewry reacted to all this oppression by an
intensification of its own activity. The Jewish nationalist movement that expressed itself throughout the
world, and especially the first Zionist Congress in 1897,
stirred the masses in Russia. They became convinced
that the only solution to their problem lay in the
establishment of a Jewish home. And yet amidst all
their suffering, there were still some Jews who hoped
that the internal problem of Russian Jewry would be
solved by emancipation. The coming of the March
Revolution, followed by the Bolshevik Revolution, of
course changed completely the problem of the Jews
in Russia.

Very important in considering the limitations under
which Russian Jewry lived, are the educational restrictions that have been imposed upon them in the last
thirty years.[2] In 1887 a percentage norm was introduced, limiting the admission of Jews to secondary and
higher educational institutions to 10% of the Christian
school population in the pale of settlement, to 5%
outside of the pale, and to 3% in the cities of St.
Petersburg (Petrograd) and Moscow. Later these restrictions were made worse and only 7% were admitted
to the educational institutions in the pale of settlement,
only 3% outside the pale, and only 2% in the capitals.
Many Jewish students, unable to enter the gymnasia
and the universities, therefore resorted to study at

[1] See *American Jewish Year Book,* 1914-15, on "Beilis Affair,"
pp. 19-89.

[2] Wegeneroff, P., *Op. cit.,* v. 2, pp. 186-187.

home and came up at the end of each year to take the examinations. In 1911 the percentage norm was extended to these externs as well. Jews were excluded from bar associations, and Jewish physicians were restricted to private practice. But the acme of stupidity of Russian autocracy may be found in the law of 1893 which, though it legalized the Jewish Heder and stopped the persecutions which this school had suffered at the hands of the police, "narrowed at the same time its function to that of an exclusively religious institution. . . . There are cases on record in which the keepers of these Heders, the so-called Melemmedim, were put on trial for imparting to their pupils a knowledge of Russian and arithmetic." [1] No better proof is needed that the thought of linking up the Jewry of Russia with the general population had not seriously entered the mind of the Russian czars. The efforts of young Jews to attain general culture and to interact with the general life, were stifled by severe educational restrictions which drove them to the universities of central Europe for education, as thousands of other Jews were driven to the shores of America in search of liberty.

D. The Inner Life of Russian Jewry

I.   The Haskalah Movement [2]

While Rabbinism and Hasidism were struggling against each other for control, a new current was gradu-

[1] Dubnow, S. M., *Op. cit.*, v. 2, p. 427.
[2] Raisin, J. S., *The Haskalah Movement in Russia;* Hurwitz, Saul Israel, *Op. cit.*, essay entitled "Ha-hasidut Weha-haskalah"; Dubnow, S. M., *Op. cit.*, v. 1, pp. 379-389; v. 2, pp. 125-138.

ally coming into Jewish life in Russia [1] which threatened both—the Haskalah. The Haskalah movement, or the movement for enlightenment, began in Germany under the influence of Mendelssohn. It spread rapidly to other parts of Europe and was followed by a gradual process of emancipation of Jewry from legal disabilities. The movement aimed at transmitting to the Jews the general knowledge, habits, and attitudes of the peoples whose neighbors they were. In Germany it resulted in the secularization of Jewish life, and later in assimilation.

In spite of all Jewish disabilities in Russia the new light coming from the West began to penetrate. "Enlightenment" attacked the fanaticism of the masses. It was opposed both to the rigorous ceremonialism of the Rabbinists and the superstitious faith which at times influenced the Hasidim. It brought rationalism into Jewish life in Russia and with it skepticism of tradition and a protest against the narrow limitations of ghetto life. It called for a widening of the horizon of Jewish life. It not only brought in a spirit critical of the old accepted values, but distinctly aimed at the creation of a new life, wider and more human.

Since there were no schools the Maskil, as the follower of this movement was called, was usually self-educated. Persecuted by a community loyal to tradition, he had to acquire a knowledge of science or foreign languages and literature in the secrecy of cellars or garrets or in the darkness of night. The Maskil sought to acquire secular knowledge since it was regarded as

[1] See pp. 148 ff.

the avenue for enlightenment, and therefore he was ready to undergo great hardships to attain his end. The example of other countries where Haskalah had resulted in emancipation deluded him, and he naïvely believed that once the Jews in Russia were possessed of secular knowledge, emancipation would follow.

To the old orthodox Jew this new movement seemed to be fraught with great danger. The rationalism of the Maskilim tended to undermine the simple belief in the traditional faith. Whether those who destroyed the old would find a new faith was to be seen in the future. Haskalah, which was helped by a tyrannical Russian government, was opposed by the masses, both because they saw in the government efforts another attempt at conversion and because they were afraid of undermining Jewish life. The struggle between the old generation and the young continued, especially as the young gained confidence as a result of the liberal measures introduced during the reign of Alexander II. This struggle was at times so bitter that it rent asunder many a Jewish family. The young felt oppressed by the life that surrounded them. They sought new life and were anxious for a brighter future. Themselves keenly conscious of exile, they went in search of freedom and light. Children left their parents, and husbands their wives, because they longed to enter a new world, to escape the narrowness of ghetto life.[1]

These children of transition did not always succeed in adjusting themselves to the new life. As an illustration, though from an earlier period, we may take Solomon Maimon who in his thirst for science left

[1] See Smolenskin, Perez, *Gemul Yesharim.*

Poland for Germany. The contrast between the new life and the old restrictive life, which he had been compelled to lead, was too great and led to disastrous results. His existence became a burden to him, and although he was a man of rare abilities he was compelled to live a life of dependence, filled with a spirit of restlessness, resulting at times in misanthropy.

Many who had lost the old faith did not succeed in finding a new one. This was the tragedy of thousands in Russia. Had these sincere attempts on the part of the Russian youth to come in closer contact with the general population been appreciated by the government, had they been treated as natives instead of as aliens, Haskalah in Russia might have reached the masses and might have effected a significant change in the Jewish educational institutions in Russia. Since the same government that sponsored new educational tendencies also encouraged political and economic disabilities, failure to win the masses was inevitable. The continued restrictions heaped upon the Jew in Russia led all those who had hoped to unite Jewry with the Russian people to despair of accomplishing their purpose and to turn their faces eastward.

II.   THE JEWISH NATIONALIST MOVEMENT [1]

The dangerous tendencies of some Maskilim, combined with the increased oppression on the part of the Russian government, resulted in a new movement of

[1] Sokolow, N., *History of the Zionist Movement.* Gottheil, Richard, *Zionism.* Dubnow, S. M., *Op. cit.,* v. 2, pp. 233-242, 324, 332; v. 3, chap. 30.

which the first literary exponent was Perez Smolenskin (1842-1885). He saw the evils of a self-effacing assimilation threatening to destroy Russian Jewry, as well as the ignorance and fanaticism of the opponents of Haskalah. In an attempt to save the youth who were passing through a period of transition he set himself the task of fighting both the assimilationist tendency of some of the Maskilim and the fanaticism of some of their opponents. He felt that the Jewish people must reconstruct its life from within. The attainment of new knowledge must go hand in hand with the maintenance of national self-respect. Smolenskin may be considered the first great Hebrew writer to preach nationalism to the Russian Jews.

The pogroms in the 80's combined with new economic restrictions to disillusion the assimilationist Jewish intelligenzia. The graduates of the gymnasia could now see how utterly impossible it was to solve the Jewish problem in the face of a hostile Russian government. Those who had not joined the gymnasia but had received the traditional Jewish training in the Heder and the Yeshibah were through the medium of Neo-Hebraic literature made conscious of the world without and realized the need for a new approach to the Jewish problem. Both of these groups were now at peace with each other. They saw that the only hope for their people lay in a national revival.

A period of intensive nationalist activity began. The "Hobebe Zion" [1] was organized. Some students in Kharkov under the leadership of Israel Belkind

[1] Lovers of Zion.

organized as the "Bilu." [1] Colonization in Palestine
began. Leon Pinsker, a prominent Russian Jew, called
upon his brothers to emancipate themselves. In contrast with the idea of civic emancipation through the
help of the Russian government he called for "auto-
emancipation," through the establishment of the Jewish people in some territory where they could live a
national life. Theodore Herzl, influenced by the anti-
semitism of Western Europe, convened the first International Zionist Congress in 1897 and became the
founder of Political Zionism.[2]

All these activities were of great importance to Russian Jewry, not merely for the intrinsic value of the
ends they sought to attain but for their immediate
effect upon the Jews. They helped a downtrodden,
persecuted people to maintain its self-respect under
most unfavorable circumstances. They stimulated
cultural activity centering around the revival of
Hebrew as a national language. They inspired the
people with new hopes and gave them courage to
struggle on against the oppression and persecution of
the Russian government.

E. The "Jewish" Environment in Eastern Europe

Jewish education in Russia and Poland would not
be properly understood if we left out of account the
influence of an intensely Jewish environment. Very
often what is considered a product of the Heder and

[1] Bilu—the Hebrew initials of "O, House of Jacob, come and
let us go!" See Belkind, Israel, *Die Erste Schritt vun Yishub
Eretz Yisrael*, v. 2.

[2] See Sokolow, N., *Op. cit.*, v. 1, chap. 48.

the Yeshibah may be more truly considered a product
of general Jewish life in Eastern Europe itself. The
daily life to which the child was subject—the home,
the synagogue, the ideals of the community—tended
to produce an intense Jewish consciousness within the
child.

The education of the child began at an early age
with the instruction given to him at home, usually by
his father, in the Hebrew alphabet. He was taught to
recite the special blessings in the morning and in the
evening before going to bed. Grace before and after
meals was the custom of the home. Parent and child
prayed three times a day. The older children joined
their parents in going to the synagogue. In many
homes the child saw his grandfather and his father rise
before dawn, and, seating themselves on the ground,
read the special midnight prayers (Tikkun Hazoth).

The entire atmosphere of the home was Jewish. The
library of Hebrew books with its very beautiful and
prominent Shas,[1] was a Jewish influence. Jewish pictures—Jacob and his sons, Moses on the mountain,
Maimonides, the Gaon of Vilna, Moses Montefiore, as
well as the Menorah and the Mizrah—were to be found
on the walls of every Jewish home, and the young boy
was accustomed to see these, to ask questions, and to
receive answers concerning them.

The celebration of Jewish holidays in the home and
in the synagogue were festivities in which the child
participated prominently. The elaborate preparations
for Passover, the beautiful ceremonial connected with
the Passover Seder, helping to illuminate the syna-

[1] A summary name for the Talmud.

gogue on Lag Be-omar,[1] made a strong appeal to the children. The tasks of decorating the house green on Shabuot, and of assisting in building and decorating the Sukkah were the delights of the child. Receiving Hanukkah Gelt and playing Hanukkah games, feeding little birds on the Sabbath when the song of Moses was read in the synagogue, eating Palestinian fruits on Hamishah Asar BeShebat, as well as receiving and distributing gifts on Purim, were all events to which the child looked forward with joy. In every home the mother baked Hallah in preparation for the Sabbath and cooked special Sabbath dishes. She lit the Sabbath candles and the entire family left for the synagogue. All of these experiences were of educative value to the child.

The particular way in which Friday evening and the Sabbath were spent in the Jewish community in Russia was a tremendous influence, leaving a deep impression in the mind of the child. The father came home from synagogue, and reciting, "Shalom Aleichem," "Peace to you, O Sabbath Angels," brought beauty and poetry into the home. The selection, "A woman of valor, who can find," was recited in honor of the mother. The chanting of Kiddush over the cup of wine, the meal especially prepared with its Sabbath dishes, the beautiful Zemirot or special chants which the entire family sang, all turned the Sabbath day into one of joy and gladness. The "Orehim," the wandering poor who were usually invited to partake of the Sabbath meals, added to this Sabbath joy by the "stories" they told of "what was going on in the world." These

[1] As was the custom in Bessarabia.

stories, too, were as a rule of Jewish interest. There was no talking of business on the Sabbath; the spirit of Sabbath rest was in the air and all felt it.[1]

Following an afternoon nap at home, the men went to the synagogue, and groups were to be seen in all its corners. Some were studying Talmud, others Mishnah, others the Ethics of the Fathers, and still others were reading the Psalms. Thus the Sabbath was not only a day of rest but also a day of spiritual activity. Hasidic life especially made the Sabbath not an austere day, but one of great joy. Such an expression as the "dear Sabbath" is an interesting reflection on the attitude to the Sabbath and a commentary on its "austerity." After supper on Friday evening, people would gather at the house of a Hasid and would sing and dance till midnight. In the late Sabbath afternoon, too, they would join in the Shalosh Se-udot in the Schtibel (the small synagogue of the Hasidim). At night at the close of the Sabbath the villagers would gather in various homes, and if a special cantor were in the synagogue that Sabbath he would be a guest of honor who would entertain and be entertained by the entire community.[2] Interesting features of these Saturday evening gatherings were the playing of a violin, as well as the singing of Hasidic melodies, both helping to develop a love for music.

Participation by the children in the life of the syna-

[1] For a description of Jewish life on the Sabbath, see Wengeroff, P., *Op. cit.*, v. 1, pp. 169-179. Also Asch., Shalom, *A Städtel*, chap. 7.

[2] Kotik, E., *Op. cit.*, v. 1, pp. 47, 48, 129. Also Katzovich, I., *Op. cit.*, p. 100.

gogue was another factor exceedingly powerful in bringing Jewish influence into their life. Carrying the Lulab and the Etrog to the synagogue on Sukkot, carrying flags on Simhath Torah, participating in the ceremony of Hosha'not, sitting up during the night of Shabuot together with the elders to read the Torah, shouting and using his Grager on Purim at the mention of Haman's name, and joining the elders in greeting with prayer and song the appearance of a new moon, all tended to make the child a participant rather than an onlooker in Jewish life.

The children also participated in all kinds of festivities that took place in the community. The community was closely knit, and it was the custom to pay many visits on holidays (Yom Tob visits). The children usually accompanied the parents and thus associated pleasant events with the Jewish holidays. There were many other joyous occasions. When a boy was born a special ceremony took place in the home of the parents. The children of the Heder and Talmud Torah were invited to recite special prayers (Keriat Shema le-enen) and as a reward they were all treated with cakes and candy. On the occasion of a Bar Mizvah, too, the children were invited to rejoice in the initiation of a new member into the Jewish community. A Jewish wedding was the occasion for inviting the poor children of the Talmud Torah to a special dinner arranged for them. Other events in the community in which the child participated were the presentation of a new "Scroll of the Law" for the synagogue, an occasion on which almost the whole village would turn

out, or the celebration of the completion of the Talmud
by some group of men in the synagogue.

From time to time, the Zaddik, the special preacher,
and the cantor would visit the community. At every
coming of such a dignitary special announcements
would be made by the beadle and the entire community
would gather to welcome them. When a committee of
the important members of the community went to the
outskirts of the city to meet a Zaddik, who was to pay
them a visit, all turned out to see the reception. The
young thus not only joined in this community gathering but were also impressed with the respect paid to
the learned and the pious. After the visitor left, "how
he sang," or the important argumentative features of
"his sermon" would be the subject of discussion by the
community for the entire week. The child heard all
of these discussions and at times participated in them.
But above all, the influence of the synagogue as a Beth
Hamidrash, or house of study, cannot be overestimated.
The following is a description given by Lilienthal of
the Bet Hamidrash that he saw:

"There I found the old, really old Jew with his
ineffable respect for the Torah, with his unfathomable
love for its study, entirely absorbed in the mazes of
the Talmudical labyrinth, entirely forgetting the world
around him. In these Bathe Midrashim every morning
after the service, several Shiurs by competent Lamddanim are read. The first Shiur is that of the Yoreh
Deah; it is attended by bankers, merchants, and scholars par excellence; then comes the Shiur of the Talmud
which is mostly visited by the Lamddanim who, diving
into the depth of the witty pilpul, spend the whole

forenoon at their large Talmudical volumes; and in the evening, after prayer, the Shiur is read on the Midrashim which, being attractive and easy and instructive at once, is visited by all the poor who, being engaged the whole day in their different business occupations, hurry in the evening into the Beth Hamidrash to listen to these instructive lectures. Here they find the inward satisfaction that having studied the Law they have fulfilled their religious duty; here they find comfort and consolation, for the Law teaches them the vanity of all earthly treasures and the rich pleasures in store for them in the future life; here they forget the sorrowful exclusion from the enjoyment of all rights and privileges, for the Law teaches them that the Jew is a member of the Chosen People, that before God exists no privilege, no favor, no exclusion." [1]

Jewish learning was closely related to Jewish life. The respect in which learning was held in Russia and Poland is evidenced by the fact that hospitality to the learned was assumed by all. At times one family would feed as many as six boys of the Talmud Torah daily; at times preachers, teachers, cantors, and rabbis were invited as guests and treated with great respect; even the very poorest people had one Talmud Torah boy at their table.[2]

Charity, or still better, the Hebrew Zedakah was a communal duty as well as an individual act of righteousness. There were all types of charity, helping the sick, redeeming the captive, clothing the poor, and

[1] Lilienthal, M., "Travels in Russia," in *Max Lilienthal*, by D. Philipson.

[2] Kotik, E., *Op. cit.*, v. 1, p. 43.

even aiding a poor maiden to matrimony. Just as Jewish hospitality and charity were considered not individual virtues, but practically community responsibilities, so honesty was regarded not a question of one's individual relation to others but one's duty to the community. Thus there was a custom that before a man left one village to move into another, he announced in the synagogue his intention to leave and requested anybody who had any claims, monetary or otherwise, against him, to state them.[1] As a rule, no one had any claims, but the announcement was made just the same.

An interesting illustration of the close relationship between the religious life and the general life of the people is to be seen in the following quotation taken from a description of Jewish life in the town of Kamenetz, Podolsk: "On the Sabbath, all the Jews, even the poorest, ate fish. . . . Fish were gotten from the local river. Seven and one-half kopeks a pound was considered a high price to pay, and if at times the price went up to twenty groschen (half kopeks) there was consternation and noise in the village against the great robbers, the fish vendors, who sell out the fish to Brisk (a neighboring town) and thereby deprive the villagers from eating fish on the Sabbath (which was considered a serious matter) ; they were threatened with corporal punishment and told that they would never be called up to the reading of the Torah in the synagogue, if they continued to export the fish from Kamenetz and in that way raise the prices." [2] The ability to prevent what was considered an unfair inflation of prices by preventing

[1] Kotik, E., *Op. cit.*, v. 2, p. 167.
[2] *Ibid.*, v. 1, pp. 72-74.

a person from being called up to the Torah is an illustration of how religion and life were interwoven. Similarly, the custom of "Ikub Ha-keriah," preventing the reading of the law in the synagogue, was resorted to as a means of redressing wrongs. When a person was wronged and did not succeed in having the wrong righted, he could thus appeal to the community. Public opinion would compel the wrongdoer to fulfill his duty. To prevent the reading of the Torah was not considered wrong. It is another concrete instance of the relationship between religion and life.

The entire life was one in which religion and learning were the important factors. The prayers and the blessings in daily life were closely related to those studied in the Heder. The study of Humosh, Talmud, Aggadah was almost a necessity in an environment of learning. Conversation would at times not have been understood if one did not know these subjects; one would have had to refrain from participating in community life without them. The coming of a new rabbi to the town meant the holding of a discussion which was really a sort of examination and in which the Lamddanim (the learned) participated. Even a child of twelve would, when free from Heder, at the end of the day, go to the synagogue to study and talk to the older Bahurim, and this conversation was often of educational value. Each synagogue usually had its groups of story-tellers who would, between the late afternoon and evening prayers, develop the imagination of the child by telling interesting stories.

Love of learning and its practice were a part of life from birth to death. The very cradle songs expressed the hope that the child would grow up to be a student of the Torah.[1] To have in one's family a Rabbi, a Dayan, or a Shohet, was considered an honor, both because of their learning and because they were "Kle Kodesh," [2] doing service for the community.

The Bar Mizvah ceremony, when the child became thirteen years old, was not only an occasion of joy and merriment but also one for learning. The special address delivered by the one who was initiated into the Jewish community was often one which showed signs of real study. The day of the Huppah (the wedding) was another serious occasion, emphasizing the religious attitude of the Jew in Russia and Poland. The following quotation is descriptive of the attitude of a young man on the day of the Huppah: "The following day, the day of the Huppah, which is considered for the bride and bridegroom a day of judgment, even greater than the Day of Atonement, I fasted, prayed much and wept. I felt the great responsibility that I was taking upon myself and I prayed to God that he grant us long life, health, sustenance and good, pious children." [3] The prayer is quite characteristic of Jewish life in Russia and Poland, as were the addresses, "Derashot," delivered by the bridegroom on this occasion, which were considered quite as important as the giving of gifts to the young couple immediately following, which was called, "Derashah Geshank."

That the environmental influence was a powerful factor in the education of the child can be seen also

[1] Wengeroff, P., *Op. cit.,* v. 1, pp. 26-28.
[2] Literally, "holy vessels," i.e., people engaged in holy work.
[3] Katzovich, I., *Op. cit.,* p. 59.

from the fact that in the country Jewish education was not nearly as successful as in the city. While in part this may have been due to the lack of actual school facilities or their inadequacy, there is no doubt that the strange, non-Jewish environment in the country was an important factor in making it more difficult to give the child a Jewish education in those parts of Russia and Poland. In the small towns and in the cities where the Jews were congregated in great numbers, the formal education in the Heder, Talmud Torah, and Yeshibah was closely related to a thorough Jewish life and was supplemented by a more powerful, informal, unconscious education.

PART II
JEWISH EDUCATION BEFORE THE HASKALAH

CHAPTER III

ELEMENTARY EDUCATION—THE HEDER

A. The Aim of Jewish Education in Russia and Poland

The aim of Jewish education in Russia and Poland was an outgrowth of the isolated position of the Jew in those countries. Separated from the rest of the population and living in a distinctively Jewish environment, the Jew had to prepare his child to live in that environment. It would have been futile to prepare the child to live in a world, which by political, economic, and social restrictions was closed to him.

The Heder, Talmud Torah, and Yeshibah, therefore, aimed to prepare the child for the social and religious life of the Jew in Russia and Poland. Since this life was regulated by Talmudic law, which was the possession of the learned, a knowledge of the Mishnah and Gemara, which constitute the Talmud, was very important. Love of learning, as an ideal, was intensified by the high regard which the Jewish people always had for Torah and for those who possessed it.[1] The Jew hoped that his son would grow up to be a "Lamddan," a scholar, or at least, "ein edeler

[1] See Book Two: *Principles of the Jewish Curriculum in America,* chap. 5.

Yid." [1]   This was impossible without Torah.   It was
Torah that refined a person, and not to possess it placed
a stigma upon the individual.   Hence the aim of the
Jewish schools was to open to the child those sources of
Jewish literature which were needed in order that he
might not be an Am Ha-arez,[1] and which were at the
same time the means of regulating Jewish life in the
ghetto.

B. Education in the Days of Jewish Autonomy

While the curriculum of the Jewish educational institutions in Russia and Poland will be found on the
whole to have shown great constancy, the same influences that changed the environment of the Jews in
those countries also affected their educational institutions and their curricula.   The educational history of
the Jews in Russia and Poland may be divided into
two parts, the dividing point being the year 1844 when,
by a special decree of the czar, new elementary schools
for Jewish children were established.   At about the
same time, Haskalah was becoming an important factor
in the life of Russian Jewry.   The scheme of Jewish
education before 1844 was on the whole uniform and
was affected by two fundamental facts: first, the condition of the Jews under the Poles; second, the condition
of the Jews under the Russians.

[1] The phrase "ein edeler Yid" might perhaps be rendered in
English, as "a well-bred man."   But in English this suggests too
great an emphasis on mere manners.   In Yiddish this phrase
implies both good manners, refinement, Torah, and general intelligence, as the phrases, "a grober Jung," and "Am Ha-arez,"
(an ignoramus), imply the lack of these.   All of these phrases
are really untranslatable.

It will be remembered that in the days of Poland's Golden Age, the Jewish people had an autonomous organization, the Kahal, which regulated all their affairs. This organization regulated education as well. When Russia became mistress of millions of Jews, Jewish autonomy practically disappeared. This change did not, however, greatly affect the Jewish educational institutions, since the separation, almost amounting to a cleavage, between the Jews and the rest of the population continued as in the days of Polish autonomy, except that conditions were worse. The common factor in both these periods is the separation of the peoples living in the countries of Poland, and subsequently Russia, from each other and the maintenance of a separate, distinct scheme of education with a curriculum iron-bound in its constancy.

When, however, under the influences coming from German Haskalah under the leadership of Mendelssohn, a new spirit began to penetrate Russian Jewry, and when, in addition, the government of Russia became interested in the secularization of Jewish learning, the curriculum of the Jewish schools underwent considerable change. The extent to which this change took place depended greatly upon the genuineness of the government's attitude and upon the extent to which it was a movement forced from without rather than a development out of the life of the people itself.[1]

Ancient Poland offered an opportunity to the Jewish people to become the much needed middle class of the country. This was in contrast with the status of the Jews in some other countries in Europe where they

[1] See chap. 7, pp. 178 ff.

had been confined to petty trading and money lending. The presence of many people who came into the country and formed a separate estate naturally resulted in an autonomous organization. The general organization of Polish society into which the Jews came allowed for relatively little interaction between various elements of the population. The ghetto, too, made interaction between Jews and the rest of the population very difficult. Bearing these facts in mind and also the fact that the cultural state of the Poles at this time was considerably lower than that of the Jews, it was but to be expected that the Jews should devote themselves to the pursuit of their studies and to the development of an educational system of their own.

At the same time the Jewish educational institutions in Poland did not spring up *de novo*. They were brought over from the other countries from which the Jews came. Thus, it is a well-known fact that Jewish educational conditions in Russia, Poland, Galicia, as well as in Germany, were practically the same before the modern period, since the Jews in Poland came in great numbers from Germany and Bohemia.[1]

[1] Professor Friedlaender, in his book on the Jews in Russia and Poland, points out that a huge wave of immigration poured into Poland at the beginning of the 16th century from various European countries, especially from Bohemia, that the Thirty Years' War drove some more German Jews into Poland, and that it may be said, "that Polish Jewry of the 16th century is the parent of present Jewry of Russia and Poland." (Friedlaender, I., *The Jews in Russia and Poland*, pp. 28-29.)

Wessely says, "But we have been accustomed to bring up our children under the care of Polish teachers." (Letter I, p. 25.)

From Germany the Jews brought their language, which developed into Yiddish, as well as their culture and communal organizations.[1] With these came the educational institutions, the Heder, the Talmud Torah, the Yeshibah, and their respective curricula.

Education, in the days of Polish autonomy, was compulsory for children from six to thirteen years of age, and under the supervision of the public authorities. The Kahal prescribed the curriculum of the Heder, at times in great detail, even mentioning the commentaries to be used in the teaching of the Bible. Jewish autonomy also regulated the kind of teachers, decided upon the relationship between teachers, and provided for special free education to orphans and for vocational education to those children who became of age and did not show abilities which entitled them to pursue further studies in the Talmud and the Codes. The Kahal determined the hours of instruction, appointed its special society known as the Hebrah Tal-

This statement shows again the close relationship between Polish and German educational conditions.

See also Güdemann, M., *Quellenschriften,* p. 19 of the Introduction.

[1] Dubnow, S. M., *Op. cit.,* v. 1, p. 43. Dubnow points out that the original wave of Jewish immigration into Poland probably came from the Lower Danube; that this was followed by a larger movement from Germany at the end of the 12th century, as a result of the Crusades, and at the end of the 14th and 15th centuries, as a result of the persecutions following the Black Death. This wave was followed by others in the 15th and 16th centuries. (Dubnow, S. M., *History of the Jews in Russia and Poland,* v. 1, p. 41.)

mud Torah, supervised the work of the Yeshibah, and selected the Rosh Ha-Yeshibah.[1]

In 1639 we find a provision in the record book of the Council representing the chief communities in Lithuania in which the rabbis are enjoined to examine the young men in the community to see whether they are continuing their studies.[2] The students are advised that even after they start to study Mishnah and Talmud, they should not cease from the study of the Bible until they know it thoroughly.[3] The teachers are also warned against proceeding to teach Mishnah before the children know the Bible.

In Homsk, "all the heads of the community are in duty bound to support no less than eighteen young men among whom there are to be a number of married men in accord with the desire of the rabbi, and boys, too, who should be taught. At least one half of these must be of the unmarried poor. The community shall support them, and the support given to the married shall be double that given to the unmarried." [4] In other statutes, provisions are made for community buying of textbooks,[5] and their distribution among poor students; if the community is too poor, it is enjoined at least to maintain one Bet Hamidrash.[6]

Perhaps the control of education and educational

[1] The head of a Talmudical Academy.
[2] "Records of the Wa'ad of Lithuania," in *Evreiskaya Starina*, 1909-1915, Article 352.
[3] *Ibid.*, 1910, Art. 353.
[4] *Ibid.*, 1912, Art. 588.
[5] *Ibid.*, 1912, Art. 589.
[6] *Ibid.*, 1912, Art. 590.

institutions by the Kahals of Poland may be best illustrated by a quotation from the original sources for the period of early Jewish history in Poland. One of the most informative documents of this kind is the Constitution of the Hebrah Talmud Torah (Society for Education) of the Jewish community of Cracow (1551-1639).

FROM THE MINUTES OF THE SOCIETY FOR "TALMUD TORAH" (EDUCATION) IN CRACOW (1551-1639)

After we, the undersigned, had been chosen by the illustrious leaders of the community of Cracow (May the Lord guard it) to supervise and improve the Holy Society of the Talmud Torah and to restore it as in the days of old, we began to search amidst the ancient writings and records and this is what we found in the record book of the year 311. (1551).

The Laws of the Holy Society of the Talmud Torah

1. This society is founded for the purpose of supervising instruction, both of the teachers of small children and of Talmud students, to see that they do not lag in their work; and to arrange that every week some one of the Society shall examine the pupils to see whether they are being properly taught, each pupil according to his capacity.

2. A teacher is forbidden to teach the Pentateuch with any commentary other than that of "Bar Mosheh" which is written in the spoken language, in order that the boy may know the commentary well; and for the student whose understanding permits, the teacher should use no other commentary than that of Rashi which is most suitable both for its simplicity and its truth.

3. It is forbidden to any teacher of small children to have more than forty in his Heder; and he shall keep two

assistants for them in order that they may be able to study with the children, one of whom shall be a young assistant to bring them to school. It is also forbidden for a Talmud teacher to have more than twenty-five pupils and he is to have two assistants who may study with the pupils and bring them to Hebrew School.

4. It is forbidden for any teacher to take pupils away in the middle of the term from another teacher doing similar work; also at the end of the term the teacher should not go to any householder (parent) to try to induce him to take his son away from the teacher he is studying with in order to bring him to his school; if, however, the parent himself comes and enrolls his son to study with him, the teacher may take him into his school. The members of the Society "Talmud Torah," shall take charge of all the above matters.

5. The Society shall engage an able teacher, a God-fearing man, to teach the children of the poor and the orphans, brought to the boys' school especially established for this purpose; the society shall also engage assistants according to the number of pupils that come.

6. The teacher and assistants shall teach the children brought to the boys' school the alphabet with the vowels, the Prayer Book and the Pentateuch with the commentaries of Bar Mosheh and Rashi, the order of prayers in their due time, manners, proper conduct, each pupil according to his understanding and degree of development; they shall also teach them the letters of the vernacular in which books are written that they may be able to read them and know morals, manners and right behavior. They shall also teach them writing in the vernacular. They shall also teach the best of the pupils the paradigms of verbs in order that they may understand the nature of the whole language, past, present, future, singular and plural,

second person, third person, regular verbs, irregular verbs
and so on, all conjugations and forms. They shall also
teach them arithmetic, addition, subtraction, multiplica-
tion and division. If one of the pupils is especially bright
and capable of undertaking the study of Halakah [1] he
shall be taught the Talmud with the commentary of Rashi
and the Tosafot.

7. If any pupil be approaching his 13th year, he shall be
taught the laws of Tefillin.

8. If a boy is 14 and is not yet ready to study the Talmud, he shall be apprenticed to an artisan or become a
servant to some householder.[2]

This document has been quoted at length because
it is one of the most important documents that have
come down to us and it throws considerable light on
Jewish education in Poland during the sixteenth century. It shows very clearly how the Heder, though a
private institution, was supervised by the community.
The community prescribed the curriculum in great
detail, limited the number of pupils per teacher, saw
to it that all children received instruction,[3] and supervised the relations between teacher and teacher.

There seems to have been an arrangement in those
days whereby the rabbi in each community was the
recipient of community funds, part of which he spent
for the support of poor students. In special provisions,
the rabbis are warned, on the one hand, not to decrease

[1] The legal portions of the Talmud. Here used to mean the
whole of the Talmud.

[2] From Güdemann, M., *Quellenschriften,* pp. 232-246.

[3] See "Records of Community of Cracow," 1604, 1606, 1615, in
Jahrbuch der Jüdisch-Literarischen Gesellschaft, v. 10.

the number of young men under their supervision, in
order to increase the amount left for their own maintenance, and, on the other hand, the local communities
are warned against curtailing the privilege of the
rabbi to increase the number of pupils if he wishes to.
Where there is an agreement with the rabbi concerning the number of students to be maintained, the agreement is subject to modification upon the consent of the
rabbi and the elders of the community. In any case,
the heads of the community are warned to do nothing
in this connection without the knowledge and the desire
of the rabbi, nor the rabbi without the sanction of
the heads of the community.[1] The foresight of the
Jewish autonomous organization in Poland may be
gauged also from the following two provisions: "A
teacher may not be accepted into any community or
country place in Lithuania unless he brings with him
a permit from the rabbi of his own city stating that
he is coming with the permission of his wife. If he
does not present such a certificate he may be permitted one half year in which to obtain it, but if he
does not succeed within that time he is to be expelled
and every possible means may be used to compel him
to leave his position in order to return to his wife." [2]
That a provision of this kind was necessary indicates
the frequency with which teachers in Poland had to
leave their home town in order to make a living.
Similar evidences of the unusual care given by the
elders of the Kahal to the instruction of the young may

[1] "Records of the Wa'ad of Lithuania," in *Op. cit.*, 1909, Art.
141.

[2] *Ibid.*, 1910, Article 260.

be seen from the provision they made that when Poland was affected with an epidemic, boys should be sent to country places for instruction. Even the absence of a Rosh Yeshibah in such a place should not deprive the children of instruction, if some learned layman could be found to teach them.[1]

The effect of Polish Jewish autonomy on education will be appreciated by any impartial student of the subject. Polish Jewry was highly intellectual as a result of its system of education, which was supervised by the community. As late as 1790, the great Polish masses were in ignorance,[2] while the Jewish masses in Poland had compulsory education throughout the days of Jewish autonomy. The educational requirements of the Jewish school were very high, particularly if we compare them with the requirements of the people in whose midst they lived. People studied in Poland not to be rabbis but for the intrinsic worth of study itself; besides, lay scholars were of considerable authority, able at times to check up decisions of law rendered by the rabbis. The ideal of the Polish mother was that her son should be a man of learning, or, if God help, a great rabbi. Literary activity was widespread. The direction in which this activity took place was, however, limited, due to the restrictions of the environment.

Even the awarding of degrees in Poland in the days of Jewish autonomy is characteristic of the attitude of Polish Jewry to learning. The degree of Haber

[1] "Records of the Wa'ad of Lithuania," in *Op. cit.*, 1909, Art. 46.

[2] See "Poland," in *Cyclopedia of Education*, edited by Paul Monroe.

(scholar) may be awarded if a man pursues at least two years of study after marriage.[1] A man well known in the community, whose conduct is worthy, may be ordained with this title by the head of the Yeshibah upon the approval of two additional Roshe Yeshibah. On the other hand, the highest degree, Morenu (our teacher), described as being equivalent to a Ph. D. degree in modern times,[2] was conferred only upon those who were at least thirty years of age, who devoted themselves primarily to study, and who had pursued studies for at least eleven years after marriage.[3] These requirements are sufficient to point out the great love for learning which prevailed. Great respect and consideration were shown to the learned. The heads of the community are enjoined to lighten the taxes of those who devote themselves to study and especially of those who maintain academies in which the young are instructed.[4]

Summarizing, therefore, we may say that the early curriculum in Poland was a result of Polish Jewish autonomy. The Kahal actually passed, as in the provisions of Cracow, upon the number of pupils in the school, upon the curricula, the schedule, and other particulars concerning instruction. The main subjects were the traditional subjects of Bible, Mishnah, and Talmud, with some of their commentaries. The ref-

[1] "Records of the Wa'ad of Lithuania," in *Op. cit.*, 1912, Art. 593.

[2] Friedlaender, Israel, *Op. cit.*, p. 180.

[3] "Records of the Wa'ad of Lithuania," in *Op. cit.*, 1912, Art. 592.

[4] *Ibid.*, 1912, Art. 607.

erence in the statutes of the Cracow Talmud Torah to the teaching of the vernacular refers not to Polish but to Yiddish. That Yiddish was the spoken language is proof of the fact that the Jews had spoken the language of the land in Germany. That the same was not the case in Poland is due to the peculiar organization of Polish society.

As the Jewish autonomous organization gradually became weaker and later altogether disappeared, the Heder became more and more private, not only in that it was organized by individuals, but in that the supervision of the community constantly decreased and finally ceased altogether. This lack of supervision undoubtedly resulted in the deterioration of the Heder. The care with which the teaching of manners, morals, and right behavior, the teaching of grammar and of the four fundamental operations of arithmetic, are mentioned in the statutes of the Cracow Talmud Torah, and the provision made for vocational education for those who are unfit to pursue Talmudical studies, will serve as an interesting contrast to the educational conditions in Russia and Poland after the decline of Polish Jewish autonomy.

The changed environment, the decline of Polish Jewish autonomy, affected the educational institutions of the Jews to a great extent. The best illustration in Russia and Poland, however, of the influence of the environment on educational institutions and their curricula, will be found if we contrast Jewish education and its institutions—the Heder, the Yeshibah, and the Talmud Torah—before and after the Haskalah. The following part of this study will therefore show:

1. What the Heder, the Talmud Torah, and the Yeshibah were, in the days before the Haskalah.

2. How these institutions changed after the rise of the Haskalah, and the extent to which these changes affected the Jewish population in Eastern Europe.

C. THE HEDER

I. INTRODUCTORY

Jewish life made necessary the evolution of an educational system so simple that it could be easily duplicated in the many new environments to which a checkered history brought it. The Heder attempted to provide this system. It was a private institution giving elementary education to Jewish children and could be established by any individual who was sufficiently versed in the Law to open a school and who received a rabbinical permit.

Though private, the Heder was in a certain sense a public institution. The private interest of the "Melammed," or teacher, made it necessary for him to take great care in the instruction given to his children, lest his number of pupils decrease during the coming semester. On the other hand, the interest of the public created a favorable attitude to those who did their work faithfully, and an unfavorable one to those who failed in their duties. The dictum, "Cursed be he who does the work of the Lord falsely," was applied to a teacher who did not faithfully perform his duties.

II. THE FIRST DAY IN HEDER [1]

Perhaps the description of the first day in Heder as given in some of the autobiographies of the Hebrew writers of Eastern Europe will serve to introduce the reader more intimately to this institution.

Lilienblum describes his first day in Heder as follows: "On the 15th day of Shebat in the year 608 (1848), my father took me in his arms and hurried me to my grandfather, who was a Melammed for little children, and there in the Heder he began to teach me 'Alef Beth,' using a big paper chart attached to a board. It was understood that the angel who throws coins of silver and copper to the little children at Heder would not forget me either." [2] Entering the child into the Heder was an occasion of festivity, as was also his promotion from a lower Heder to a higher Heder, at which time special parties were arranged. The rich people made such parties very elaborate so that the child was impressed by the fact that an additional step had been taken in his Jewish education.[3]

Another description of a first day in Heder is interesting, because of the special attitude which it reflects. It is the description given by M. A. Günzburg in his autobiography, *Abiezer:*

"Wrapt up in my mother's arms I came to the Heder for the first time. The Melammed ingratiated himself with me and assured me that I would learn the whole

[1] Wegeneroff, P., *Memoiren einer Grossmutter,* v. 1, pp. 127-128.

[2] Lilienblum, M. L., *Hatot Neurim.*

[3] See pp. 80 ff.

Torah almost while standing on one foot if only I would keep my eyes on the book and pay attention to the alphabet chart which he had in front of him.

"There my eyes were opened and I saw a new heaven and a new earth. The Melammed told me at length inane stories about the angel who bores holes in walls and throws coins to the children who know their lesson, and stories of a similar nature that either tend to disgust or appear as a joke to a child who was brought up by an intelligent father, whose understanding is sufficiently developed to have a high conception of the angels of God, and who would never dream of troubling them for the sake of silver and copper coins which have their root below in the earth."

The unfavorable attitude of the writer to the institution he describes is very evident, but it should be remembered that the literature on the Heder of Eastern Europe was usually written by people who were interested in changing the Heder and therefore constantly emphasized its unfavorable aspects. This writer's supersensitiveness to the Melammed's kind assurances that he would learn if he would but make the effort, and his attitude to the pretty little legend which Jewish children are told, that the angel rewards with sweets and coins those who study diligently, are merely an expression of dissatisfaction on his part with some of the unfavorable aspects of the educational system and with some of the superstitions of the day which he justifiably condemns. However, it is clear that entering the child into the Heder was a great event. At least it appeared great to the family and was fully impressed as such upon the tender mind of the child.

III.   THE PHYSICAL ASPECTS OF THE HEDER

What were the physical accommodations and the general appearance of this institution to which the child was introduced at the early age of three or four?

Solomon Maimon in his autobiography gives the following description of the Heder which he attended: "The school is commonly a small, smoky hut and the children are scattered, some on benches, some on the bare earth. The master in a dirty blouse, sitting on the table, holds between his knees a bowl in which he grinds tobacco into snuff, with a huge pestle like the club of Hercules, while at the same time he wields his authority. The assistants give lessons, each in his own corner, and rule those under their charge quite as despotically as the master himself. Of the breakfast, lunch and other food sent to the school for the children, these gentlemen keep the largest share for themselves. Sometimes the poor youngsters get nothing at all; and yet they dare not make any complaint on the subject, if they will not expose themselves to the vengeance of these tyrants. Here the children are imprisoned from morning to night, and have not an hour to themselves, except on Friday and a half holiday at the new moon." [1]

In another somewhat exaggerated description of the Heder rendered in verse,[2] the one room school of the Melammed is depicted. The entire family lives in that room, and all the household tasks are performed there. Uncleanliness is an accompanying feature. The pupils

[1] Maimon, S., *Autobiography,* pp. 34-35.
[2] Adler, M., *Goral Ha-melammedim,* pp. 3-18.

are described as poor, sickly, and unclean. A general
lack of order in the physical appearance of the room
encourages a similar carelessness on the part of the
pupils. Broken windows, broken furniture, torn books,
darkness in general, a poor equipment that could inspire but little respect in the mind of the pupil, seem
to be characteristic.

Although there is no doubt that the physical conditions of the Heder were by no means favorable, the
descriptions given in both the sources referred to are
undoubtedly exaggerated. In both cases the aim was
distinctly to draw an unfavorable picture of the old
Heder. Solomon Maimon, who was a product of the
old Heder and found difficulty in adjusting himself to
the new life and education in Germany, could not but
deprecate the kind of training that he had received
in his early days. It is true, however, that most writers
on Eastern European Hadarim, present an unfavorable
description of their physical appearance.[1]

A slightly less unfavorable description of the Heder,
though not as typical, is given by Lilienthal. In describing the Heder in Vilna (1840) Lilienthal says:
"These were long, spacious rooms on the first floor
whose ceilings were not very high, whose walls were
more black than white; long tables were standing along
the walls surrounded by very common benches upon
which sat the poor children, sometimes numbering one
hundred and more. The number of teachers, with
hungry emaciated faces, amounted to four or five. All
were teaching at once, so that the noise and confusion
made by the teachers and pupils were insufferable. At

[1] See for example Linetski, I. J., *Das polische Jüngel*, p. 9.

a table in the midst of the room sat the principal, and the rod—the supreme ruler of this little empire—was lying by his side. The air we inhaled when entering the room was damp, warm, and unhealthy, and I pitied the little creatures who were forced to pass the gay and joyful days of childhood in such an abode."

Lest the reader get the impression that these physical conditions were restricted to the Heder alone, it might be well to quote the following description given of the Dame Schools in England during the nineteenth century:

"The Dame Schools are apt to be close, crowded and dirty. 'The usual scene of these schools,' says Mr. Winder, in reference to Rochdale, 'is a cottage kitchen, in which the mistress divides her time between her pupils and her domestic duties. The children sit round the room, often so thickly stowed as to occupy every available corner, and spend the greater part of their time in knitting and sewing. At intervals the mistress calls them up, one or two at a time, and teaches the alphabet and easy words, the highest proficiency attained being the power of reading a little in the New Testament.' " [1]

The truth of the matter is that although the physical features of the Heder were bad, they were by no means as bad as a resident in this country would imagine. The difference between the homes of the children and the Heder was not great, although the latter may have been somewhat inferior to the home due to the presence of many people in one room. In mild weather, too,

[1] See Monroe, Paul, "Dame Schools," in his *Cyclopedia of Education*.

only those children remained within who were under the immediate care of the teacher at the time. The rest were out in the yard, playing freely in the open air, under the supervision of the assistant.

IV.   THE CURRICULUM IN THE HEDER [1]

a.   *The Elementary Heder*

There were three types of Hadarim in Russia and Poland. The first was the Heder Dardaki or the school for the youngest children. To this school children came at the age of three or four. The parents were usually very busy (the father engaged in study and the mother in earning a living), and some of the burden of caring for the children was taken over by the Heder. Sometimes this Heder was known as the Heder Irbubyah, the mixed Heder, so called because it contained both boys and girls.[2] Both of these were for the very young and were organized as follows: One group consisted of the very beginners who studied the letters of the Hebrew alphabet. The second group consisted of those who had already learned the alphabet and who studied syllable formation. The third and highest group was comprised of those who were able to read more rapidly, and were ready to begin the study of the Pentateuch. As soon as the child was able to put the letters together into words, the prayer book was used as the textbook, in order that he might

[1] See Lifshitz, A., "Ha-heder," in *Ha-tekufah,* v. 7; also Ginzberg, Louis, *The Primary School.*

[2] The elementary Heder was as a rule the only one that also admitted girls.

be "religiously active." This enabled the child at an early age to participate in synagogue life, which was one of the characteristic features of the ghetto environment.

The teacher who took charge of this Heder usually had two "Behelfers." [1] These assistants helped in the instruction and performed certain services incidental to the Heder, such as bringing the youngest children to school, carrying their lunch, taking them home, playing games with them, etc. Before the child learned how to read he was under the care of the assistant during the greater part of the day, only coming to the teacher's table for a few minutes of reading (letters, vowels, and syllables) three times daily. But as soon as he learned how to read he was seated at the long table of the Melammed the greater part of the day. A great deal of time was spent in learning to read mechanically and rapidly. In that respect the Heder was successful. Translation of the prayer book was not deemed necessary, since it was assumed that the child would understand the meaning of the prayers after he had studied the Bible and the Talmud. Although it is true that many children knew enough Hebrew to understand many of the prayers, there were some, nevertheless, who, not having attained much knowledge of the Bible and Talmud, forever remained ignorant of the prayers. The blessings for food as well as special blessings for certain occasions, such as for thunder, lightning, etc., were taught, and these blessings were actually used in daily life. As soon as the children learned how to read rapidly, they engaged in daily prayers which were

[1] Assistants.

recited in the Hadarim. In some cases the study of the Humosh was also started in this elementary Heder. This was usually done towards the end of the child's stay in this school. Although there was no fixed period for the course in the elementary Heder, it usually took between two and three years for the children to reach the stage where they could enter the next highest school, the Humosh Heder. The method of instruction was poor,[1] and it was therefore difficult for the child to learn. It necessitated a long time to learn to read. Yet the stay of the child in Heder was pleasant. The younger assistant, who was always with the children, played games with them and in general made their life at Heder interesting.

b. *The Humosh Heder*

The second type of Heder is the Humosh Heder. To this school the child came after he had completed the course in the more elementary Heder; in other words, after he had learned how to read fluently.

On entrance to this Heder a party was arranged, presents were given to the child, the parents were invited, and an interesting ceremony took place. One child was appointed "Makshon," [2] and the hero of the day, standing on the table, answered his questions which were somewhat as follows:

"What is your name, child?"

"I am no longer a child, but a young man who has begun the study of Humosh in a propitious hour."

"What is Humosh?"

[1] See chap. 4, pp. 93-94.
[2] Questioner.

"Humosh is five."

"What five? Five cakes for a cent?"

"No, the five books of the Torah that God gave to Moses."

"And what book will you study?"

"I will study Leviticus which deals with sacrifices."

"Why do you want to study about sacrifices?"

"Because sacrifices are clean and I am a clean Jewish child. Let therefore the clean come and busy themselves with the clean."

"And why is the 'Alef' in the word 'Wayikra' small?" [1]

"Because I am a small boy and I will study the Torah. Alef means 'to study' and the Torah can't exist except for him who is humble in the study of it and not falsely proud."

"If so why are you proud?"

"God forbid, I am not."

"Then why do you stand upon the table?"

"I will take your advice and get down." [2]

This ceremony was followed by great merriment. The giving of presents and all kinds of dainties to the child and the "Mazzol Tob" greetings helped to make this day as impressive as possible, so that the child remembered it for a long time.

The subjects of study in this Heder were Humosh and the Commentary of Rashi. At times other parts of the Bible were taught and distinct chants were

---

[1] The Alef, the last letter of the word "Wayikra," is printed small in the Pentateuch.

[2] Adapted and abridged from "Ha-heder" by A. Lifshitz in *Ha-tekufah*, v. 7, pp. 332-333.

reserved for the Humosh, for the Prophets, and for the Psalms, respectively. The children were seated on both sides of the long table engaged in study from morning till night. The study usually began with the Book of Leviticus, which deals with sacrifices, the subject matter of which is certainly not such as would interest a beginner. The reason given for beginning with this book in preference to others is similar to the one mentioned in the document of the Middle Ages, the *Hukke Ha-torah*, previously quoted,[1] and also that the study of the Law of Israel should precede that of the History of Israel.[2] In more recent times the teaching of Leviticus was discontinued, although it was used as the first lesson in the introduction to the study of Humosh. Later the portion of the Bible which is read in the synagogue weekly was taught to the child. Not every part of the Sidrah was studied but only such portions as the child could learn well in one week, even if it was only a single chapter. To the young children the rest of the Sidrah remained a closed book unless some of the stories were told to them by the assistant, but as they grew older they began to study the entire Sidrah. The aim was to develop general familiarity with this source and an extensive Hebrew vocabulary, rather than to teach grammar or history or interpretation of the Bible.

After the child had mastered a part of the Humosh, he began the commentary of Rashi. All studied Rashi, the commentator par excellence. The frequent quotation of Rashi in conversation made him an essential

[1] See chap. 1, p. 9.
[2] Ginzberg, Louis, *Op. cit.*

subject of study. At the same time, also, his use of the Aggadah and the Halakah, served as an introduction to the study of the Talmud. Toward the end of the week a review took place and on Friday the special synagogue chant for the reading of the Torah and the Haftarah [1] were taught. The five scrolls, too, were studied at the appropriate part of the year, each with its characteristic chant.

In some of the Hadarim, the historical books of the Bible were also taught and in others the Prophets and Hagiographa were introduced, though usually little time was left for them. The historical books were studied because they were more easily taught and the Book of Psalms, because it was so frequently used in the Bet Hamidrash, but as a rule pupils were expected to study the Prophets by themselves. On the Sabbath, too, the child came to Heder to study the Ethics of the Fathers or "Borki Nafshi." [2] Occasionally, before the holidays, the special laws concerning the holidays, as well as any special liturgical poems which would be read in the synagogue, were taught. The stories of the holidays were told to the child. In such ways the Heder was related to life. In some cases the children who were well advanced in the Humosh Heder also began the study of Talmud in the same school. This was one means by which the teacher, who had a personal, economic interest in his pupil, succeeded in holding him for a longer period.

[1] The portion of the Prophets read in the synagague on the Sabbath at the conclusion of the reading of the Pentateuchal portion for the week.

[2] Psalm 104.

c.   *The Talmud Heder*

The third type of Heder was the Talmud Heder.[1]
The child usually entered this school at the age of ten,
at times earlier.   This Heder was divided into three
groups.   The first was the beginner's group.   The
second consisted of those who studied Gemara with the
commentary of Rashi and the third consisted of those
who also studied the Tosafot.   The studies were
arranged weekly.   At the beginning of the week the
teacher explained the portion to be studied, and the
students spent the rest of the week reviewing by themselves, afterwards repeating aloud while all listened
to the recitation.   On this occasion the teacher had an
opportunity to make all additional explanations and to
elaborate on the subject.   The textbook was the Talmud itself.   Rarely were any introductory books used.
The difference in gradation lay in the explanation of
the teacher.

The study usually began with "Nezikin" (the laws
of damages), and the highest point was reached when
the Tosafot was taught.   The object was to enable the
child to study the Talmud by himself, and in Lithuania
it was customary to expect the child to know his portion of Talmud by heart.   The emphasis in the curriculum was given to the Talmud and this fact aroused
considerable protest especially from those who were
shocked at the neglect of the Bible and Mishnah
resulting therefrom.

The study of the Talmud was, however, important

[1] For Talmud Heder, see Kotik, E., *Meine Zikronot,* v. 1,
p. 56.

because it helped most to open up to the student all the literature that he was to read. The student who knew Bible and especially Talmud could proceed by himself to understand Jewish literature: the Siddur, the Mahzor, the Commentaries, the Codes, the ethical books, homiletical writings, casuistic writings, and the philosophical writings. In this Heder, too, the Pentateuch, Rashi, and the five Scrolls were studied, but only a few hours weekly. As in the Humosh Heder, before the holidays the laws pertaining to them were usually taught, but Prophets and Hagiographa were more rarely studied. The Sabbath program consisted of the study of the Ethics of the Fathers or Midrash. Before Bar Mizvah, the laws of Tefillin were taught, as well as a special address that was interwoven with Halakah and Aggadah.

The curricula of the Hadarim varied in some respects in accordance with the desires of the parents, who naturally exerted considerable influence on the Melammedim. Thus, in some Hadarim, writing of both the square characters and script was taught. The child learned how to write "Shürah Grüss," and how to write a letter in Yiddish. In most cases, however, it was left for a special writing teacher, since writing was not considered sufficiently important to form a regular subject in the curriculum of the Heder. No attempt was made to develop style or the ability to write well. The four fundamental operations in arithmetic were taught, but secular languages were usually omitted from the curriculum of the Heder since these subjects were mainly concerned not with the study of the Torah but with the general economic life, from which the

Jew was for the most part excluded. In some Hadarim the elements of Hebrew etymology were also taught but this was infrequent. History and ethics were not taught in the Hadarim as special subjects. A good deal of ethical instruction came as a result of the teaching of various portions of the Hagiographa as well as the Ethics of the Fathers studied on the Sabbath. The stories of heroism told of men like Akiba and the martyrs of the Middle Ages served to inspire the youth with Jewish idealism. Jewish literature was deemed sufficient to cover ethical teaching. The humane tendencies of the Halakah, and especially the beautiful tales of the Aggadah, served not only to develop the imagination of the child but also to give him ethical instruction.[1] Grammar was not studied in the old Heder; it was left to the individual initiative of the students, and later when the teaching of grammar became a characteristic of Haskalah education, its study fell into disrepute because it was associated with the Maskilim, many of whom were opposed by the masses. The codes, too, rarely formed a subject of study in the Heder. They were left primarily for the Yeshibah.

It should be noted that as a result of the teaching of the Bible, the study of Rashi, the Ethics of the Fathers, and the Talmud, the child attained a considerable knowledge of Hebrew, although language, as such, was not a part of the curriculum. To these studies may be added the reading of ethical books. Every student read by himself, and most boys read the legends concerning the rabbis and the Zaddikim

[1] See Ginzberg, L., *Op. cit.,* pp. 23-24.

as well as any ethical books that they were able to get. The main object, however, was to bring about the ability on the part of the student to study the Talmud by himself. When this ability was attained, he was graduated to the Yeshibah or Bet Hamidrash.

D. The Teaching of Secular Subjects

The teaching of secular subjects should be especially considered, since it will enable the reader to see more pointedly the contrast between education before the Haskalah and education under the influence of Haskalah. As a rule, secular subjects were not a part of the Heder curriculum. There may have been a Heder here and there where secular subjects were taught, but it was the exception rather than the rule.

The Jews did not feel the necessity for secular subjects of instruction, since they were not free to participate in the general life. In the enclosed life of the ghetto there was little need of anything outside of distinctive Jewish learning. Besides, secular studies were too closely related to the weekday life, to be included as a part of Torah which was the chief subject of the Heder, and a tradition of long standing prevented these from becoming a part of the Jewish curriculum. This tradition became almost universal as a result of the utter separation of the Jewish people from their neighbors in Russia and Poland.

Yet we find here and there illustrations of people whose course in Heder was considerably wider than was usual. Thus a pupil of Solomon Luria describes his studies in his commentary [1] as including Bible, philosophy and religio-philosophical writings, Kabbala, arithmetic, geometry, and astronomy.[2]   M. A. Günzburg, in his autobiography describes the education of his father as including Talmud, Codes, Bible, Hebrew, grammar, natural history, history, Polish, German, logic, geography, arithmetic, algebra, and optics.   Since his father lived in the 18th century, this course of study may well be considered another exception to the usual education of those days.   In the 19th century, Lilienblum's teacher had a copy of the translation of the Bible in Russian,[3] which his pupils used at times. He, himself, succeeded in learning from his father the general rules of arithmetic and a smattering of physical geography.[4]

The difficulties of getting a general education in the 18th century in Poland are described in the autobiography of Solomon Maimon (born in 1754).   The result was self-teaching, which was wasteful and difficult.   Maimon, himself, could satisfy his thirst for knowledge by studying several languages from the numbers on the pages of certain Hebrew books, but in order to study science he had to go to Germany, as did many others who sought to widen their field of knowledge.

[1] *Monoah Ha-lebabot* to the book *Hobat Ha-lebabot* by Bahya Ibn Pakuda.

[2] Quoted in Güdemann's *Quellenschriften,* pp. 88-90, giving the studies of Rabbi Monoah Hendel b. Shemarjah in Poland (16th and 17th centuries).

[3] Showing the influence of the Haskalah.   See chap. 6, pp. 166 ff.

[4] Lilienblum, M. L., *Op. cit.,* pp. 14-15.

In general it may be said that the study of secular subjects was rare. •Occasionally some Hadarim taught arithmetic. But the students of the old Heder who attained a broad education did so not because of it, but in spite of it.[1] The Russian government not only failed to encourage such instruction but discouraged it, even to the extent of penalizing teachers who introduced such studies into their Hadarim.

[1] See Appendix A for curricula in certain Hadarim.

CHAPTER IV

ELEMENTARY EDUCATION (CONTINUED)

A. The Method in the Heder

I. General Features

THE Heder, after the days of Jewish autonomy, lacked a fixed curriculum, fixed hours of instruction, and consistent organization. There was no attempt to grade children by age or to promote them regularly. Promotion came whenever the teacher deemed it fit. These facts are merely illustrations of the general uncertainty of method which was a characteristic of the Heder, for not all teachers pursued the same methods. The method of one teacher was to win the children over with love and kind words. Others were too strict and implanted fear into the hearts of the children, at times, developing falsehood in them by asking them to do things that they could not be expected to do.[1]

There are, however, certain features of method which were prominent in the Heder and were common to most Hadarim. Some of these features are favorable, others unfavorable. Teaching was individual in character. Since there were only a small number of pupils,[2]

[1] See Günzburg, M. A., *Abiezer,* p. 30.
[2] For number of children in Heder, see p. 106.

it was possible for the Melammed to teach about four children at a time. Hence he was able to pay individual attention to each pupil and to take a personal interest in his progress. Another very favorable feature was the close relationship that the method of the Heder bore to the life of the environment. The whole life in the Heder was religiously Jewish. The child learned in Heder what he had to do at home or in the synagogue and, at times, life in Heder was but a reflection of these institutions. The simplicity of the teacher's method may also be considered a favorable feature. Thus, as an illustration, the teacher may have been unable to differentiate between formal history and story-telling, but the stories that he did tell were told impressively. He would tell his stories sympathetically, and at times, in his simple way, stir the children to tears. The stories were realities to the pupils and were remembered in later days after the pupil had grown up and had long left the Heder.[1]

The intimacy of relationship between teacher and pupil made it possible for the teacher to consult the commentaries in the presence of the pupil when a point of difficulty arose. In fact, this had a good psychological effect in impressing upon the mind of the young the need of further knowledge even on the part of the learned.

As against the favorable features mentioned, there were a number that were unfavorable. In the first place, there were the long hours of the Heder. The program of the day was usually as follows: Morning prayers, study from about nine to one or two, one

[1] Ginzberg, Louis, *The Primary School,* pp. 22-23.

hour for dinner, and then study again until eight or nine in the evening, depending upon the age of the boys. In the summer, study ceased at about sundown; in winter, study continued after dark and the child went home at night. The evening prayers were recited in the Heder, the boys duplicating the life in the synagogue. The program of the day differed on Friday, when, in winter, the children were permitted to leave at two, and in the summer at about three or four. Even the Sabbath was not a totally free day. The child had to appear either for his weekly examination, which took place at home in the presence of the father and the teacher, or had to go to the Heder to study the Ethics of the Fathers in the summer and "Borki Nafshi" in the winter. As a result of these long hours, whatever individual study was necessary took place in Heder and no homework was given. In fact, the greater part of the week was spent in reviewing the new chapter of the Bible or the new portion of the Talmud which had been introduced and fully explained at the beginning of the week.

Secondly, the Heder placed undue emphasis upon memory work, and according to the testimony of some writers the punishment administered by the teacher varied inversely with the memory of the pupil.[1] At times, too, the punishments of the Heder were severe.[2] Although the intimacy of relationship between teacher and pupil made the teacher's approval the motive for good work, corporal punishment was widespread, as was also the "Keena." This punishment consisted of

[1] Günzburg, M. A., *Op. cit.*, p. 18.
[2] See Kotik, E., *Meine Zikronot*, v. 1, p. 167.

placing the boy in a corner of the room with a dunce cap on his head and riding a broom. For some of the bigger boys this was so serious a penalty that they preferred corporal punishment to it.[1] It should be pointed out, though, that here, as in other phases of method, there were many individual differences and that the "cruel" punishments of the Heder are mostly exaggerations.

II. THE METHOD OF TEACHING READING, BIBLE, AND TALMUD

a. The Teaching of Reading

The general aim in teaching the prayer book and the Bible in Heder was not so much an understanding of their content as a general familiarity with the sources. The teaching of mechanical reading [2] was the first subject of instruction and began with the alphabet, which the child learned from large charts until he knew it forwards and backwards, with the vowels and without the vowels.[3] Then came the syllables and later the reading of words. The textbook used was the prayer book. A great deal of the study depended upon the memory and upon unceasing repetition. Visual appeal was used whenever it was found of help. Thus the child was told that the Bet (the second letter

[1] For cruel punishments in Heder, see Maimon, S., *Autobiography*, p. 32.

[2] The ability to read Hebrew, though not understanding the content of what is read.

[3] In Hebrew the vowels are special signs placed under the consonants to make syllables.

of the alphabet, which means a house) has its mouth open and the Pe (the mouth) has its mouth closed.[1] Not only were names of the letters taught, but also their meaning, their form, and their position. The fact that the phonetic method[2] was not used was, however, a source of difficulty, and the learning of the letters by names caused the teaching of reading to be extended at times to two years, whereas today a child can be taught to read Hebrew in a few weeks. Constant repetition was the only means of attaining fluency, but the lack of interest in the process was somewhat overcome by the singsong accompanying the reading of the prayers.

b.   The Teaching of Bible

The teaching of Bible began, as a rule, at the age of five or six. It was taught usually for two years and at the beginning the translation method was used.[3] This translation was at first taught word by word, i.e., "Wayomer"—and he said "El" to "Moshe," a man whose name was Moses. Later this word for word translation was supplemented by combining the separate words into phrases (Hibbur), so as to give

[1] Ginzberg, Louis, *Op. cit.,* pp. 15-16.

[2] The names of the letters and the vowels were learned by the child. For the child to combine the sound of a consonant with a vowel is relatively easy, but to combine a letter which he knows by name with a vowel which he knows by name is exceedingly difficult.

[3] This does not mean that the study of the Pentateuch was abandoned at the end of two years but that it ceased to be the main subject of study.

the child a connected idea of the content of the story read. Although the teaching began with translation into Yiddish, this was abandoned after the child had attained fluency in the Pentateuch, and the text was just read and difficult words were explained by the child or, if necessary, by the teacher. Instead of translation, the child pursued only Hibbur, which combined translation with interpretation, often including related legends. The commentary of Rashi was used as a source for interpretation. The Humosh was studied by Sidrah, that is, by the portion of the week. The textbook was the Bible itself, and short editions were in disrepute. Since the entire Sidrah was too long to be covered in one week, especially by the younger children, the child could learn only a part of it and then had to proceed to the next Sidrah as soon as a new week began. For this reason the child did not get a connected story from the instruction he received. On the other hand, one of the chief advantages of this method was that it related the study to the Jewish life of the ghetto. In the Heder the child studied the very portion which was read in the synagogue on Sabbath, and on Monday and Thursday of that week. That Sidrah, too, with its commentaries, was studied by the adults on Saturday, and the itinerant preacher used it for his text. In the synagogue the adults studied it, and it frequently entered into their conversation. Later on the child succeeded in studying the entire portion of the week and became well acquainted with the Humosh. It should be remembered that the teacher not only translated the Bible for the children, but also interpreted it, using his own knowledge, the Commentary of Rashi, and Jewish legends as helps. Some of the abler Melammedim also succeeded in making their instruction more concrete by drawing pictures (e.g., of the Tabernacle in the wilderness, the garments of the high priest, etc.).

Another favorable aspect of the method of teaching Bible in the Heder, were the special chants reserved for different books. The Sidrah of the week had its chant. The Prophets had a chant of their own. Some of the Five Scrolls read in the synagogue at different times of the year had their own characteristic melodies, which the child learned when he studied their content. At times, too, poetic introductions were added as an explanation of the text. As an instance, one may take the "Song of Songs" which had a very pretty chant of its own, and which was given this elaborate introduction, in Yiddish:

The Song of Songs which is Solomon's,
The Song of all Songs.
Other songs have been sung by a wise man,
This song was sung by a wise man, the son of a wise man.
Other songs have been sung by a King,
This song has been sung by a King, the son of a King.
Other songs have been sung by a righteous man,
This song has been sung by a righteous man, the son of
    a righteous man.
By whom?
By Solomon, son of David, King of Israel!

A very interesting feature in connection with the teaching of the Pentateuch is the attitude to questions asked by the children. Modern pedagogy has pointed out the value of the problem method in teaching. In the Heder, too, the teacher would stimulate the child to ask questions, at times even suggesting that, "Rashi in commenting on verse so and so, implies a question. See whether you can discover it." However, questions that would affect belief and tradition were scrupulously excluded.

The method employed in teaching the Commentary of Rashi was similar to that of the Pentateuch. It was taught portion by portion. The younger boys learned less, the portion being increased as the student grew older and more advanced in the study of the subject.

However, one should not conclude that Bible study in the Heder was altogether satisfactory. Far from it. The Pentateuch was taught, but as a rule, not well taught. The Prophets and Hagiographa were almost always neglected. Even in the early days of Jewish autonomy, we find a warning given in the constitution of the community of Cracow that, "The teacher of the Talmud Torah shall not begin Gemara with any pupil unless he has been tested for three weeks by the three main supervisors to see if he is fit and adapted to the study." [1] There was a decided tendency to neglect the Bible and to hasten to the study of the Talmud. We learn from another source that, in the 17th century in Germany and Poland, it was customary for parents and teachers to neglect the study of Bible and to admit children at very tender ages to the study of the Talmud, on the

[1] Güdemann, M., *Quellenschriften,* p. 235. See also Wettstein, F. H., *Kadmoniyot Mipinksaot Yeshanim,* p. 6.

ground that it sharpens their minds from their very youth.[1]

Wessely, a disciple of Mendelssohn, whose ancestors came from Poland, testifies that he did not study the Bible and Mishnah in school, but that on admission to Heder at the age of five, he was at once introduced to the study of the Talmud. He started with the tractate of "Kiddushin," dealing with the laws of marriage, studied until he was nine, and not until he was ten did he come in contact with some one who taught Hebrew grammar. From the new teacher he learned to understand the Pentateuch and the Prophets.

He criticizes this system of study under which the Bible is neglected and under which people hasten to the study of the Talmud, in the following words:

"We do not pay attention at all to the study of the Bible since we live upon the Mishnah and the Talmud and do not turn from them to the right or to the left. Tell me what fault have we found with those parts of the Mishnah and with those sayings of the Talmud which command us to teach the Bible to our children and to study it ourselves? We have our learned Rabbi [2] who said that a child should study the Bible at five, the Mishnah at ten and the Talmud at fifteen. And who, pray, has permitted us to transgress the words of our ancestors and to upset this order of studies as we do by bringing in our children at the age of five, and introducing them to the Talmud, and what is worse, by immediately accustoming them to casuistry,

[1] Güdemann, M., *Op. cit.*, p. 213, from writings of "Leone del Bene in Ferrara," in the 17th century.
[2] Rabbi Judah Hanasi.

and teaching them every week questions and answers which serve only to confuse the tender mind of the child?" [1]

No wonder then, that he concludes bitterly, "By my life, I did not know what the Torah contained. The Torah, from Genesis to the very end was a treasure hidden from me." [2]

That this neglect was widespread may be judged from the many protests against it. Thus Rabbi Isaiah Horowitz says, "And ye shall teach your children in this order. The boy shall begin to study the Bible and shall not turn from it till he will have completed the study of the Torah, Prophets and Hagiographa. He shall not skip from chapter to chapter following the portion of the week, but he shall study consecutively. And he shall not leave any portion until he knows the meaning and interpretation of the words and the explanation of the verses. It is also good for him to learn a large portion of grammar while he is still young, for then the teachings are inscribed in his heart and they remain in the memory forever." [3]   This quotation is significant, not only for the illustration that it gives of the neglect of Bible, but also of the tendency to hurry over the portions that were taught without teaching them thoroughly, all with the object of quickly reaching the study of Talmud. In similar

[1] Wessely, N. H., *Dibre Shalom We'emet*, Letter 2, p. 55.
[2] *Ibid.*, Letter 2, p. 87.
[3] Margoshes, S., *A History of the Curriculum of the Jewish Schools in Germany from the Middle of the 17th to the Middle of the 19th Century,* chap. 1, note 23.   A quotation from the Shelah, p. 134.

manner, Rabbi Jacob Emden criticizes the method in Poland which attempts to teach the boy the whole of the Torah, "while he stands on one leg," without giving him the necessary basis for it, a knowledge of the Bible. Wessely summarizes the evils arising from this tendency to hurry to the study of the Talmud in the following quotation:

"The boy studies the Pentateuch before he is even at home in the prayer book. At best he studies only a fraction of one portion of the week and then of another. Thus he continues for an entire year with the result that when the next year comes around the boy has forgotten all that he has learned of the portion of the week of last year, so that he is left without the knowledge of any phrase in the Bible. Then after he has gone through two or three such cycles, he immediately begins the Mishnah, only to learn one or two chapters of the Tractate Berakot. Thereupon he begins the study of the Talmud which he follows in similar fashion. One week he studies one or two Halakahs, the next week he has already jumped to another Talmudic subject. Moreover, he skips over Rashi and begins the Tosafot, in spite of the fact that he is only eight or nine years old and not mature as yet for the study of the Tosafot. Thus he continues till Bar Mizvah, bereft of all knowledge of the Law, so that there are few indeed who are familiar with the Pentateuch, let alone the Mishnah." [1]

That all these protests were of no avail is evidenced by the fact that even as late as the days of the writer,

[1] Güdemann, M., *Op. cit.*, p. 92: Von Moses b. Aharon aus Mähren "Kezad Seder Mishnah."

the study of Bible was neglected in his own Heder in order the more quickly to reach the study of the Talmud. Here and there one may find an exception as in the case of Lilienblum,[1] whose teacher made sure that he was well versed in the Pentateuch and Prophets before starting the Talmud. He began the study of Talmud at eight,[2] was able to attempt a page of Talmud by himself at the age of ten, and at fourteen understood and read intelligently and without help the difficult Commentary of Rabbi Samuel Edels, known as Maharsha. His education was, however, different from that of other boys. He was also taught some grammar and was able to write to his future father-in-law letters full of abbreviated words, which at that time was an indication of erudition. But in the majority of cases Bible instruction suffered while the greatest part of the time was given over to Talmud.

c. The Teaching of Talmud [3]

In Poland, and later in Russia to a lesser extent, the Talmud was the chief subject of study. In the words of Maimon, "The study of the Talmud is the chief object of a learned education among our people. Riches, bodily advantages, and talents of every kind have indeed in their eyes certain worth, and are

[1] Lilienblum, M. L., *Hatot Neurim,* p. 11. But even in his case we learn that he began the study of the Latter Prophets for the first time at the age of twenty. *Ibid.,* p. 34.

[2] The study of the Talmud was usually begun at a very early age in Russia. The writer began at seven.

[3] See Lifshitz, A. M., "Ha-heder," in *Ha-tekufah,* v. 7, pp. 316-319.

esteemed in proportion, but nothing stands among them above the dignity of a good Talmudist. He has the first claim upon all offices and positions of honor in the community. If he enters an assembly he may be of any age or rank, everyone rises before him most respectfully, and the most honorable place is assigned to him." [1]

There were three aims in the study of the Talmud. The first was the mastery of the language of the Talmud, the second was an understanding of its content, and the third a grasp of its method and style. It was impossible to arrange an order of study that would apply to all the three aims equally. Hence the one chosen was the third, that of a grasp of method and style of the Talmud. In the course of study the child would gradually learn to recognize the method of the Talmud, and from the recurrence of the discussion he would learn to understand the principles involved. Difficult as the subject was, it was made clear and concrete, so that the children understood what was taught.

The method of teaching was that of translation as in the case of Bible, and as in that study, translation was abandoned when the child attained a fair knowledge of the subject. The instruction given was individual as a rule, except several times a week when the teacher read the Shiur [2] before all the students, explaining as he read. Otherwise, all the students studied individually. Individual instruction would naturally lead to a lack of attention on the part of the other pupils and made it necessary to have very few

[1] Maimon, S., *Autobiography,* p. 45.

[2] The portion of Talmud assigned for a given period of study.

students in the Talmud Heder. The method pursued lent itself particularly to the development of the mental abilities of exceptional children, while the sudden jump from one subject of discussion to another without preparation made the duller students drop out. In this way the Talmud Heder became an institution primarily for exceptional children, since some elements in the Gemara that the children were really expected to know, were not taught.

The study of Talmud began at an early age, usually at seven or eight. Rabbi Jacob Emden says, "With all this my father hoped to have me enter another school after I was three years old so that in my fifth year I had already finished learning the Tractate Berakot." [1] Solomon Maimon was introduced early to the study of the Talmud by his father who told him that, "He who understands the Talmud, understands everything." [2] This early introduction of children to the study of the Talmud, many parts of which they could not understand, resulted in developing a distaste for the subject. A good illustration is the case of Maimon, who, when he broke with the old life of his early days, spoke of the Talmud as a book in which "absurd questions are discussed with the highest efforts of intellectual power." That this is an unfair view of the Talmud is understood by anyone who has studied the subject and is acquainted with the general aim of Talmudic Judaism, with the humane tendencies of the Halakah, and with the parts of the Talmud known as the Aggadah, replete with poetic ideas and senti-

[1] Margoshes, S., *Op. cit.,* chap. 1, note 37, from Megillat Sefer.
[2] Maimon, S., *Op. cit.,* p. 26.

ments and words of wisdom that inspire the reader. However, the undue emphasis upon Talmud too often produced a violent reaction and Maimon, having been duly warned by his father not to read any books except the Talmud, managed at the early age of seven to complete the reading of a textbook on astronomy.

Each student of Talmud had to go through three stages in order to reach a stage of independence in this important study. The first stage was that of translation. Here, with the help of a teacher, he studied the Talmud, slowly translating word by word and learning perhaps, at the beginning, no more than a half page or a page during the week. The second stage was reached when the student was entrusted to study a page of Talmud by himself, with the aid of the commentaries and to read it before the teacher, to have his mistakes corrected, and to receive help in difficult passages. The third and highest stage was reached when the student was able to engage independently in disputation with other students. Such disputations were very frequent, particularly in the 16th century, and contributed a great deal to the development of the method in the study of the Talmud, known as Pilpul or casuistry, of which more will be said in the chapter dealing with the Yeshibah.

B. The Personnel of the Heder

I. THE MELAMMED [1]

The most important person in any educational system is the teacher. In considering the Jewish edu-

[1] See Wengeroff, P., *Memoiren einer Grossmutter,* pp. 73-85.

cational institutions of Russia and Poland, it is very important, therefore, to know the various types of teachers or Melammedim who taught in the different schools that we have considered. In the early days of Jewish autonomy in Poland, the Melammed was subject to considerable supervision by the elders of the community. In some cases, as we already know, the curriculum, the method, the hours of instruction, and the remuneration were fixed by the Kahal. When, however, Jewish autonomy declined, the Melammed, who was always a private teacher undertaking a private venture, became responsible only to himself and the parents of the children. The type of Melammedim, therefore, degenerated. Since there was no supervision, one could find here and there Melammedim who were incapable of the difficult work of instructing the young. There was nothing to prevent people who lacked even the necessary knowledge, from coming into the field of teaching. If there was in addition a lack of natural ability to get along with young people, or as in some cases, even, a dislike for young children, instruction became unpleasant both to teacher and pupil. Those who were unfortunate enough to come under the influence of these poor teachers never forgot them. Some teachers failed with the younger children because of natural inability, with the older children because of lack of knowledge. But since there was no supervision and no special technique to be attained, the Hadarim continually multiplied under the private initiative of the Melammedim.

The system of remuneration, too, did not tend to improve the quality of the teacher. The Melammed's

income depended upon bargaining. He was paid by
the semester, and in addition received "holiday money"
as a special gift from some or all of the parents. The
income was usually limited. According to Kotik [1]
(1850) the total income of the teacher was usually
sixty to one hundred rubles a term. Those who
received one hundred were considered rich teachers.
The teachers of the elementary Heder had about sixty
to eighty children, usually three years of age, and
received one ruble per semester per child. The rich
paid one and a half rubles. In the Humosh Heder
there were from twenty to thirty children, each of
whom paid about three rubles. In the beginners'
Talmud Heder there were about fifteen to twenty
pupils who paid four rubles per semester. The rich
paid five. The next highest Melammed, who taught
Gemara, usually had a still smaller class consisting of
about twelve children who paid six to seven rubles
per semester. The Heder in which the children studied
Talmud with Tosafot had about ten pupils who paid
about ten rubles each.[2] These sums were at times
paid by the poorest people who were barely able to
make a living and, modest as they seem, entailed
making all kinds of sacrifices for the education of their
children. Children were rarely, if ever, excluded for
non-payment.

Although the children paid for light [3] and for books,

[1] Kotik, E., *Op. cit.*, v. 1, p. 58.

[2] *Ibid.*, pp. 58-59.

[3] Since the children also studied at night during the winter,
lamps had to be used and money for kerosene was paid by the
children.

the meager earnings of the Melammed were insufficient
to pay his small rent and the wages of his assistant.
Even these earnings were not secure since the parents
might at any time fail to return their children to the
same Heder, when the new semester began. The
Melammed, therefore, had to engage in other occupations, such as matchmaking, which in Eastern Europe
might well have been considered at certain times dependent upon learning, since learning was a great
factor in the selection of the bridegroom. Some
teachers settled economic disputes, others engaged in
some special Jewish work, such as the making of
Mizrahim, Mezuzahs, or Zizit. Withal, the wife of
the Melammed usually had to help by keeping a little
store or by selling at a stand in the market; otherwise
the modest economic demands of the teacher's family
could not be met.

Under the above system of remuneration the child
very often brought the teacher's pay to school or the
teacher came to collect it from the parent in person.
This state of affairs naturally resulted in lessening the
pupil's respect for the teacher. There was also the
factor of competition which multiplied the number of
Melammedim, and although this tended to prevent
illiteracy, it did not elevate the position of the teacher.
Added to these factors was the fact that nearly everyone could be a Melammed, especially for the elementary and Humosh Heder. These facts combined
to lower the prestige which the Melammed otherwise
had.

The regular Sabbath examination,[1] which was held

---

[1] Kotik, E., *Op. cit.*, v. 1, p. 56.

in the afternoon at the home of the parents and in the presence of the teacher, had its advantages and disadvantages. On the one hand, it helped to maintain a sense of responsibility on the part of the teacher, who was anxious to show to the parent how well the pupil learned. On the other hand, the parent would at times rebuke the teacher in the presence of the pupil, thus bringing about a loss of respect on the part of the young for their teachers.

In exceptional cases the Melammed was a teacher because he could do nothing better. Perhaps he had failed in business or did not succeed in becoming a rabbi and therefore he became a Melammed and was in constant poverty.

It may be said, however, that in most cases the Melammed was capable of the work that he undertook in his community. It is true that he had no pedagogic training and had to depend upon his natural ability to get along with young people. Nevertheless, the chief requirement, which was that he be a man of knowledge, faithful, and religiously devoted to the work in which he was engaged, was usually met. Though he was free from teacher's examinations and from special preparation, his position in the community and his knowledge of the great responsibility that he was shouldering in carrying on the work of God, made him a fit person to teach children. What he lacked because of his ignorance of child psychology, child hygiene, and general secular studies, he often made up by his love for the child, his friendship to the family, and by his simplicity and devotion.

The position which the Melammed held in the community increased his sense of responsibility. In the small community he performed some of the functions of the rabbi. He gave advice on various problems and at times would even answer questions of ritual. He was so well acquainted with some of the families that he was considered a member of the group. He visited the parents on Sabbaths and holidays and participated with them in their joys and sorrows.

The relationship, too, between the teacher and pupils was a very friendly one. The intimate acquaintance with the parents of the pupils helped to bring this about. Under such intimacy the child readily responded to the approval and disapproval of the teacher, and the Melammed's simple sincerity left a lasting impression on the mind of the child.

II. THE ASSISTANT [1]

Another personality in the Heder that should be considered is the Behelfer, or assistant. Of these there were two kinds, the junior assistant and the senior assistant, who were employed in the elementary and Humosh Heder. The Talmud Heder had no assistants. The junior assistant brought the children to and from Heder, at times carrying two or three youngsters on his back at once. It was he, too, who brought food to the children. He also brought them to the synagogue and taught them the necessary responses to the prayers. He would get his maintenance in accordance with the custom of boarding around ("eating days").[2] This

[1] See Wengeroff, P., *Op. cit.,* v. 1, p. 71.

[2] He was extended the hospitality of some family in the town or village for a given day in the week. In this way he had sev-

meant that he was the guest of a different family in the village every day of the week, which was the scheme also in vogue for the support of wandering students. On New Moons, on Hanukkah, on Purim, and on other holidays he received gifts from the parents. At times he would do certain odds and ends for them, such as carrying gifts on Purim, or purifying the dishes for the Passover. He was always in close touch with the children, played with them, made their gragers, flags, and trendles. He was usually unmarried and young, and when he married he turned to other sources of livelihood.

The older assistant taught the children reading and reviewed the Pentateuch with them. Instruction in portions of the Pentateuch that the Melammed had not yet taught was not entrusted to him. On the other hand, in country places the assistants were very often the teachers where they were also part of the family. There they taught and also performed various services around the house. At times the country people felt the need for an assistant who could teach secular subjects. Such assistants they found especially in the days of Haskalah, when young men left their parents in order to pursue their secular studies free from family restrictions.[1] At times, special fairs were arranged in some places at which the assistants could be hired.

In general the assistants contributed in no small way

eral families at whose house he "ate days"; at times, too, he may have had a free day—a day on which he went hungry because he had no family to go to for his meals.

[1] For separation of families for sake of Haskalah, see Kotik, E., *Op. cit.*, v. 2, p. 46.

to the joy of the children in Heder. This was especially true of the young assistant who was always with the children, playing with them as well as caring for their physical needs.

C. The Extra-Curricular Activities of the Heder

The fact that the Heder was a one-room school, which served also as habitat for the Melammed and his family, resulted in a good many inconveniences. The child was in Heder from the early hours of the morning until eight or nine o'clock in the evening, and this made instruction in one room exceedingly undesirable. The long hours of instruction, coupled with the fact that children started at the age of three, at times affected the health of the children.

But rigorous as these long hours may have been, it should not be imagined that the child attended Heder unwillingly. While at times this may have been the case, life in the Heder was on the whole attractive and Heder remained a source of pleasant memories in later life. Life in the Heder was very different from life in a modern school. Simple in its organization, and without any supervision, the Heder was not subject to many rules. The relationship between teacher and pupil was usually a very friendly one. Extra curricular activities that centered about festivals or occasions of festivity helped to increase this intimacy and to sweeten the days that the child spent at Heder. Story-telling after a tiring lesson was a feature well loved by the children. Some of the stories told by the Melammed, who may not have been exact in details of information, nevertheless served to stimulate the imagination of the child and to develop within him an attachment to the Bible as well as to the heroes about whom the stories centered.

The singing of songs and the playing of games under the supervision of the Behelfer were also a source of joy. The games played were usually "Nuts" and "Buttons." The life that surrounded the child also served as a source from which the child drew his imitative games. The children played "Teacher and Heder," "Synagogue and Leaders," "Rabbi and Congregation," etc. Some of the other games played during the free periods showed the influence of the studies the children had engaged in. "David and Goliath," "Israel in Egypt," "Building the Temple," "Joseph and His Brethren," "Ahasuerus and Haman," and "Romans and Israelites" were among the favorite games of the children. A number of special feasts took place during the year. One such feast took place at the end of the winter, when study at night ceased and the children began to leave the Heder at the end of the day. Other occasions for a party were when a child began to study the Pentateuch, or when a tractate of the Talmud was completed, or Lag BaOmer. The child engaged in all of these activities together with his teacher and Behelfer. On Lag BaOmer eve, the children would go to the synagogue and help in preparing the illuminations. The Holiday of the Scholars would thus be impressed upon them. The following morning they would go out into the fields with bows and arrows which the assistant had already prepared, and spend the entire day out-of-doors. In some places it was customary for the teacher to take the children to the river and to teach them how to swim. The indoor games during the holidays of Hanukkah, the special party that was made on Hamishah Asar, and jollity on Purim and Sukkot added to the joy of the children. The making of the trendles and playing with them, the preparation of flags for Simhat Torah, and even the special visits for prayer paid to the home where a newborn baby had come were all related to the Heder and added color to its activities. The carved swords for Tishah Beab and the special "skate" on the ice known as the "Wayomer David," [1] were all of educational as well as recreational value and helped to add interest to life in the Heder.

The days when the children were free from Heder, such as the holidays, the free periods between the two semesters, and the days of the new moon which were set aside as half holidays, were all occasions of joy to the children, not only because they meant relief from burdensome tasks, but also because they were interwoven with the life they lived in the Heder. The games they played during these periods would also be based on some of the knowledge they acquired in school. As an illustration one may take the day before Tishah Beab, when a war between two groups of boys in the same Heder or between two groups of different Hadarim would be styled the war of the Romans against the Judæans.

[1] Wayomer David—derived from the fact that the position of the skater was similar to that of the supplicant as he recited that particular prayer in the synagogue.

See Ginzberg, L., *Op. cit.,* p. 26.

Although the discipline and punishment may have been severe in some Hadarim, the atmosphere of the Heder was on the whole a pleasant one. The fact that the meals were brought to the children in the Hadarim resulted in developing a spirit of sociability in their midst. The assistants, unlike those described in Maimon's *Autobiography*, as depriving the children of the food brought to them, were very often kindly persons who not only ate with the children, but participated in their games, told them stories, made special toys for them, and in general enabled them to lead a happy life while under their care. Even going home at night in winter, with lanterns and burning candles in their hands, which might ordinarily seem a rigorous experience for children of tender ages, was an occasion of joy, as all the children were out together singing Hebrew or Yiddish folk-songs, merrily marching home through the muddy streets of the Russian villages. All in all, these varied child activities surrounded the school with a glory not easily forgotten by those who once attended it.

D. THE TALMUD TORAH

The Talmud Torah in Eastern Europe was an elementary Jewish school for the children of the poor. Its aim, curriculum, method, and organization were the same as those of the Heder previously discussed. Whatever differences there were between these two institutions arose from the fact that the Talmud Torah was a philanthropic venture.

Since the Talmud Torah was a philanthropic institution, it was under the care of the elders of the community. During the days of Jewish autonomy, when the Heder was supervised, the Talmud Torah also received special attention. The needs of the poor were carefully provided for, as a result of the high regard for learning. After Jewish autonomy ceased, however, the Talmud Torah was as unsupervised as the Heder. The utter neglect into which most of these schools fell reflects the lack of supervision in education, after the days when the Kahal ceased to exist.

Thus, the Odessa Talmud Torah, before Haskalah influence penetrated, is described as a narrow, old shanty, stuffy and crowded. The Talmud Torah in general before the Haskalah was, according to Kantor,[1] "a half ruined shanty in which an ignorant Melammed half teaches, half maims, a group of little, hungry, poorly-clad children." The subjects of instruction were exclusively Jewish and the methods of teaching "prehistoric."[2]

In 1782 the Lemberg Talmud Torah [3] is said to have accommodated forty-three pupils. Of these, seven children studied the alphabet, twelve were able to read words, study short prayers, and read the prayer book. Occasionally some of the children in this division also began to study the Pentateuch. Thirteen children actually studied the Pentateuch, a little Hebrew writing, and occasionally began the study of the Talmud

[1] Kantor, J. L., "The Talmud Torah," in *Russki Evrei*, 1880, no. 30.

[2] Shayel, "Odessa Talmud Torah," in *Russki Evrei*, 1880, nos. 34, 36, 37, 43.

[3] See Braver, Abraham J., "Mifkad Ha-hadarim be-Lebub Beshenat, 542" in *Reshumot*, v. 1.

while still in this division. The highest group, consisting of eleven pupils, studied the Talmud and its commentaries. From this division, too, children were taken out to be apprenticed, with a view to vocational preparation.

The above Talmud Torah was under the supervision of the Hebrah Talmud Torah,[1] or the community society for education, which supervised the instruction here as well as in the Hadarim. This society drew its financial support from the "Kuppah" or charity box, from which it received one sixth of the total collection on Monday and Thursday, as well as from membership fees.

A description of a Talmud Torah one century later is given by Katzovich in his autobiography.

"I enter a low, dirty hut that is about to come down; about twenty boys shabbily dressed, dirty looking, almost in rags, are shouting in unison, and in the middle of the room is to be seen a man, beard and ear-locks uncombed. An old greasy cap covers his head that seems to grow feathers instead of hair. He is dressed in a long woolen Tallit Katon, reeking with perspiration, and hanging down over an exposed chest covered with long hair. Upon seeing me he remains standing with his 'leather noodles' (cat o' nine tails) in his hand, frightened as a hare. . . .

"I ask him what is taught in the Talmud Torah. He answers as usual, Ibri, Pentateuch and the chanting of the Sidrah. With his permission I examine the children. The Pentateuch is studied in Yiddish translation, word by word, without any understanding of the

[1] See pp. 65 ff.

content. No one knows the significance of a holiday. No one knows even a word of Hebrew. Writing is never taught, Russian and arithmetic are not even mentioned." [1]

The curriculum of the Talmud Torah in Krivoe Rog, Russia (1890), mentioned in the above quotation, is characteristic of the education received by most Talmud Torah children where Haskalah influence did not change the institution. Rarely did a child that left the Talmud Torah ever get beyond the translation of the simple portions of the Pentateuch or the mere mechanical reading of Hebrew. And even this meager education was so poorly supervised that only at the end of the term, and in the better Talmud Torahs on an occasional Sabbath, were the children examined publicly. For these reasons the Talmud Torah gradually fell into disrepute.

Here and there we may find an exception to the rule with regard to the kind of education received by the children in the Talmud Torahs. As an illustration of the exceptional Talmud Torah, we may consider that in Kamenez, Podolsk. In that school there were about twenty boys who were studying Talmud under two teachers. As is usual in the case of poor children, the pupils were supported on the scheme of "eating days." The boys were divided into two classes: beginners in Talmud and advanced students who studied the Tosafot. There were three trustees in charge who gathered contributions, chiefly in country places, every Hanukkah. The physical facilities, too, are described as being fair and the boys are dressed almost as well

[1] Katzovich, I. A., *Sechzig Jahr Leben*, pp. 299-300.

as the children of the ordinary householders. Every Sabbath, learned men in the village were brought by the trustees to examine the children.[1]

The description given of the Kamenez Talmud Torah is to be considered the exception rather than the rule. The discussion of the Heder need not be repeated here, as the Talmud Torah was really a free Heder for the poor. Unfortunately, it was not only *for the poor* but also a *poorer* educational institution from all points of view.

The Talmud Torahs well deserved the disrepute which has in time become attached to them, since most of them were, from the point of view of their physical equipment, unfit as educational institutions. In addition, supervision, curricula, and methods were by no means such as to warrant their being effective media of educating the child.

It should be remembered, however, that in part the meager results of Talmud Torah education may be accounted for by the economic condition of its pupils. Whereas parents who could afford to pay for the education of their children usually made it possible for them to continue their studies till they were married,[2] the children of the poor who attended the Talmud Torah were often apprenticed at an early age. It is also worthy of note that, although the results of Talmud Torah education were not successful, the lack of supervision was due to the breakdown of Jewish autonomy,

---

[1] Kotik, E., *Op. cit.*, v. 1, pp. 64-65.

[2] And then the father-in-law usually arranged that his young son-in-law should continue to study the Talmud for a couple of years after marriage.

a circumstance which was beyond the control of the Jewish community. Jewish autonomy was officially abolished by a decree of the Russian government in 1844.[1] However, unsuccessful as the Talmud Torah may have been, its mere presence in every Jewish community is an indication, not only of the high regard for learning, but also a reflection of the attitude that philanthropy must supply people with more than bread alone.

E. Private Instruction

The extent of private instruction in Eastern Europe is unknown, but that there was considerable private instruction cannot be doubted. In the cities the rich would get private teachers for their children as a luxury, and in the small villages and country places the poor would do the same as a necessity, since there were not enough children in one village to organize a Heder. In country places the teacher usually lived with the parents of one of his pupils, that being his reward for his services to that family. His additional income was received from the parents of other children who were sent to the same home for instruction. His total income consisted of about thirty or forty rubles per semester, plus his board and lodging.

This teacher usually came from some town and went home to see his family two or three times a year on the occasion of the holidays.[2] Unfortunately, some of

[1] Dubnow, S. M., *History of the Jews in Russia and Poland,* v. 2, p. 59.

[2] See "Fischel, the Teacher," by S. Rabinowitz, in *Yiddish Tales,* translated by Helena Frank, in which an excellent description of such a type and the life he led is given.

these teachers did not know much, as a result of which the children in the country often remained ignorant of Jewish knowledge.[1] The instruction usually consisted of reading, Pentateuch, Rashi, Prophets, Hagiographa, Talmud, and, only at rare times, Zohar.[2]

In the 19th century, during the sixties, the country teachers were of a higher type. In justice to them, it should be said that some were the bearers of culture in the country places. The nature of the instruction that they gave and the environment in which they found themselves, brought them into very close contact with the family and made them of lasting influence in the life of the people.

F. EDUCATION OF GIRLS

The education which girls received depended more upon the home and upon the Jewish environment than upon any formal educational institution. Without any special school for training in household arts, the Jewish girl learned how to bake, how to cook, and how to take care of the home. The Jewish influence of the home was sufficient to teach the future mother all the important customs and ceremonies, and to develop within her the virtues of industry, thrift, modesty, chastity, and charity. That the Jewish mother was a source of good influence in the education of the children is a tribute to the thoroughly Jewish environment of the country.[3]

However, girls were admitted in some Hadarim, and

[1] Kotik, E., *Op. cit.*, v. 2, pp. 126, 207, 209.
[2] Katzovich, I. A., *Op. cit.*, pp. 21-23, and 38.
[3] Sachs, A. S., *Choruwe Welten.*

both sexes studied together. There were also some special women teachers known as "Rebizins." The subjects taught were usually reading of the prayer book, blessings for special occasions, Pentateuch, and writing Yiddish. But the Humosh Heder and the Talmud Heder were never reached by the girls. The little reading of Hebrew and Yiddish that they were taught was developed by subsequent reading of the famous "Ze'enah U-re-enah," the Yiddish adaptation of the Pentateuch, which is interwoven with a great deal of legend and folklore. This book exerted a tremendous educational influence upon the Jewish women of Eastern Europe, who spent their Sabbath day reading it. This applies also to some other ethical books that had been translated from Hebrew into Yiddish. The books that were read by the mother or grandmother also had a Jewish influence on the children. At times the youngsters were present when these stories were read aloud in prayerful chant. From these books, too, were taken the stories that grandmother told to the little children who listened to them with avidity. However, most of the women did not know how to read or write well. They were very rarely taught Russian, and the Jewish education that they received, as pointed out before, depended mostly upon the home influence and upon the Jewish environment.

G. Summary and Critique

The Heder and Talmud Torah were educational institutions for children of elementary school age. All the writers on the subject agree that from the point of view of their physical facilities the Heder and Talmud Torah were altogether inadequate. Solomon Maimon, Lilienthal, Smolenskin, all agree that the small room, dark, dirty, and crowded, was not a fit place for school. The fact that the entire family of the teacher lived in that room and that it served at once as school, parlor, bedroom, dining room, and kitchen could not but make it, from our modern point of view, an impossible place for children. On the side of curriculum and method, too, the Heder left much to be desired. The lack of grading, the individual instruction which caused a waste of time on the part of children waiting for their turn, the fact that the child was there all day, were difficulties that the Heder did not overcome. The curriculum at times depended upon the desires of the parents, each of whom wanted to prescribe for the teacher the curriculum to be used in the instruction of their children. These shortcomings of the Heder were even intensified in the Talmud Torah, especially after Jewish autonomy ceased.

The method in vogue by which certain studies [1] were emphasized and others were neglected naturally resulted in a failure to give an all-around education even within the field of Jewish study itself. But the Heder and Talmud Torah failed not only in giving an all-around Jewish education. They failed even more in respect to secular education, a failure, however, not due to their own negligence. The utter separation of the Jewish people from the community life in which they lived, a separation which was forced upon them

[1] Rudayev, M. J., "Matarat ha-hadarim ha-metukkanim," in *Ha-zefirah*, v. 29, no. 183.

by persecution and economic and political restrictions, made it unnecessary for them to give their children a well rounded secular education. For this reason, too, the Heder and the Talmud Torah did not prepare the child for any calling in life.[1] The occupations or professions that the Jewish child might pursue were so limited by restrictive laws as to make attempts of the Jewish educational institutions to provide such training, futile. Why prepare for an occupation or a profession which your religion precluded you from pursuing?

It should not, however, be thought that the Heder and Talmud Torah failed in the purpose for which they were organized, as a result of all these difficulties. On the contrary, they succeeded in developing the kind of Judaism that was needed in a country where ghetto life was forced upon the Jew. The emphasis upon the Talmud and upon the Codes connected with it was due to the fact that in Eastern Europe these served as a means of regulating the inner life of the Jews and hence were important in the curriculum. Not only the rabbi, but also the layman, who was in any way connected with Jewish self-government in ancient Poland, had to know Talmud and the Codes to be able to act intelligently. At times the layman would even criticise the decisions of a rabbi in matters of law. Only a thorough knowledge of the sources of law would enable him to do that. In small villages that could not afford to keep a rabbi, the learned layman very often took his place, giving advice on ritual matters and at times answering questions that a rabbi would otherwise answer.

[1] Lilienblum, M., *Op. cit.*, p. 29.

Remembering, therefore, that the aim of the Heder was to produce what was known as the "edeler Yid" by opening to the child the main sources of Hebrew literature, the Bible, the Mishnah, and particularly the Talmud because it regulated life, we might well conclude that the Heder achieved its purpose. That this education was a narrow one cannot be the fault of the Jewish people, who were artificially hedged in by a government that showed its greatest ingenuity in inventing restrictions upon restrictions with which to torture one of the earliest peoples that lived under its jurisdiction. That this limitation upon Jewish education was not due to an unwillingness on the part of the Jews themselves to receive secular education may be judged from the rapidity with which the Jews flocked to the general educational institutions as soon as they were thrown open to them. Here, if anywhere, we can see the influence of the environment in shaping the curriculum of educational institutions. The Heder and the Talmud Torah, as described in the preceding pages, were but a natural consequence of the social conditions under which the Jewish people lived in Russia and Poland, and, although they did not prepare the child for a vocation, they enabled him to participate effectively in the social and religious life of the Jewish community of the ghetto.

CHAPTER V

HIGHER EDUCATION—THE YESHIBAH

A. Introductory

THE Heder and the Talmud Torah were the elementary educational institutions of Eastern Europe. The Yeshibah was the higher educational institution. If anyone wished to write a panegyric on Russo-Polish Jewry, he could do no better than describe its intellectual life and particularly its center of gravity, the Yeshibah. The education which its students received was not only an intensive one, which made for profundity of knowledge as well as for depth of mind, but also an extensive one which affected large numbers of the population. According to an estimate of Dr. Louis Ginzberg,[1] there were about five Yeshibah students to each one thousand of the Jewish population. In the countries of western Europe there are about two university students to each one thousand of the population.[2] In America the ratio is one to four hundred of the population.[3] The Yeshibahs were found in such

[1] Professor of Talmud at the Jewish Theological Seminary.

[2] Margoshes, S., *A History of the Curriculum of the Jewish Schools in Germany from the Middle of the 17th to the Middle of the 19th Century,* chap. 1, note 65.

[3] In the study made, professional schools and agricultural and technological schools were included. See "College Attendance," in *Cyclopedia of Education,* edited by Monroe.

great numbers throughout Russia that Smolenskin in describing his fictitious city in *Keburath Hamor* says that there was scarcely a home that did not house a Yeshibah student at least one day during the week.

In his *Leb Tob* Rabbi Isaac ben Eliakum (1600-1700) of Posen repeats the warning of the Talmud [1] that a Jew should study the Torah not for the sake of reward nor for the sake of becoming a rabbi, nor even for a reward in the world to come, but for its own sake. This emphasis upon study of the Torah, for its own sake, combined with the social prestige which a knowledge of Torah afforded, were undoubtedly the most important factors in producing a great number of scholars among Polish Jewry.

A rather lengthy quotation,[2] but perhaps one of the best on the Yeshibah, from the work of Rabbi Nathan Hannover, a chronicler of the 17th century, will help the reader to get a concrete idea of the nature of the institution and its organization in the early days of Polish-Jewish autonomy.

"In no country was the study of the Torah so widespread among the Jews as in the Kingdom of Poland. Every Jewish community maintained a Yeshibah, paying its president a large salary, so as to enable him to conduct the institution without worry and to devote himself entirely to the pursuit of learning. . . . Moreover, every Jewish community supported college students (bahurim), giving them a certain amount of money per week, so that they might study under the direction of the president. Every one of these bahurim

---

[1] *Talmud*—Tractate Nedarim, p. 62.

[2] Güdemann, M., *Quellenschriften,* pp. 176-178.

was made to instruct at least two boys, for the purpose of deepening his own studies and gaining some experience in Talmudic discussions. The (poor) boys obtained their food either from the charity fund or from the public kitchen. A community of fifty Jewish families would support no less than thirty of these young men and boys, one family supplying board for one college student and his two pupils, the former sitting at the family table like one of the sons. . . . There was scarcely a house in the whole Kingdom of Poland where the Torah was not studied, and where either the head of the family, or his son, or his son-in-law, or the Yeshibah student boarding with him, was not an expert in Jewish learning; frequently all of these could be found under one roof. For this reason every community contained a large number of scholars, a community of fifty families having as many as twenty learned men, who were styled Morenu or Haber. They were all excelled by the Rosh-Yeshibah, all the scholars submitting to his authority and studying under him at the Yeshibah.

"The program of study in Poland was as follows: The scholastic term during which the young men and boys were obliged to study under the Rosh Yeshibah lasted from the beginning of the month of Iyyar until the middle of Ab (approximately from April until July) in the summer, and from the first of the month of Heshwan until the fifteenth of Shebat (October to January) in the winter. Outside of these terms the young men and the boys were free to choose their own place of study. From the beginning of the summer term until Shabuot and from the beginning of the winter term until Hanukkah all the students of the Yeshibah studied with great intensity the Gemara (the Babylonian Talmud) and the commentaries of Rashi and the Tosafists.

"The scholars and the young students of the community, as well as all interested in the study of the Law, assembled daily at the Yeshibah, where the president occupied a chair, while the scholars and college students ˙stood around him. Before the appearance of the Rosh Yeshibah they would discuss questions of Jewish law, and when he arrived everyone laid his difficulties before him and received an explanation. Thereupon silence was restored and the Rosh Yeshibah delivered his lecture, presenting the new results of his study. At the conclusion of his lecture, he arranged a scientific argumentation (called Hilluk),[1] proceeding in the following way: Various contradictions in the Talmud and the commentaries were pointed out and solutions were proposed. These solutions were, in turn, shown to be contradictory, and other solutions were offered, this process being continued until the subject of discussion was completely elucidated. These exercises continued in summer at least until midday. From the middle of the two scholastic terms until their conclusion, the Rosh Yeshibah paid less attention to these argumentations and read instead the religious codes, studying with the mature scholars the Turim with commentaries, and with the (younger) students the compendium of Alfasi. . . . Several weeks before the close of the term the Rosh Yeshibah would honor the members of his college, both the scholars and the

[1] Or Pilpul.

students, by inviting them to conduct the scientific disputations on his behalf, though he himself would participate in the discussion in order to exercise the mental faculties of all those attending the Yeshibah.

"Attached to the president of the Yeshibah was an inspector, who had the duty of visiting the elementary schools, or Hadarim, daily, and seeing to it that all boys, whether poor or rich, applied themselves to study and did not loiter in the streets. On Thursdays the pupils had to present themselves before the trustee (gabbai) of the Talmud Torah, who examined them in what they had covered during the week. The boy who knew nothing or who did not answer adequately was by order of the trustee turned over to the inspector, who subjected him, in the presence of his fellow-pupils, to severe physical punishment and other painful degradations, that he might firmly resolve to improve in his studies during the following week. On Fridays the Heder pupils presented themselves in a body before the Rosh Yeshibah himself, to undergo a similar examination. This had a strong deterrent effect upon the boys, and they devoted themselves energetically to their studies. . . . The scholars, seeing this (the honors showered upon the Rosh Yeshibah), coveted the same distinction, that of becoming a Rosh Yeshibah in some community. They studied assiduously in consequence. Prompted originally by self-interest, they gradually came to devote themselves to the Torah from pure, unselfish motives." [1]

The above quotation gives a rather favorable de-

[1] Translation from Dubnow S. M., *History of the Jews in Russia and Poland,* v. 1, pp. 116-119.

scription of the Yeshibah and its method, the Hilluk or Pilpul which was its characteristic. We shall see later how such a favorable attitude is not always expressed by other writers on the Yeshibah.

B. Life at the Yeshibah

It is possible to get a better conception of the institution through an acquaintance with the life which the students led in it, the order of studies, the curriculum, and the method. Lilienblum [1] describes his own Yeshibah life and his program for the day somewhat as follows:

At ten o'clock he went to the Bet Hamidrash where the Yeshibah was located. There he studied the Talmud for about three hours in true casuistic fashion. After dinner he continued his study at the Yeshibah, the subject, however, being Hoshen Mishpat (Codes). This he continued until about five o'clock. After that, till about ten in the evening, the students reviewed by themselves the lessons which they had learned during the day with their teacher. At ten o'clock the students went home and Lilienblum tells us that he continued to study the Talmud by himself till the early hours of the morning, not getting to bed until about three or four o'clock, after extended prayers.

In general, life at the Yeshibah was not easy. The number of students at the Yeshibah varied between one hundred and two hundred.[2] These students were usually wandering scholars, as a rule not studying at

[1] Lilienblum, M. L., *Hatot Neurim,* pp. 28-29.
[2] See Smolenskin, P., *Hatoeh Bedarke Ha-hayim,* v. 1, part 1, p. 266. See also, Katzovich, I. A., *Sechzig Jahr Leben,* p. 50.

the Yeshibah in their own town. Very often, in fact, there was no Yeshibah in their own town, and they had to go far to attain the knowledge they sought. They lived at the Yeshibah, sleeping on the hard benches in the house of study, using a sack of hay for a pillow and a cloak for a covering. Their food was provided in accordance with the usual scheme of "eating days" and many a hungry student came back to the Yeshibah late at night and tried to forget his hunger in the study of a page of the Talmud. The simplicity of their demands is well described by one of them who says that after suffering hunger for two days he succeeded in buying for himself two pounds of bread for one kopek, cheese for one kopek, and a sour pickle, and he feasted upon these, considering it a kingly repast if he succeeded in adding a baked potato to his meal.[1]

The Yeshibah usually consisted of a long room or several rooms in which the pupils were seated around long tables. Others stood near their lectern. Usually they would sway to and fro, chanting the Talmud they studied with its characteristic chant. At night candles were used in addition to the synagogue lamp, although these were considered a luxury, students often trying to steal them from the beadle.

The students of the Yeshibah lived on friendly terms with each other and developed close social relationships. A brighter student would very often help a duller one and would receive his spiritual reward by hearing his pupil recite the lesson correctly before the master, the Rosh Ha-Yeshibah. This social life helped

[1] Katzovich, I. A., *Op. cit.*, p. 53.

them to bear the hardships that they underwent as did also the high regard in which the learned man was held in Eastern Europe. In fact, it has been pointed out that at the yearly fairs which were held in Poland, at which learned discussions would take place and to which the heads of the Yeshibahs brought their most distinguished students, the merchants would come to choose husbands for their daughters from amongst these students. He who was most learned had the best opportunity to be chosen the son-in-law of a rich man and to live a life of comfort for at least a few years during which he would be able to devote himself to the study of the Talmud.[1]

C. The Curriculum of the Yeshibah

Although the curriculum of the Yeshibah can be summarized by saying that it consisted of the study of the Talmud, its commentaries, and the codes arising therefrom, one really fails, from that statement alone, to conceive the wealth of material that a student had to study. In the will of Rabbi Jonah Landsofer (17th century) there is a statement which is illustrative not only of the material that was included in the curriculum but also of the attitude with which some of the people regarded these studies.[2] The material would be vast if nothing more were included than the long list of commentaries. But even more interesting is the statement that a short cut through the Talmud should include the "Tosafot, with Maharsha, R. Asher,

[1] See Kotik, E., *Meine Zikronot,* v. 2, p. 124.
[2] See Appendix B.

Rif, Ran, Rambam, Tur, Bet Joseph and Shulhan Aruk." [1]

Another description of the Yeshibah curriculum is that of the one in Vilna, given by Lilienthal in his "Travels in Russia." [2]

"The boys, when I entered the room, were rocking their bodies and 'Peot' [3] over their Gemaras, and while continuing the peculiar chant that accompanies the Talmudical study, they squinted at the strange intruder who dared to disturb them. . . . Upon my inquiry concerning the subjects of tuition, he (the teacher) told me that the boys ranging from ten to twelve years of age are instructed in this class in Humosh but more particularly in Gemara and that the Talmudical chapters treating of the civil law are taught, they being the most fitted to sharpen the intellectual faculties of the youngsters. They visit the school from morning until eight and nine o'clock in the evening, and every Friday a strict examination is held in the lessons of the week, so that on Saturday afternoon, when examined by their parents, they may do credit to the school and to themselves. In the next room the study of the Humosh is already laid aside and the 'Leienen,' study by one's self of certain lessons of the Talmud, begins. The commentaries of the Tosafot, Maharsha and others are added to the plain reading of the Talmudical text and the scholar is initiated into the labyrinth of the Pilpul. In the higher

[1] Quoted in Güdemann, M., *Quellenschriften,* pp. 133-134.

[2] Lilienthal, M., "Travels in Russia," in *Max Lilienthal, Life and Writings,* by Philipson, D., pp. 285-286.

[3] Earlocks.

classes called Halakah Tosafot, the students are kept day and night at their folio volumes, sometimes not undressing for a whole week, and sleeping only a few hours on their hard benches."

In the old Yeshibah at Odessa there was uniformly one curriculum which consisted primarily of Talmud, the Commentaries, and the Codes. Here and there, there may have been a student who also studied Russian by himself and who attracted the attention of others to that study at the same time; but he was the exception rather than the rule.[1]

D. The Method of the Yeshibah

The method of instruction at the Yeshibah was very similar to the method of teaching Talmud to advanced students in the Talmud Heder. The head of the Yeshibah gave an assignment which had to be prepared for the next day when he called upon one of the students to recite. On this occasion, the student showed to what extent he grasped the method of the Talmud as well as its content. Everybody listened attentively, and the head of the Yeshibah had the opportunity of making his remarks, at times correcting wrong interpretations or making clear difficult passages.[2]

But most characteristic of the method of the Yeshibah, was the Pilpul [3] or the casuistry which accompanied all its instruction. Rabbi Samuel Edels (16th century), famous as Maharsha, a commentator on the Talmud, says, in criticism of the method in vogue,

[1] Katzovich I., *Op. cit.*, p. 54.
[2] *Ibid.*, p. 50.
[3] For description of Pilpul, see p. 128.

"Whoever understands better the crooked casuistry at the disputations of the present time is accorded greater respect." [1]

So widely was this pilpulism spread that many of the great rabbis opposed it on the ground that it prevented true information and emphasized mental trickery instead.   Amongst those prominent in attacking this method were the Maharal of Prague, Rabbi Isaiah Horowitz, his son Sheftel, Rabbi Hayim Yair Bacharach, and many others. [2]

Pilpulism was so well developed that at the disputations the participants at times asked questions and gave answers which neither the questioner nor the answerer understood but which made an impression upon the audience.   At times, in the heat of the discussion, invective would be used as is evidenced by the fact that Rabbi Sheftel warns against it.   We see, therefore, that the method of the Hilluk or Pilpul which was so favorably described by Rabbi Hannover in the quotation previously given, is not always approved by other writers.   In fact, a very severe condemnation of this method is given by the well-known preacher Solomon Ephraim of Lenchitza (d. 1619). This quotation is too famous to be omitted and will serve as a summary of the attitude of those who were unfavorably disposed to the pilpulistic method.

"The whole instruction at the Yeshibah," he writes, "reduces itself to mental equilibristics and empty argu-

[1] Güdemann, M., Op. cit., p. 77.   Originally found in Ein Ya-akob, Baba Mezia, folio 7.

[2] See Margoshes, S., Op. cit., pp. 25-26, chap. 1 and notes thereto.

mentations called Hilluk. It is dreadful to contemplate that some venerable rabbi, presiding over a Yeshibah, in his anxiety to discover and communicate to others some new interpretation, should offer a perverted explanation of the Talmud, though he himself and everyone else be fully aware that the true meaning is different. Can it be God's will that we sharpen our minds by fallacies and sophistries, spending our time in vain and teaching the listeners to do likewise? And all this for the mere ambition of passing for a great scholar! . . . I myself have more than once argued with the Talmudic celebrities of our time, showing the need for abolishing the method of Pilpul and Hilluk, without being able to convince them. This attitude can only be explained by the eagerness of these scholars for honors and Rosh-Yeshibah posts. These empty quibbles have a particularly pernicious effect on our bahurs, for the reason that the bahur who does not shine in the discussion is looked down upon as incapable, and is practically forced to lay aside his studies, though he might prove to be one of the best, if Bible, Mishnah, Talmud, and the Codes were studied in a regular fashion. I myself have known capable young men, who, not having distinguished themselves in Pilpul, forfeited the respect of their fellow-students, and stopped studying altogether after their marriage." [1]

E. Special Subjects of Study at the Yeshibah

Another subject of study in the Yeshibah, though not a regular subject of the curriculum, was the Kab-

[1] Quoted in Dubnow, S. M., *Op. cit.,* v. 1, pp. 119-120.

balah or mystic lore.[1] This study represented the reaction of mysticism to legalism. It was the attempt
to approach the divine through feeling and imagination, rather than through learned discussion and
reasoning. It involved people in the search for "mysterious" interpretations of the Bible, and in its practical results led to stimulation of the imagination and
to asceticism. In the Yeshibah this was reflected in
the study of the Zohar and the reading of other mys-
tical books. So widespread was this study that complaints were made against the numbers of the unfit
who entered upon it. Thus one complaint is as follows:
"Each one jumps at the study of the Kabbalah, which
captures the eye, and not only the initiated attempt
it, but even the ordinary men who cannot tell their
right hand from their left, who walk in darkness, who
do not know how to explain a Sidrah or even a chapter
of the Pentateuch with the commentary of Rashi,
hasten to the study of the Kabbalah." [2] On the other
hand, we find some rabbis advising that after a student has studied the Bible and Talmud sufficiently, he
should devote himself "with reverence and fear, with
holiness and purity,[3] to the study of the Kabbalah."

Besides the Kabbalah, there were few special subjects studied at the Yeshibah. Nevertheless, the students pursued some subjects of study which were not
in the official curriculum. The study of Ibn Ezra
included mathematics. The books of Maimonides

[1] See Ginzberg, L., "Kabbalah," in *Jewish Encyclopedia.*
[2] Margoshes, S., *Op. cit.,* chap. 1, note 94.
[3] Rabbi Isaiah Horowitz in *Shene Luhot Ha-berit,* Tractate
Shabuot. Quoted in Margoshes, S., *Op. cit.,* note 92 to chap. 1.

involved philosophy and medicine, while the *Seder Ha-dorot* [1] and the *Zemah David* [2] provided the Yeshibah bahur with historical information. Rabbi Israel Samosz [3] advises the need of overcoming any discrepancies between the Talmud and mathematics, geometry, and optics, since these sciences rest on a firm foundation. In this way, although the official curriculum of the Yeshibah stressed the Talmud, the Commentaries, and Codes, which were so closely related to the environment of the Jew, the actual studies pursued by the students covered a much wider range of knowledge and gave them more of a general education than their curriculum implied.

F. The Yeshibah of Volozhin

One of the most important Yeshibahs in Russia will serve as a typical illustration of that educational institution. The Volozhin Yeshibah was not only important because of the great number of students who attended it, but also because of the influence that it had upon other institutions and because of its fame for scholarship. Many intelligent young men of all strata of Jewry came to study at Volozhin. A description of the activities of that Yeshibah will therefore help us to see more concretely the higher educational institution as a type.

In his "Travels in Russia" Lilienthal describes this institution and its physical facilities. "It was a spa-

[1] By Jehiel Halpern (1670-1746).
[2] By David Gans (1541-1613).
[3] In his introduction to *Nezah Yisrael* (pub. in 1741), quoted in Güdemann, M., *Quellenschriften,* pp. 194-195.

cious stone building containing several large halls in which the students were studying. The furniture was of the most ordinary description. Rough long tables, surrounded by barren wooden benches, some long shelves filled with a large Hebrew library, an Aron Kodesh, with a few Sifre Torah and a pulpit for the reader was all the furniture within these halls." [1]

In these simple halls the students continued their studies of the Talmud and the Codes, day in and day out, swaying their bodies, to and fro, as they studied.

The program of the day began early in the morning with prayers. Presence at the services was compulsory, and at the beginning of the week was followed by an announcement of the program of the week by the Rosh-Yeshibah. Following that the students had to prepare themselves for the regular Shiur which was later explained by the teacher. In the afternoon they studied by themselves till the time of evening prayers. This study usually lasted until about eight o'clock in the summer time and till ten o'clock in the winter time. [2] After supper, many a student returned to the Yeshibah and remained there for the rest of the night studying the Talmud, getting only a few hours' sleep on the hard benches as dawn approached. Others would come home and spend their evening, as little of it as was left, in secular studies, in this way supplementing the thorough Talmudical training that they received at the Yeshibah.

At meal time these students were received with joy

[1] Lilienthal, M., "Travels in Russia," in *Max Lilienthal, Life and Writings,* by Philipson, D., pp. 348-349.

[2] Hurwitz, M. M., *Derek Ez Ha-hayim,* p. 111.

by the particular family with whom they boarded, the table was prepared, the meal was on the table, and the student began a simple repast while the women of the house excitedly said to the other members of the house, "Sh—, do not disturb him, the Yeshibah Bahur is eating." When through, he recorded the cost of his meal, usually about six or seven kopeks, and went back to the Yeshibah to continue his studies.

This scheme of support was different from what it was in most other Yeshibahs. As we have previously seen, in most cases the students were supported on the scheme of "eating days." This was not the case in Volozhin. Here the founder, Rabbi Hayim, appealed to the Jews throughout the country, and his appeal was responded to with generosity. Yearly collections were made for the Yeshibah, and these collections were sufficient to maintain the students. Of course their demands were modest. Out of the four hundred students that were at Volozhin, about sixty were married men and three hundred and forty unmarried. The married men received two to three rubles weekly. The boys received sixty to seventy kopeks weekly. This was sufficient to support them without being dependent upon getting a "day" at a different family as was done in other Yeshibahs.[1] This scheme of support made this Yeshibah more popular than others and helped to increase the number of students, since Volozhin was the one place where the students did not have to worry about their daily food.

The subjects of study were primarily the Talmud

[1] See Hurwitz, M. M., *Op. cit.,* p. 108. See also *Ozar Ha-sifrut,* Third year, p. 15. Also "Arba-ah Olamot," in *Hakerem.*

and the Codes. Here, as throughout Eastern Europe, the aim was to teach the sources rather than to develop principles or points of view. The discussion of the Talmud was followed, and the laws of the Codes were studied, without any attempt to formulate principles.[1] Secular studies were not included in the curriculum of the Yeshibah till the days of the Haskalah period when the introduction of the teaching of Russian was made compulsory for the Yeshibah. Many a young man would, after twelve to fourteen hours of study in the Yeshibah, go home to study reading or writing in the secular languages. In this way it came about that there was considerable general culture among the students.

Finally, under the pressure of the Russian government, compulsory measures were attempted in order to change the curriculum of the Yeshibah. These measures failed, and the Yeshibah of Volozhin was closed by the Russian authorities in 1892.

G. Summary

Jewish education in the ghetto environment faithfully attempted to fulfill its aim through its educational institutions. The Heder developed the man who attained sufficient knowledge to read the Bible with its Hebrew commentaries or to read various other Hebrew books. The Yeshibah developed the Lamddan, the lay scholar, and the learned rabbi. The Yeshibah emphasized that which the ghetto required—a knowledge of the sources of Jewish literature. To the extent that Pentateuch, Mishnah. and especially Talmud and

[1] See *Hakerem,* p. 65.

the Codes were the means of regulating the life of the people, they were of importance in the education given to the child in Russia and Poland. The curriculum of the Yeshibah was intensive, and concentrated in the study of the Talmud and the Codes. This emphasis was constant for centuries until a new wave of ideas brought about by the coming of Haskalah—enlightenment—penetrated the thick walls of the ghetto and permitted rays of light from without to play upon its oppressed inhabitants.

PART III

JEWISH EDUCATION UNDER THE INFLUENCE OF HASKALAH AND JEWISH NATIONALISM

CHAPTER VI

JEWISH EDUCATION OF THE HASKALAH

A. HASKALAH IN GERMANY

THE Haskalah movement in Russia can hardly be
understood without a knowledge of its source, Germany, and Mendelssohn, its leader in Germany. The
hopes of emancipation on the part of the Jews in Germany were reflected in new intellectual pursuits on
their part. Moses Mendelssohn was the expression of
a new intellectual movement which aimed at bringing
the Jews in close touch with general culture. As an
exponent of both Jewish knowledge and secular knowledge, Mendelssohn contributed greatly toward the
secularization of culture and toward the widening of
the mental horizon of the Jew. His translation of the
Bible into German was a significant event and stimulated the Jews to study the German language and
literature, with the view of becoming a part of the
general population.

Under the influence of Mendelssohn, the Jewish Free
School of Berlin was organized (1778).[1] This was

[1] Kohler, M. J., "Educational Reforms in Europe in Relation
to Jewish Emancipation," in *Jewish Forum*, v. 2, pp. 704-715,
775-788. See Ritter, I. H., *Geschichte der Jüdischen Reformation,* chap. 4.

the first Jewish school in Germany in which French
and German were taught as well as Hebrew and to
which Christian pupils were admitted. The presence
of Christian teachers in the school and the mingling of
the Jewish and Christian school population were facts
quite unusual in those days.

At the same time the Toleration Edicts of Joseph II
of Austria (1781) gave an impetus to the establishment
of modern German Jewish schools as well as to the
attendance of Jews in the public schools. In this way,
under the influence of contact of peoples and cultures,
the curriculum of the Jewish school in Germany underwent a fundamental change.

As is pointed out by a writer on the curriculum in
Germany, "When the secularization of European culture went hand in hand with the idea of tolerance,
allowing not merely for a one-sided show of cultural
force, but instead for a free interplay of intellectual
powers, the conditions were created for that intimate
contact between the Jewish culture on the one hand
and the non-Jewish culture on the other, which, as
always, as in Alexandria, Babylon, Spain and Italy had
been productive of a change in the Jewish cultural
ideal." [1]

The following is a summary of the changes which
resulted in the curriculum of German Jewry, and it
will be interesting to compare these with those resulting from the Haskalah movement in Russia. [2]

[1] Margoshes, S., *A History of the Curriculum of the Jewish
Schools in Germany from the Middle of the 17th to the Middle
of the 19th Century,* chap. 2, p. 3.

[2] *Ibid.,* chap. 3, pp. 13-19.

1. The secular studies gradually encroached upon the time of Jewish studies.
2. The study of the Talmud was gradually decreased and later altogether eliminated.
3. Bible was studied with the German translation of Mendelssohn and given more emphasis than previously, when, as we already know, Bible had been slighted for the sake of Talmud which was the end-all of the curriculum.
4. Hebrew was studied as a separate subject apart from Bible, and considerable stress was laid on grammar which had previously been neglected.
5. Religion was introduced as a special subject, and the catechism was taught—something which is characteristically un-Jewish.
6. Moral instruction was introduced as a separate subject and taught by a method not hitherto employed in the Jewish school. Verses of the Bible were memorized, moral lessons "drawn" from stories, etc.
7. Jewish history, a new subject, was introduced but only Biblical history was taught and the biographical method was used.
8. General subjects were taught—German reading and writing, French reading and writing, English (sometimes taught) for its commercial value, Latin (in a few schools), arithmetic, penmanship, nature study, geography, universal history, drawing, singing of secular and patriotic songs, bookkeeping (as leading to commercial vocations), manual training, and horticulture.

The aim of these schools was to introduce the Jews to, and develop within them a love for, German culture. How well they succeeded in attaining this aim may be judged from the following statement:

"Less than half a century after the Jews had been scolded for not participating in the culture of the German people and attempts had been begun to educate the Jewish youth, Jewish activity in all fields of German cultural endeavor was so great that bitter cries arose against the Judaizing of German culture." [1]

The old Jewish school in Germany gradually disappeared and by the end of the first half of the 19th century almost all Yeshibahs in Germany had disappeared.[2] The new schools took their place, or the Jews attended the general educational institutions to which they were freely admitted as the years went by. The Jewish school in Germany became a supplementary religious school for the teaching of religion, Biblical history, translation of the Hebrew text of the Bible, and sufficient Hebrew to understand the prayers. The emancipation hopes in Germany had revolutionized Jewish educational conditions in that country.

B. The Beginning of Haskalah [3] in Russia

Hopes of emancipation in Russia and the example of German Haskalah led to the rise of a similar movement in Russia. The Jews of Russia, downtrodden and oppressed, hoped that their country, too, would follow the example of Germany and Austria and that the only requirement for civil equality would be their assimilation of general culture. That this was not the case they soon learned from the sad experiences that

[1] Margoshes, S., *Op. cit.,* chap. 3, p. 9.

[2] *Ibid.,* chap. 3, p. 55.

[3] See Raisin, J. S., *The Haskalah Movement in Russia.* Also Wengeroff, P., *Op. cit.,* v. 2, pp. 5-22.

followed. No wonder, then, that Haskalah in Russia was not nearly so revolutionary as in Germany. In Germany Haskalah led to complete assimilation. In Russia Haskalah led to Jewish nationalism.

The hopes that were stirring the hearts and rousing the minds of Jews everywhere are well reflected in the words of Wessely. Anxious to convince the Jews of the need of coming closer to the people that surrounded them, he overestimated the tendencies on the part of the rulers to treat their Jewish subjects like human beings and even included the Czarina of Russia in his enumeration of rulers who were humanizing in their influence.[1]

Wessely, who was one of the most important followers of Mendelssohnian enlightenment in the field of education, gives a description in his "Words of Peace and Truth," of the shortcomings of the old education and the new changes that the movement for enlightenment was trying to bring about. After a description of the evils of the old curriculum which, he points out, are the same in Germany as in Poland, he states the reason why the Jews have failed to introduce secular studies into their curriculum.

His analysis of the reasons clearly places the responsibility upon the unfriendly environment in which the people lived and is worth quoting as an interesting illustration of the fact that the environment affected the curriculum and that this effect was recognized by a writer on education.

"But know ye, that *we* are not guilty of this. . . . but the *nations* that were before us for more than a

[1] Wessely, N. H., *Dibre Shalom We-Emet,* Letter 2, p. 94.

thousand years . . . for they have done evil to us, through the decrees of their kings and advisers, and because of ulterior motives, have risen against us to cut us off and to lower us to the very earth; they have issued evil decrees that are contrary to good sense, they have rebelled against the laws of humanity, for they have lowered us in the dust and throttled our spirit within us. As a result the hearts of our people have become darkened and they have ceased to study secular subjects, seeing that our people are dealt with heavily and that in the eyes of their rulers they are considered beneath the state of humankind. Therefore they despised everything under the sun, seeing that they had no share or inheritance in all the good with which God had endowed his creatures from one end of the world to the other, and in the bitterness of their hearts they have forsaken those studies, the object of which is a knowledge of the laws of the heavenly and terrestrial bodies, to trace the course of the constellations, to study agriculture, to go into the depths of the seas, to build cities and towers, and to learn the laws of people and the ways of government. For, they said, why do we need all this? Are not the inhabitants of our own land our enemies? Our advice they do not accept, our energies they do not utilize; fields and vineyards we have not; let us therefore leave off these studies . . . and let us interest ourselves only in those things that bring eternal life, which are the laws of God and his commandments." [1]

But now that the benevolent rulers are removing the difficulties that were in the way of emancipation

[1] Wessely, N. H., *Op. cit.,* Letter 1, pp. 9-10.

the Jew must respond by changing his education. "The education of Jewish boys is divided into two parts, the first part deals with the education of man, comprising such studies as are needed for one who styles himself man and without which one does not deserve to be classed as man. The second part deals with the law of God, comprising laws of God that transcend all human faculties and which were known to Moses only by prophecy, laws which are binding only upon us as Children of Israel." [1]

Wessely then urges the study of German, history, geography, arithmetic, geometry, astronomy, zoölogy, botany, physics, anatomy, medicine. He deplores the fact that Hebrew has not been taught grammatically and that "religious instruction has not been properly organized." [2] He advises the introduction of textbooks for the teaching of religion and ethics, morals and manners, the use of the catechetical method, and the study of the Bible with Mendelssohn's translation. [3] He urges the minimizing of instruction in Talmud sufficiently to allow time for other studies that are important to develop the child into an intelligent and worthy man. [4]

That these tendencies in Germany would influence the Haskalah movement in Russia was to be expected. At the beginning of the 19th century, "Berlinerdom," the forerunner of "Haskalah," entered Russia. The Berliner was a man who "arrayed himself in a short

---

[1] Wessely, N. H., *Op. cit.*, Letter 1.
[2] *Ibid.*, Letter 1, p. 2.
[3] *Ibid.*, Letter 2, p. 63.
[4] *Ibid.*, Letter 2, pp. 64-68.

German coat, cut off his earlocks, shaved his beard, neglected the religious observances, spoke German or the language of the land, and swore by the name of Moses Mendelssohn. The culture of which he was the banner bearer was a rather shallow enlightenment, which affected exterior and form, rather than mind and heart." [1]

Russian Jewry had no great Russian culture to be attracted to in the early days of German Haskalah. Hence it followed German culture. This meant the study of German, which could not possibly have the favorable results upon Jewry in Russia that it had upon Jewry in Germany. Yet many Jews in Russia began to read Schiller and study him in true Talmudic fashion. [2]

These changes came slowly into Russian Jewish life. At the time that in Germany the old forms of Jewish life were giving way to the new, Russian Jewry maintained itself unchanged. Secular culture was hardly permitted to enter. Rabbinism and Hasidism were struggling against each other. But it was a struggle of scholasticism against mysticism, of casuistry against simplicity of faith. It was a struggle as to the kind of a Jew one should be.

Within the folds of Jewish life, however, "one could even detect a certain amount of toleration towards the anathematized 'secular sciences,' though this toleration was limited to the realm of mathematics and

[1] Dubnow, S. M., *History of the Jews in Russia and Poland*, v. 1, p. 384. See also Kotik, E., *Meine Zikronot*, v. 2, pp. 148-152.

[2] Wengeroff, P., *Memoiren einer Grossmutter*, v. 2, pp. 30-31.

partly that of natural history." [1] Rabbi Elijah of
Vilna introduced the method of textual criticism and
substituted it for the many "castles of casuistry in the
air," that had been in vogue. He also studied logic,
grammar, and geometry [2] and "permitted his pupil
Baruch Shklover to publish a Hebrew translation of
Euclid's Geometry" (1780). Yet the dread of philosophy was as great as heretofore and the incompatibility
of free research with Judaism was looked upon as an
inviolable dogma. The Jewish mind continued to
move within "the four ells of the Halakah and was
doomed to sterility." [3]

Efforts at secularization of Jewish literature and
education were nevertheless made. Mendel Levin
translated into Hebrew some popular works on medicine and travel. Tobias Feder published some moraliz-
ing treatises, satires, and odes.[4] Mordecai A. Günzburg
(1796-1846), one of a group of Vilna Maskilim, as
these bearers of enlightenment were called, translated
into Hebrew Campe's *Discovery of America* and
Politz's *Universal History*. He wrote a history of
the Franco-Russian War of 1812 in Hebrew.[5] These
were the first books on secular subjects written in pure
Hebrew.

[1] Dubnow, S. M., *Op. cit.*, v. 1, p. 381.
[2] Fünn, S. J., *Safah Lene-e-manim*, p. 133. See also Hurwitz,
Saul Israel, *Me-ayin le-ayin*, pp. 184 ff; also Jawitz, Wolf, "Mig-
dal Ha-meah," in *Keneset Israel*, edited by S. P. Rabinowitz, pp.
130-145.
[3] Dubnow, S. M., *Op. cit.*, v. 1, p. 381.
[4] *Ibid.*, v. 1, p. 388.
[5] *Ibid.*, v. 2, pp. 133-134.

"A Jewish author of a book in the Russian language appears in the person of Loeb Nevaknovich as early as 1803." [1] Isaac Baer Levinsohn, the Russian Mendelssohn, knew the Russian language and came in contact with the current of Russian thought as far as Jewish matters were concerned. In his famous work, *Teudah BeYisrael*, he discusses some questions fundamental to Russian Jewry, such as:

1. Is it permissible to study languages other than Hebrew?
2. Should one engage in secular studies?
3. If permissible, what advantages might these bring?
4. If there are advantages, are they not counteracted by harm done to religion as a result of these? [2]

In this argument the author of course concludes that the study of Bible and Hebrew demands a knowledge of grammar, that our sages studied it, that the rabbis always urged the study of the language of the country in whose midst the Jewish people lived, that the great men of all ages engaged in secular studies, and that many great Jews made their contributions in languages other than Hebrew. [3]

All these men who translated, wrote, and in every possible way urged the study of secular subjects and the study of Russian were the harbingers of the change that was to come upon Russian Jewry and to

[1] Wiernik, P., "General Educational Problems and the First Modern Schools," in *Jewish Forum*, v. 1, no. 7, p. 389.

[2] See *Teudah BeYisrael*, by I. B. Levinsohn, Int., p. 14. See also Fünn, S. J., *Op. cit.*, pp. 151-154.

[3] See also Teitelbaum, Mordecai, *Harab Mi-Lodi Umifleget Habad*, for what Rabbi Schneur Zalmon (1747) studied.

culminate in the second and third quarters of the 19th century.

This change was soon reflected in the Neo-Hebrew literature of Russia and in changes in the educational institutions. J. L. Gordon depicted in his poetry the glorious days of emancipation and called upon the Jew to interact with his fellow men in his famous dictum, "Be a man without, a Jew within your home." He attacked Rabbinism and favored the secularization of Jewish culture. Mendele Mokher Sefarim, father of modern Yiddish and "grandfather of Neo-Hebrew literature," and others satirized the inner life of Russian Jewry and the half-hearted attitude of the government which stimulated reactionary groups.

Educationally this movement was reflected in the rise of new schools and in changes in the old. Instruction in Russian, in vocational education, in citizenship, in agriculture was urged. A curriculum advocated for a school system in Vilna includes reading, prayers (translation and explanation), religious precepts, Pentateuch with commentary, writing, Prophets, grammar, Mishnah, Russian, arithmetic, German; for gifted children, a more intensive study of Bible, Mishnah, and Talmud, higher mathematics, geography, and history, and for the less able, training for vocations.[1]

C. The Introduction of the Crown Schools

The changes that were introduced in the Jewish educational institutions of Russia came not only on the initiative of the Maskilim but also as a result of the

[1] See Kaufman, Arkadya Aaron, "Miktab Al Debar Ha-hinuk," in *Pirhe Zafon,* pp. 43-61.

stimulus of the government. The so-called Crown Schools that were organized by the government were the new institutions that were intended to meet the needs of Jewry looking to a changed Russia. By a special imperial edict issued on November 13, 1844, arrangements were made for the establishment of the following new schoools: (1) elementary schools of the first grade or elementary city schools; (2) second grade schools or district schools; (3) rabbinical schools for the training of teachers and rabbis. The organization of these schools was to be undertaken by the Ministry of Public Instruction.[1] At the same time, the Jewish schools hitherto existing were placed under the supervision of this Ministry.

The general aim of these schools naturally would be to secularize Jewish education and to enable the child to come nearer to the general Russian environment. A rabbinical commission was set to work on a program of studies for the government schools (1843). Some Jewish teachers were to be imported from Bavaria, Prussia, and Austria where enlightenment had already started, and "Learned Jews" were to supervise the new schools that the government founded. The government schools would naturally be under the supervision of the state inspectors who, together with the Learned Jews, would be responsible for the general and the Jewish aspects of the curriculum pursued. The entrance requirements were a reading knowledge of Hebrew, knowing by heart the most frequently used prayers, and a knowledge of two books of the Pentateuch. The cost of the schools was to be met through

[1] *Spravochnaya Kniga,* pp. 45-46.

a special tax on the candles lit in Jewish homes on Friday evening. The Jews who attended these schools were to be given privileges similar to the privileges of those who attended the general schools. Military service was to be lessened and in exceptional cases altogether abolished.

Coming, however, as these schools did, from a government that was known to be cruel to the Jews, that had entered upon a policy of compulsory conversion, that had expelled thousands from various parts of the country, and that taxed the people heavily and excluded them from human rights, it was natural for the schools to be regarded with suspicion by the masses of Jewish people. The unfavorable response to them will therefore be less of a surprise to us, than the fact that in spite of the attitude of Nicholas and his government toward the Jews, there were some people who spoke enthusiastically in favor of them. Many a progressive helped the government in its efforts and appeals were made pointing out, even exaggerating, the good intentions of the government in founding the Crown Schools and the two seminaries in Vilna and Zhitomir.[1] Nicholas was even declared by some of these to be a benefactor of Russian Jewry, and many progressives desirous of general education hailed the coming of the Crown Schools. But under the circumstances it could not be expected that the masses would overcome the mental attitude that was created by the many examples of severe oppression displayed by Nicholas. As a result the urging of the Maskilim was of little avail. Even the work of Isaac Baer Levinsohn in his *Teudah*

[1] Gurland, Jacob, *Kebod Habayit*.

BeYisrael, which was written to prove the advisability
of the Jews entering the schools, was of little help.[1]
The Jews regarded all the Maskilim as heretics and
refused to accept their advice or to enter the government schools. Rabbinism was strongly intrenched, and
it was well that it was so, or it could not have prevented Jewry from disrupting under the unfavorable
conditions of Nicholas I. It used strict measures
against youths who set out to imitate the customs of
the Berliners. The slightest deviation from custom was
looked upon with much suspicion and regarded as a
means of helping the government to de-Judaize the
Jews. Talmudism and pilpulism reigned supreme
especially in Lithuania, and a study of extraneous
sciences meant persecution or excommunication for
the offenders.

Hasidism, too, with its mysticism and miraculous
stories of the Rabbis could hardly be open to extraneous knowledge. "Hasidism and Zaddikism were, so to
speak, a sleeping draught which dulled the pain of the
blows dealt out to the unfortunate Jewish population
by the Russian government; but in the long run the
popular organism was injuriously affected by this
mystic opium. Its poison rendered its consumers in-
sensible to every progressive movement and planted
them firmly at the extreme of obscurantism, at a time
when the Russian ghetto resounded with the first appeals calling its inmates toward the light, toward the
regeneration of inner Jewish life." [2]

[1] See p. 154.
[2] Dubnow, S. M., *Op. cit.,* v. 2, p. 125.

D. THE WORK OF LILIENTHAL

In considering the introduction of the new schools into Russia, mention should be made of the work of Max Lilienthal whose brilliant career in Russia suddenly ended when he learned what the intentions of the Russian government really were.

In 1840 Lilienthal, a young German Rabbi, was called to Riga to take charge of a modern Hebrew school. His experiment was very successful. He knew German, was a "modern," and was very popular at that time in Riga. The first public address that he delivered made a profound impression. Lilienthal was praised by the Czar and by Uvarov, the Minister of Public Instruction.[1] In 1841 Lilienthal went to meet Uvarov in St. Petersburg (Petrograd). At this meeting a discussion took place concerning the problem of regenerating the Jews of Russia. Lilienthal expressed his opinion as follows: "Let the Emperor at once proclaim the emancipation of the Jews and then let him issue any ukase whatever to begin the work of Jewish reform in earnest, to cut short the exclusive study of the Talmud, and although totally unacquainted with the character of the Russian Jews, I dare to vouch that ten years hence they will surpass the most sanguine expectations of the Imperial Government." [2] To this contention Uvarov answered that the Jews must first win the favor of the Emperor by showing that they are worthy of emancipation. Further discussion then led

[1] Wiernik, P., "Max Lilienthal," in *Jewish Forum,* v. 1, no. 8.
[2] Lilienthal, M., "Travels in Russia," in *Max Lilienthal, Life and Writings,* by Philipson, D., p. 197.

to the suggestion of introducing special schools for the Jewish population where secular studies would be taught and where, at the same time, the children would receive a Jewish education at the hands of Jewish teachers.[1]

Lilienthal had a series of such conferences and had occasion, as he tells us in his "Travels," to point out to the Minister of Public Instruction that if it should turn out that the educational scheme of the government was a pretext for proselytism, the Jews would undergo the greatest suffering, but they would under no circumstances give up their religion. Lilienthal seems to have left Uvarov convinced that the intentions of the Russian government concerning the Jews were sincere. He then began to correspond with leaders of enlightenment in Germany and obtained a list of about two hundred people who were subsequently to come to Russia to undertake the work of enlightening Russian Jewry.[2] Lilienthal then proceeded to make a tour to convince the Russian Jews of the advisability of attending the Crown Schools and of co-operating with the Russian government in its plans. The elders of Vilna warned Lilienthal concerning the intentions of the Russian government in these words: "You are a stranger; do you know what you are undertaking? The course pursued against all denominations but the Greek proves clearly that the government in-

[1] Lilienthal, M., "Travels in Russia," in *Op. cit.,* p. 194.

[2] Lilienthal also wrote to Samuel David Luzzato for a program of the Rabbinical College in Padua which was under his direction (1841). See *Igrot Shadal,* published by Shealtiel Isaac Graber (Przemysl, 1882), v. 4, pp. 733-734.

tends to have but one church in the whole empire; that
it has in view only its own future strength and great-
ness and not our future prosperity. We are sorry to
state that we put no confidence in the new measures
proposed by the ministerial council and that we are
looking with gloomy foreboding into the future." [1]

To this statement of the Vilna elders, Lilienthal answered, "All that I can promise you as your co-religion-
ist, is that I shall not go a step further in promoting
the plans of the government before having obtained
the assurance that nothing will be undertaken against
our holy religion, that I shall lay down my office as
soon as I shall become convinced of the contrary and
that no offence on the part of my brethren shall excuse
me from breaking this promise I am making to you in
this solemn hour." [2]

When Lilienthal came to Minsk, he found the people, Hasidim and Mithnaggedim alike, united to defeat
him.[3] It was to be expected that Lilienthal would find
it difficult to convince a people, subjected to compulsory conversion by means of militarism, who could
not but regard these schools as a means of helping in
the process. After failing to convince the people of
Vilna and Minsk,[4] Lilienthal told Uvarov frankly of
his failure and suggested that a conference be called
of the representatives of the Jews themselves and that
in this way the confidence of the people would be won.
Lilienthal then toured the country once more to urge

[1] Lilienthal, M., "Travels in Russia," in *Op. cit.*, p. 264.
[2] *Ibid.*, p. 206.
[3] *Ibid.*, p. 306.
[4] Fünn, S. J., *Op. cit.*, pp. 171-172.

the election of delegates to such a conference.[1] This time he was greeted cheerfully in Vilna and Minsk, as well as in other cities of Russia.[2] The diary of Lilienthal concerning his travels in Russia suddenly breaks off at this point but the general events that followed are well known. In 1844 the government issued two decrees, one of which was public and called for the establishment of Jewish schools. The other was confidential and stated that "the aim pursued in the training of the Jews is that of bringing them nearer to the Christian population and eradicating the prejudices fostered in them by the study of the Talmud— and that as soon as the Crown Schools have been established in sufficient numbers, attendance at them would become obligatory, that the superintendents of the new schools should only be chosen from among Christians."[3] The government also realized that many Maskilim were to be found in Russia itself who would be glad to help in the execution of the policy, not knowing of the true intentions of the government. As a result, they gave up the idea of importing teachers from Germany, a fact which must have caused considerable difficulty to Lilienthal who had previously invited about two hundred men to come to Russia.[4]

[1] Fünn, S. J., *Op. cit.*, pp. 172-174.

[2] The members of the Rabbinical Conference were: Rabbi Menahem Mendel of Lubawitch of the Hasidim; Rabbi Isaac Ben Hayim of the Volozhin Yeshibah; Israel Heilpern and Bezalel Stern. Lilienthal and Mandelstamm also participated in the conference.

[3] Dubnow, S. M., *Op. cit.*, v. 2, p. 58.

[4] Wiernik, P., "The New Learned Jew," in *Jewish Forum*, v. 2, no. 6.

This, combined with the fact that, in spite of assurances of Uvarov that there was no desire to convert the Jews, the government continued the process of conversion through militarism and did not keep faith with Lilienthal, resulted in his sudden leaving for the United States (1848), in this way fulfilling the promise that he had made to the elders of Vilna.

E. Leon Mandelstamm

After the sudden departure of Lilienthal to the United States, Bezalel Stern, principal of a modern Hebrew school in Odessa, was made curator of education of New Russia. He died shortly after entering office, and Leon Mandelstamm was appointed "Learned Jew" instead. Mandelstamm himself is an interesting example of the Maskil of those days. His early education at the hands of his father was based upon Mendelssohn's translation of the Bible, the use of which was considered heresy at the time. The child pursued the usual course of study in Talmud and was considered an "Illui" [1] at the age of twelve.[2] He studied sciences, modern languages, and Hebrew poetry and acquired some ability to speak Russian. Philosophy, mathematics, and philology were studied one after another. Contrary to the desire of his relatives, he continued to study Russian after his marriage, and left home to prepare himself for entrance into a university. After a number of difficulties because of his accent and because the road to education was not easy for a Jew, he was finally given special permission to

[1] A prodigy.
[2] Wiernik, P., "Leon Mandelstamm," in *Jewish Forum*, v. 1.

enter the Moscow University.[1] Mandelstamm, the first Jew to receive a diploma from a Russian university, acted as secretary of the rabbinical conference and took the place of Lilienthal when the latter left. He supervised the schools and the rabbinical seminaries and disbursed the funds for school expenditures. He prepared school books and translated the Bible into Russian.

Some of the progressives hailed Mandelstamm as they had hailed Lilienthal before him, but the masses of the people could not get themselves to see the educational activity of the government divorced from the oppression and the cruelty which it continually inflicted upon the people, and therefore rejected anyone who was associated with the new educational schemes of the government. In 1857 Mandelstamm, too, suddenly gave up his work with the government. The reason for his resignation is not known.

F. The Society for the Diffusion of Enlightenment amongst the Jews of Russia

One of the important factors in the process of secularization of instruction amidst Russian Jewry was the Society for the Diffusion of Enlightenment amongst the Jews of Russia. Here and there in a community there was an individual, perhaps, who was a "modern," studied the Prophets instead of studying only or primarily the Talmud and medieval Jewish philosophy, and tried hard to learn Russian and German secretly. But on the whole the opposition to the Haskalah and especially to the Crown Schools was great. The

[1] See Appendix C.

schools were opposed on principle by some people and
for economic reasons by the Melammedim who feared
them as substitutes for the Hadarim.[1] When schools
were opened they were in many instances, "desolate,
no one attended them and only the poor brought their
children thither." [2] The Christian principal who was
usually appointed to organize a school came to the
leaders of the community and urged them to get a
student body. The poor or the orphans were usually
enrolled, parents being at times paid for sending their
children. Thus, in a city of ten thousand Jews only
twenty-seven pupils were in attendance (1852). The
principals were often embarrassed and reported as
attending many pupils who had left.

But, with the increase of liberties under Alexander
II, the need became felt for an organized effort to
spread Haskalah amidst the masses. The Society for
the Diffusion of Enlightenment was organized by the
Maskilim, "to help in the spreading of culture amidst
Russian Jewry, to stimulate them to engage in secular
studies and to assist young men who seek knowledge." [3]
Its aim was to help the Jews to attain secular education in anticipation of the longed-for emancipation.
Here and there they would help a student financially,
thus enabling him to pursue his studies. They would
use their influence to arrange the studies in the Jewish
schools so that there would be time both for religious
and for secular studies. On one occasion they sent

[1] Rosenthal, J. L., *Toldot Marbe Haskalah BeYisrael,* Int. to
v. 1, p. 10.
[2] *Ibid.,* Int. to v. 1, p. 11.
[3] *Ibid.,* Int. to v. 1, p. 9.

letters to the rabbis requesting them to see to it that
the Melammedim taught secular subjects in the
Hadarim. They requested the rabbis to speak in
praise of Haskalah, to improve the condition of the
Hadarim and the Yeshibahs, to invite special teachers
for secular subjects where necessary, to organize
libraries of Hebrew and Russian books, and not to
ordain anybody as a rabbi until he had learned to
speak, read, and write Russian correctly. But their
direct influence upon the hundreds of educational institutions, the Hadarim and the Yeshibahs, was not
great.

A concrete idea of some of their activities can be
formed from the minutes of their meeting on February
8, 1864, where a special committee on "spreading a
knowledge of Russian and secular subjects amidst the
Jews of Russia," reported. This committee advised:

1. The reprinting of textbooks for the study of Russian for
   beginners, published by the government in 1857.
2. Publication of a history of the Jews in Russia.
3. Stimulation of as many Jews as possible to write on
   Jewish subjects in Russian, and helping them in the
   publication of such writings, either in periodicals or in
   book form.
4. The publication of books in Hebrew so that the masses
   may understand them, on the following subjects:
   nature study, arithmetic, geography, general history,
   Jewish history, and special monographs.
5. The circulation of Yiddish periodicals among some of
   the educational institutions.
6. The organization of some libraries where useful books
   might be acquired and read.

7. The distribution of the funds of the Society as follows: ⅜ for assistance to students, ⅛ for the spreading of Russian language and secular subjects, ⅛ for general expenses, and ⅜ for the permanent fund for the society.[1]

Helpful as all these activities may have been, the Society could not include in its program the founding of new schools to any extent, both because of lack of funds and because of government restrictions. The help given to students prepared future workers in the cause of the Haskalah, and was an item which was within the limits of the Society's budget. The Society helped many a student to a general education and many schools with necessary books, and at times even assisted in the founding of new schools. It stimulated the spread of Russian literature and the translation of the Bible and the prayer book into Russian, but complaints were made again and again of the ineffectiveness of its work, and while the Society constantly expressed the hope to the people that emancipation would follow these activities, the people insisted that only emancipation can bring about true enlightenment.[2] While the Society grew considerably, its budget for so large an undertaking was even in its very best years, insignificant, and its influence could not have been great. In 1864, the first year of the Society, its expenses were 4515 rubles; in 1865, 11,202 rubles; and in 1884, the last year of its existence, 27,832 rubles.[3]   The relative

[1] Rosenthal, J. L., *Op. cit.*, v. 1, pp. 2-4.
[2] *Ibid.*, v. 1, pp. 31-88.
[3] *Ibid.*, v. 1, opposite p. 208, chart on expenditures.

ineffectiveness of the Society once more proved the impossibility of spreading enlightenment amongst a people that was constantly oppressed by an "unenlightening" government.

G. THE CURRICULUM IN THE NEW SCHOOLS

What were the actual curricula in the Crown Schools, in the schools influenced by the Society for the Diffusion of Enlightenment amongst the Russian Jews, and in the schools generally influenced by the Haskalah?

As previously pointed out, German influence could readily be traced in the curriculum of the new schools. When the Polish Jews came under the domination of Prussia, attempts were made to introduce general culture into their midst. The Wilhelmschule was opened in Breslau (1791) for that purpose. The subjects of study in that school were the German language, the writing of German, Hebrew, the writing of Judeo-German, French, Polish, history, geography, nature study, natural history, arithmetic, drawing, and moral instruction.[1] This was the first modern Jewish school in that part of Poland which came under the dominion of Prussia.

There seems to be some disagreement, however, as to which was the first modern school in Russia. The writer believes that the first modern Jewish school in Russia was established in 1808.[2] Nathan Glicksberg

[1] Margoshes, S., *Op. cit.,* chap. 2, pp. 29-32.
[2] Warsaw was the capital of the independent Duchy of Warsaw at the time and came under the dominion of Russia on Feb. 8, 1813.

and Isaac Davidson sent a petition to the Board of Education of Warsaw (May 2, 1808), to found a city high school for the teaching of ethics, Polish, French, German, Hebrew, letter writing in Polish, calligraphy, arithmetic, bookkeeping, geography, nature study, and history. They stated that some individual Jews in Warsaw would pay for the support of the school till the community learned to appreciate the value of the school. This, it should be remembered, was done in the same year in which the Jews in Warsaw were robbed of political and civil rights (Oct. 17, 1808), to which they were entitled under the constitution of the Duchy of Warsaw.[1]

The school opened on June 20th, 1808. But the authorities were afraid to entrust the responsibility of teaching Polish to these two men, for whom, however, as their letters show, they had the highest respect. They therefore ordered the addition to the staff of a Polish Catholic teacher by the name of Tchechovsky, who himself knew little Polish. In a letter to the authorities written in bad Polish, this teacher subsequently complains that he was discharged and that a new teacher was taken in who had taught in another school and had corrupted his pupils by bringing them to saloons and giving them whiskey to drink, and that, furthermore, he never paid for the whiskey he drank. This attitude on the part of the authorities, who preferred these incompetent teachers to the men who were responsible for the organization of the school and in whom they themselves had expressed confidence, could hardly result in encouraging the Jews to secularize

[1] Dubnow, S., *Op. cit.,* v. 1, pp. 299 ff.

their schools. How long this school existed is unknown, but probably not after December, 1810.[1]

In 1813 Joseph Perl opened a school in Tarnopol,
Galicia. Tarnopol belonged to Russia at that time
and this may therefore be considered the second school
of its kind in Russia.[2] Joseph Perl's school had the
following curriculum: (a) Hebrew, reading, translation of Hebrew into German, religion and ethics, reading Judeo-German, writing Hebrew, translation of the
Bible, Talmud, Jewish ceremonies, Hebrew spelling and
composition, Hebrew grammar, and reading of ethical
treatises; (b) reading and writing German, penmanship, ethics, mental arithmetic, Polish, German, grammar, spelling, drawing, manual training, history of
commerce and industry, commercial arithmetic, bookkeeping, natural history, geography, and French.[3]

According to others, the first Jewish school for
secular education in Russia was established in Uman
in the Gubernia of Kiev about 1822, probably by
Hyman Hurwitz who had come from England, but
little is known of this school.[4] The following incident
is, however, too interesting and significant of the seri-
ousness with which the Russian government approached the problem of Jewish education, to be
omitted. Hurwitz addressed the Central Government

[1] From the magistrate's archives of Warsaw, No. 159, quoted
by E. N. Frank in *Ha-tekufah,* v. 4, pp. 480-488.

[2] It was recovered by Austria in 1814. See note 4, in Philipson,
D., *Op. cit.,* p. 14. See also Fünn, S. J., *Op. cit.,* p. 150.

[3] Margoshes, S., *Op. cit.,* chap. 3, p. 62.

[4] Wiernik, P., "General Educational Problems and the First
Modern Schools," in *Jewish Forum,* v. 1, p. 390.

at St. Petersburg, asking it to grant him permission to open this new school in which subjects would be taught in accordance with the "system of Mendelssohn." The Central Government requested local government authorities to investigate the integrity of the applicants. Unfortunately for the petitioners at that time, a Jewish criminal by the name of Mendelssohn had escaped the local prison. In view of the fact that teaching had to be "according to the system of Mendelssohn" who, as they "knew," was a man of low character, the petition was refused. Moreover, the petitioners were in danger of being imprisoned for associating with such a character. With great difficulty they extricated themselves from being involved in a criminal offence.[1]

A Russian Jewish school that we know more about was that established in Odessa under Sittenfeld and later supervised by Bezalel Stern, who, we recall, joined the Rabbinical Commission in 1843. The curriculum of that school consisted of Bible with German translations and the commentary of Mendelssohn, Hebrew language, grammar and rhetoric, Talmud, ethical books, Russian, French, German, the grammar of these languages, and Melizah,[2] mathematics, physics, rhetoric, Russian history, history of the world, geography, and bookkeeping.[3] It is interesting to note that German, the translation of the Bible into German, and the use of Mendelssohn's commentary were practically universal, showing the influence of the German

[1] In *Voskhod,* v. 4, p. 130.
[2] Melizah—the ability to write flowery language and rhetoric.
[3] Fünn, S. J., *Op. cit.,* p. 151.

Haskalah movement. As in Germany, Talmud was neglected, although it was at first included to satisfy the conservatives, only to be abandoned later at the first opportunity. The school under Sittenfeld in Odessa was considered one of the best schools in Russia. It was closed in 1874.

The next school to be considered is that of which Lilienthal took charge at Riga. It was this school and the work of Lilienthal in it that drew the attention of the government to him. The curriculum of the Riga school consisted of reading, Hebrew, calligraphy, study of Russian and German, arithmetic, prayers, Bible with Mendelssohn's translation, Hebrew grammar, geography, history of Russia in relation to the history of the world, and the Jewish religion.[1] In 1879 the same school had as its subjects of study: religion, Hebrew, German, Russian, Latin, French, arithmetic, geometry, general and Russian history, natural sciences, geography, calligraphy, and singing.[2]

All the schools above mentioned were private schools but in one form or another were influenced by the Haskalah movement. The St. Petersburg school will give us an illustration of a school organized by the Society for the Diffusion of Enlightenment amidst the Russian Jews. Its curriculum consisted of: Russian, Russian grammar, literature, arithmetic, geography, botany, zoölogy, mineralogy, penmanship, drawing, and, in the girls' school, German.[3] The Jewish subjects

[1] See Ehrlich, Adolf, *Entwickelungsgeschichte der Israelitischen gemeindeschule zu Riga*, p. 5.

[2] *Ibid.*, p. 27.

[3] See *Spravochnaya Kniga*, pp. 153-155.

contained reading and writing of Hebrew letters and words, simple translation into Russian, Hebrew literature and grammar, memorizing Hebrew poems, translation from Russian into Hebrew, study of the Pentateuch and Rashi, study of the former and latter prophets [1] and Hagiographa, the order of prayers, and the translation of the most important prayers. Religion was taught as a separate subject. In connection with this subject, the sources of Jewish religion were also taught through chosen selections from the Bible, the Talmud, the Yad Ha-Hazakah, and the Shulhan Aruk. Jewish history was taught beginning with the early period down to modern times.[2]

A school that might be considered typical of the Crown Schools is that established by the government at Vilna. Its curriculum is the curriculum of the Crown School in Russia. It contained Bible, prayers, Hebrew language, grammar, Biblical history, customs, and ceremonies in addition to the secular subjects that were similar to those of other schools.[3]

In contrast with the Hadarim, their dilapidated condition, their unsanitary aspect, the teacher pedagogically unqualified, the distaste of the children for the school, the new school and the new curriculum were a boon to the Jewish children of Russia. It will be well to close this description of the new school and its curriculum with the description of an eye-witness of

[1] The former prophets include the books of Joshua, Judges, Samuel I and II, Kings I and II. The latter prophets include Isaiah, Jeremiah, Ezekiel, and the twelve minor prophets.

[2] *Spravochnaya Kniga,* pp. 122-125.

[3] *Ibid.,* pp. 127-129.

a modern school in Vilna. This school was organized in 1840 and the director of it was N. Rosenthal. The subjects of study in it were Talmud, Bible, Hebrew, Russian, German, French, arithmetic, geography, and special ethical works which were taught on the Sabbath.[1] Of his visit to the school during his stay in Vilna, Lilienthal gave the following description:

"In the afternoon I visited the elementary school established by Messrs. Klatzko and Rosenthal. What a mighty contrast to the dark and dirty Hadarim I had visited in the forenoon. . . . Large, clean and commodious stairs led to fine apartments in which some eighty or ninety children were assembled. A fine group of teachers had been appointed and though all of them were Polish Jews I found them to be men of thorough learning, capable of conversing fluently and correctly in the Hebrew, Russian, Polish, German and French languages. The school furniture was of the finest kind, the arrangements through all the departments complete, and the scholars looked healthy and happy. I examined the classes in the different subjects of instruction and found them to be far advanced in Hebrew grammar, in translation of the whole Bible, and well posted in the chapters of the Talmud they had learned. They wrote German quite correctly; some of them had gone through the elementary rules of French grammar and being at that time still unable to examine them in their vernacular I was assured that the Russian and Polish languages were quite familiar to them. The boys were all dressed in clean, nice Schubetzes tied to the vest with fine, silk girdles, and on their head the

[1] Fünn, S. J., *Op. cit.,* p. 168.

Yarmulke, the usual and continual covering of the Polish Jew. The teachers were all self-made men. In hidden nooks, unobserved perhaps even by their own wives, at the late hour of midnight when all were asleep, they had to study by themselves primary branches of the German and French languages, by laborious self study to acquire the knowledge through which they became so eminently useful to the rising generation. They were specimens of thousands of martyrs to science and knowledge; their history is always the same and it is a pity that they did not enjoy a full and regular education; they would have become brilliant stars on the horizon of European science." [1]

[1] Lilienthal, M., "Travels in Russia," in *Op. cit.,* pp. 288-290.

CHAPTER VII

JEWISH EDUCATION OF THE HASKALAH AND OF NATIONALISM

A. The Rabbinical Seminaries

WITH the founding of the Crown Schools, two seminaries were founded, one in Zhitomir and one in Vilna. The aim of these was to train teachers and rabbis to teach in the Crown Schools and supervise the instruction. A brief account of the curriculum of the Vilna Seminary will be sufficient to illustrate the type of instruction.

The Vilna Seminary was divided into three departments, containing nine classes. The first department consisted of three preparatory classes, the second department consisted of four rabbinical classes, and the third department was for specialization and consisted of the pedagogical faculty and the rabbinical faculty. In 1858 the seminary had about two hundred and fifty students, fifty of whom were assisted by government funds. There were eighteen teachers of whom twelve were Jewish and six Christian. The pupils entered the school at the age of ten and had to submit a health certificate before they were admitted. Instruction lasted from 8:30 to 2:30 daily except Friday and Saturday. The day began with prayers for the czar and for success in studies.

The curriculum, which was very elaborate, was as follows: Russian language and literature, history of Russian literature, grammar, general history, history of Russia, geography, drawing, Bible with commentaries and German translation, Mishnah with commentaries, Talmud with commentaries, Maimonides, Rosh, Alfas, Tur, Yoreh Deah with the Shakh, Eben-Ha-Ezer with the Bet Shmuel, Codes, Hayye Adam, Jewish history, principles of religion, ethics, homiletical books, Hebrew, Aramaic, German, arithmetic, algebra, geometry, mathematical geography, and calligraphy.[1]

But even in this institution the intentions of the government as judged by its administration seem not to have been of the best. Thus, in a letter written to the Society for the Diffusion of Enlightenment, the Jewish teachers of the seminary complain that the government pays higher salaries to Christian teachers of general subjects than it pays to the Jewish teachers who devote more time to the school. This they point out is not only unfair but also breaks down the discipline of the school and impairs the respect of the pupils. They point out that the people, who already distrust the institution because it is a government institution, will distrust it even more, seeing that even the followers of enlightenment are thus treated by the government.[2]

The rabbinical schools both at Vilna and at Zhitomir were closed by the government in 1873 because they did not achieve the object for which they were established. They did not accomplish for the great masses

[1] Gurland, J., *Kebod Habayit,* pp. 25-40.
[2] Rosenthal, J. L., *Op. cit.,* v. 2, pp. 28-31.

of Russian Jewry what the government was anxious to accomplish. How could they, if the government was not sincere in its intentions and the masses of Jewry sensed its insincerity?

B. REASONS FOR THE REJECTION OF THE GOVERN-
MENT SCHOOLS

In the large communities the number of Crown Schools was not sufficient to meet the needs of the population. At the same time the schools that existed were attended by only a small number of Jewish children, and even these entered only after they had received some training at the Heder or the Yeshibah which prepared them to meet the entrance requirements of the school. Even the attitude of the Jews during the days of Alexander II, during the era of reform, did not prevent the great majority from attending the Heder. So small was the attendance in the Crown Schools that it is claimed that the per capita cost in these schools at times amounted to 1500 rubles yearly.[1]

The reasons for the rejection of these government schools by the population are many, some inherent in the nature of the schools and others resulting from the attitude of the Jews or of the government. To begin with, the general curriculum of the schools was inadequate. The child only learned the reading and writing of Russian, elements of grammar, and the four fundamental operations of arithmetic. Since as a prerequisite these schools demanded a knowledge of

[1] Dubnow, S. M., *Op. cit.*, v. 2, p. 175. Also, Rosenthal, L., *Op. cit.*, v. 2, p. 74.

Hebrew reading, a knowledge of some prayers by heart, and the ability to translate Genesis and Exodus, it was necessary for the child to attend the Heder, or to receive some private instruction, before coming to the Crown School. To the Heder, too, the child would have to return for a study of the Mishnah, Talmud, Rashi, and the Commentaries, subjects which were not taught in the Crown Schools. Instruction in the general subjects of the curriculum was also inadequate, hence those who were interested in giving their children a secular education failed to make use of these schools, since upon the completion of a five-year course at these schools, the children were able to enter only the third year of the gymnasium.

Furthermore, the schools did not function properly in that they failed to prepare the Jewish child for the kind of life he was to lead. Aiming to produce an enlightened man at a time when most ways of living were closed to the Russian Jew, regardless of the enlightenment that he possessed, was hardly an effective way of preparing the child for life. The child was not prepared to enter any definite calling. From the point of view of the relation of the curriculum to the environment, the schools were inadequate.

From the point of view of method, too, they were not altogether satisfactory. The lack of a Russian translation of the Hebrew prayers made it necessary to teach the translation in German. This became the more difficult as the children confused German and Yiddish and had to study two languages, neither of which they knew. The linguistic difficulty was increased by the inclusion of other languages in the curriculum. Religion, too, which was taught as a separate subject in these schools, could not be attractive to the child. The process of living a religious life in the home was much more educative than the study of the "Hayye Adam." [1] To aggravate the situation there was added to these difficulties of curriculum and method the fact that the child was dismissed for the afternoon, whereas in the Heder he had been kept the entire day. The Russian Jewish parent, who found it difficult enough to make a living under the unfavorable circumstances in his country, and was therefore always busy, appreciated the Heder's supervisory care over his boy for the entire day.[2]

It will help us to find out what was wrong with the schools if we examine the suggestions that were made for their improvement by the Society for the Diffusion of Enlightenment. These suggestions are also an interesting reflection of the Haskalah tendencies with regard to the subjects of the school curriculum. The following suggestions were made:

1. That a preparatory class be organized in the first grade school consisting of a one year course.
   a. During the first term the subjects of instruction shall be: the Hebrew alphabet, Russian, German, syllabication, and reading.
   b. During the second term one half of the Book of Genesis is to be taught in Yiddish translation, practice in reading, and the beginning of writing in these three languages (Hebrew, Russian, and German).
2. The curriculum of the school proper should be:

[1] A code of laws.
[2] Rosenthal, J. L., *Op. cit.*, v. 2, pp. 69-70.

a. First year: Genesis and Exodus, translated into German; nouns and verbs in Hebrew, grammar, catechism, writing in the three languages, Russian grammar, translation from Russian into German and from German into Russian, the four fundamental operations of arithmetic.

b. Second year: Leviticus, Numbers, and Deuteronomy, in German translation, catechism, Hebrew grammar, Jewish history in German, Russian grammar, translation from Russian into German and vice versa, arithmetic up to fractions, and geography.

c. Third year: Prophets and Hagiographa, catechism, Hebrew grammar, Jewish history, Russian grammar, short compositions in Russian, arithmetic, geography, and a short history of Russia.[1]

All in all the schools were not above criticism from the point of view of organization, curriculum, and method.

But had these intrinsic reasons been the only reasons, the schools would not have been so emphatically rejected by the great majority of Jewry. The attitude of the Jews, however, also played a part in this rejection. The old has tremendous power, and orthodox Jewry showed itself strongly entrenched against any innovations. In a commentary on the will of Rabbi Moses Schreiber [2] the author quotes the following advice: "But the books of Moses Mendelssohn you are not to touch, then your feet will never stumble.

[1] For a discussion of the general attitude to the Crown Schools and the reasons for it, see Rosenthal, J. L., *Op. cit.*, v. 2, pp. 93-96.

[2] Akiba Joseph ben Jehiel, *Leb Haibri*, being a commentary on the will of Rabbi Moses Schreiber (1763-1839).

The Bible with the commentary of Rashi and with the commentary of the Ramban [1] you may teach your children." This advice not to teach Mendelssohn's commentary is characteristic of the fear with which the old Jew regarded the coming of the Berliner into Russian Jewish life. The orthodox Jew who wanted to give his child a secular education was very much afraid that the new school would lead to a break between him and his child, that it would lessen the religious bond and would take the child away from the fold. The great fear was that education without human rights would necessarily lead to baptism, and this fear was intensified by direct government efforts at conversion. In fact, the schools were accused of breaking up the family life, of destroying sacred customs, and of having failed to conceive their function as that of harmonizing Jewish studies and actual life.[2] No wonder then that the rich Jews gave their children private instruction and only the poor who could do no better sent their children to attend these schools, a fact which would naturally react upon other well-to-do parents and keep them from sending their children to an institution that was regarded as charitable in its character.

Another factor in the attitude of the Jew to the new schools must have been the influence of the Melammedim. These men, who had for years been devoting themselves to Jewish education, and who found in this their source of livelihood, could not but see in the new

[1] Rabbi Moses ben Nahmon, a Spanish Talmudist who lived during the 13th century and also wrote a commentary on the Pentateuch.

[2] Rosenthal, J. L., *Op. cit.*, v. 2, p. 74.

schools a personal economic danger. The propaganda of the Melammedim would naturally result in prejudicing parents against the Crown Schools.

But by far the most important factor in the rejection of the government schools was the attitude of the government itself. The first and the most important reason for their rejection was the very fact that they were organized by the government. The attitude of the people was expressed in the motto, rejecting these schools, which was on the lips of old and young alike, "Znat ne Znayem, Shkoly ne Zhelayem." [1] The phrase "Znat ne Znayem" is an indication that the people were so suspicious of the government, that any measures initiated by it could not even receive the consideration that an otherwise rational proposal would deserve. Under the circumstances, government sponsorship was sufficient to condemn them. It was clear that the government not only aimed at giving the Jews a general education, but also at supervising Jewish education.[2] Here and there government attempts at conversion were very evident. The personality of the teachers was too often such as not to inspire the parents with confidence, especially since the parents were suspicious of the actions of the government.

In a letter to the Society for the Diffusion of Enlightenment (March, 1864), the Rabbi of Minsk reports that there is a "first grade" school for boys in Minsk, but that this school is not attended by any of the pupils of the middle class or the well-to-do. They maintain

[1] We do not know—We do not care—We do not want the schools.

[2] Rosenthal, J. L., *Op. cit.*, v. 1, p. 128.

private teachers to teach their children Russian, German, and occasionally the Bible with Mendelssohn's translation and Hebrew grammar. Most of the instructors, however, are not well versed in these subjects. They follow the desires of the parents, who are interested primarily in the study of the Talmud and its commentaries, and the parents would rather entrust to these the education of their children than to the Haskalah School. The Hebrew School is therefore composed of about fifty-two children of the poorer classes; some of these read Russian with understanding; they are also able to write Russian and to read and write Hebrew and German, although their knowledge of German is rather limited. The director of the school is a Pole, and the writer states that the number of students, "would increase seven-fold," if the director were a Jewish graduate, properly trained in one of the higher educational institutions, so great was the fear of conversion. Incidentally, the subjects of instruction, in addition to the above-mentioned, are: Rambam, Hayye Adam, calligraphy, and it is reported that the teacher of Bible has a peculiar method, "of teaching grammar for the first half of the year, and leaving the second half for the study of the Bible." [1]

If we bear in mind the picture previously given of the reign of Nicholas I, we can hardly be surprised that the Jews rejected the schools coming from such a government. "A system of conscription which annually wrenched thousands of youths from the bosom of their families, the barracks which served as mission houses, the method of stimulating and even forcing conversion

[1] Rosenthal, J. L., *Op. cit.*, v. 2, pp. 18-19.

of recruits, the establishment of Crown Schools for the same covert purpose, the abolition of communal autonomy, civil disfranchisement, persecution; all were set in motion against the citadel of Judaism. . . . The hand which dealt out blows could not disseminate enlightenment." [1]

C. The Influence of the Haskalah on the Heder

Beyond the establishment of about one hundred Crown Schools and the two rabbinical seminaries at Vilna and Zhitomir, the influence of the Haskalah penetrated Jewish education only to a very small extent. Most of the Hadarim remained unaffected while the rest were not affected in a fundamental way.

Kotik, in his Memoirs, describes a teacher who was more lenient than the others, knew how to read Russian. but did so secretly, and was able to explain some simple scientific facts. This man is typical of the teacher in the Heder somewhat influenced by the Haskalah. As soon as the father of Kotik learned that the teacher was imparting this general knowledge to his pupils he was afraid that his son would turn out to be a disbeliever and immediately changed to another school. The further enlightening of the pupil had to continue through the secret study of Moreh Nebukim, Kuzari, Behinot Olam, and Hobat Ha-Lebabot. [2]

The government began to supervise the Hadarim and the Melammedim (1865) with the intention of crushing out the "pernicious influence of the Talmud," but government supervision was of little avail. Even

[1] Dunbow, S. M., *Op. cit.*, v. 2, p. 111.
[2] Kotik, E., *Op. cit.*, v. 1, pp. 289-291, 298-299.

subsequent attempts to supervise the Hadarim were dropped by the government since it was unsuccessful in its efforts.

Here and there the Hadarim were affected by the Haskalah. A private Heder showing Haskalah influence was that organized by Dr. T. Luria in Warsaw. Children were admitted at the age of six or seven, an age later than that at which children usually entered the Heder. A prerequisite for entry was the reading of Hebrew and Russian, showing the influence of the entrance requirements of the Crown Schools. The subjects of study were Hebrew, grammar, translation into Russian, prayers, Bible, Jewish history up to the destruction of the first Temple, and parts of the former Prophets.[1]

Another Heder, of a Maskil catering to the pupils of the well-to-do, was described to the writer by an eye-witness. This Heder existed in Donoyevtzy, Podolia, at about 1895. Its curriculum contained Bible in Yiddish translation, study of the Talmud, but less than in the old Heder, the Haskalah literature, such as the works of Gordon and Mappu, the writing of compositions in Hebrew and in some cases translation from Yiddish into Russian, the writing of letters and the study of Hebrew grammar.[2]

In general, Haskalah aimed at making the Heder more of a social and public institution.[3] It sought to bring in reform in the equipment, in the teachers' ap-

[1] *Spravochnaya Kniga,* p. 130.

[2] Described by Mr. Zevi Scharfstein, instructor of the Teachers' Institute of the Jewish Theological Seminary.

[3] Katzovich, I. A., *Sechzig Jahr Leben,* p. 124.

pearance and knowledge, in the sanitary conditions, and in the method. It tried by raising the pay of teachers to eliminate the outside occupations in which the Melammedim were usually engaged because of insufficient remuneration. It resulted, however, in few pedagogic improvements. True enough, the study of the portions of the week which resulted in constant skipping of parts of the Pentateuch and failed to give the child a unified view of the Bible was severely criticized, but beyond that and the objection to the translation into Yiddish and the desire for Mendelssohn's translation, little progress was made. The Heder remained an all day school for the teaching of Jewish subjects.

Under the influence of the Haskalah, the importance of Talmud decreased and the Bible was made the center of the curriculum. The study of Hebrew grammar was introduced and a good deal of time was spent on Melizah, letter writing, and acquiring beautiful expressions for future use. Where Talmud was taught some reforms were suggested, such as not to start with the portion dealing with the laws of damages, or to eliminate the portions dealing with the laws of women or to eliminate casuistry. Religion was introduced as a separate subject and religious questions were discussed from the point of view of the Haskalah. In this way Jewish catechism was introduced and in some cases became the end-all of the Heder.

But on the whole the influence of the Haskalah on the Heder was negligible. The Maskilim sent their children to the gymnasia and had little influence in changing the Hadarim since they were private institutions. The masses were almost untouched by Haskalah. It did not reach many of the Hadarim, and those which it did reach were affected but slightly. Even the government regulations were disregarded, and the orders issued in 1893 by the government concerning hours of instruction and school accommodations were evidently not heeded, since to the knowledge of the writer the Heder which he attended seven or eight years later was not in accord with the rules of the government. The fact of the matter really was that the Russian government was not interested in the Jews in any way whatsoever,[1] so that even whatever efforts it made were quickly abandoned where resistance was shown. That resistance was to be expected, is evident from the conditions under which the Jews of Russia lived.

D. The Influence of the Haskalah on the Talmud Torah

The influence of the Haskalah on the Talmud Torah was twofold. It was changed from within, due to the desire of the Maskilim, whose influence could affect the communal institutions, and from without as a result of the desire of the government. The government regulations for the Talmud Torah beginning with the decree of Nicholas in 1844 could but result in making these institutions more modern, but as in the case

---

[1] Thus a Jewish school of handicrafts in Zhitomir was closed in 1884 by the Russian government, in order that the Jews might be less able to compete with their Christian neighbors for whom there was no such school. This school was certainly a result of Haskalah.

of the Crown Schools, the stamp of the government made the masses suspicious. Nevertheless, the changes instituted should not be overlooked.

The decree of Nicholas in 1844 provided that there be one teacher for every twenty-five pupils in the Talmud Torah and that children above eight be taught Russian. The curriculum, too, was made more general than it had been hitherto, and public examinations were instituted, thus throwing the institutions open to the view of outsiders.[1] Generally, the subjects taught were, in addition to the Jewish subjects, Russian reading and writing, penmanship, and arithmetic.

The following was the curriculum of the Talmud Torah of Odessa: (a) Jewish subjects: reading, writing, grammar, customs and ceremonies, Pentateuch, Prophets, history, dictation, translation from Russian into Hebrew, and religious instruction. (b) General subjects: Russian, arithmetic, natural history, geography, grammar, German, Latin, and special instruction in patriotism, similar to that given in religion.[2]

Another important factor was the attempt on the part of the Maskilim to introduce vocational education, especially for children whose aptitude did not permit them to continue their other studies. An illustration of such a Talmud Torah is the Trade School of the Vilna Talmud Torah, authorized on the 10th of March, 1890. The purpose of this school was the practical teaching of trades in metal and wood. It consisted of a one year course and the subjects taught

[1] *Spravochnaya Kniga,* pp. 50-57.
[2] *Ibid.,* p. 125.

were practical geometry, drawing, elements of physics, mechanics, and technology. There was no instruction in the school on Sabbaths or on Jewish or legal holidays, but instruction continued throughout the year in general and in Jewish subjects, except in the summer when general subjects were not taught.[1]

The Talmud Torah "Adat Yisrael" in St. Petersburg had as its curriculum (in 1865): religion, ethics, Russian, German, Hebrew, arithmetic, nature study, physiography, writing, drawing, gymnastics, thus showing very distinctly the influence of the Haskalah [2] on the Talmud Torah.

But the influence on these Talmud Torahs should not be exaggerated. Although it is true that here and there young men and women, Maskilim, were the cause of transforming the old Talmud Torah, and in some places courses in Russian were introduced and the old curriculum gave way to the new, this transformation was slow in some places, and never reached many others. Thus on April 5th, 1876, the Talmud Torah of Minsk is voted one hundred rubles by the Society for the Diffusion of Enlightenment on condition that it introduce the study of Russian as one of the subjects in the curriculum. But the Talmud Torah is described as having equipment which is not suitable. As for the Russian that was taught, it is reported that it would have been difficult for a non-Jew to make himself understood in Russian in spite of the study of Russian in the school. The money is finally given to the Talmud Torah on condition that Russian continue to be

[1] *Spravochnaya Kniga,* p. 71.
[2] Rosenthal, J. L., *Op. cit.,* v. 2, p. 81.

taught, though not necessarily by a non-Jew, thus making provision for some one to teach the subject who can, if necessary, make himself understood in Yiddish.[1] Here again, as in the case of the other institutions influenced by the Haskalah, the influence may have affected the institution somewhat, but, if it did, it was only in the case of a comparatively small number of Talmud Torahs in the country. Most of the Talmud Torahs remained as in the days of old, places physically unfit for the instruction of the young and equally defective from the point of view of their spiritual equipment.

E. THE INFLUENCE OF THE HASKALAH ON THE YESHIBAH

The influence of the Haskalah on the Yeshibah was even less than on the Talmud Torah. Here the Maskilim could be of little influence since the Yeshibah was also more or less a private undertaking. The government issued its decrees, but those who sent the young to the Talmudical academies heeded little the decrees of the government or the desires of the Maskilim. What the government intended may be seen from the Rules on the Yeshibah of Volozhin authorized December 22, 1891.[2] The subjects of instruction in accordance with these rules were to be: Russian, arithmetic, and calligraphy, in addition to the Jewish subjects regularly taught. The director of the Yeshibah was to have a command of the Russian language and to have a diploma from a district school.

[1] Rosenthal, J. L., *Op. cit.,* v. 1, p. 128.
[2] *Spravochnaya Kniga,* pp. 64-68.

The institution was to be under the supervision of the director of public schools, who was to see that the desire of the government was carried out. Smolenskin in his novel, *Ha-toeh Bedarke Ha-hayim,* describes how one such inspector came to the Yeshibah to see if the teachers did their work properly, and when he learned that the order to teach in the language of the land had not been followed, he threatened to close up the Yeshibah. Other requirements were that the general subjects be taught sometime between nine and three, that no more than ten hours be devoted to study, that there be no study at night, that the Yeshibah be a place for study only, and that no gatherings for prayers be held there. The Yeshibah in Odessa included in its curriculum grammar, Hebrew, Bible, Talmud, Codes, the Russian language, German, mathematics, and literature. This curriculum, which is wider in scope than the curriculum that was current in most Yeshibahs, may be ascribed to the influence of Haskalah.

But on the whole, it may be said that beyond the introduction of the teaching of Russian [1] in these schools the Haskalah or the government had little effect. Haskalah was more effective upon the spirit of the individual, who here and there, observing the tendency of the new times, studied Russian or German secretly in an attempt to become a "cultured" man. As for the official observance of the governmental decree, the incident previously mentioned in Smolenskin's novel turned out to be literally true. The Yeshibah of Volozhin was closed by the Russian gov-

[1] And often that, too, was fiction.

ernment in 1892 for not observing the regulations of the government.

F. THE INFLUENCE OF THE HASKALAH ON THE EDUCATION OF GIRLS

Under the old system, the Jewish education of girls was very limited. The ability to read the Hebrew prayers and to write a Yiddish letter was the extent of their education. As a result, when the young Jewish women joined the general schools and received a secular education, they were more easily estranged from their people. They had not attained a sufficient amount of Jewish culture to stay within the fold.

The Haskalah appreciated the need of giving the Jewish woman training that would prepare her to be the enlightened first teacher of the child at home. As a result, under its influence special Hebrew schools for girls were established. The subjects of instruction were similar to those in the other Haskalah schools.

In a school for girls in Bakhmut the subjects taught were: reading of prayers, grammar of the Russian, Hebrew, and German languages, arithmetic, reading, interpretation of books of ethical value, dancing, and handiwork. The Hebrew school for girls in Tchernigov (1862) had a curriculum containing Russian, Hebrew, German, French (as an elective), arithmetic, Jewish history, and manual work.[1] The Hebrew school for girls in Kishinev in 1864, subsidized by the government, included in its curriculum, Russian, German, and Hebrew, reading and writing, Russian history, Jewish

[1] Rosenthal, J. L., *Op. cit.*, v. 2, p. 63.

history, arithmetic, geography, sewing, dancing, and music.[1]

In Minsk (1864) there were two schools for girls, and in these they studied German, arithmetic, Russian, religion, writing, French, and playing the piano. The girls in this school were reported to know Russian well.[2]

Along with the establishment of these schools for girls there came some professional schools of which ten are listed in the various governments of Russia.[3] These schools were mostly trade schools preparing the girls for millinery, basketry, dressmaking, and occasionally to be saleswomen. In general, Haskalah recognized the important function that woman has as the first teacher of the child, and attempted to prepare her to fulfill that function properly.

G. SUMMARY

In summarizing the influence of the Haskalah on Jewish education in Russia, it will be well for us to note some important facts concerning the extent of this influence. From an extract of a report presented in 1899 by the School Commission to the Society for the Diffusion of Enlightenment among the Jews in Russia, we learn that in Lithuania, out of a total of 93,874 children of school age only 2994 or 3.2% attended the middle or lower schools. In all the educational institutions of the fifteen governments of the Pale, the settlements which were the most thickly populated

[1] Rosenthal, J. L., *Op. cit.,* v. 2, p. 32.
[2] *Ibid.,* v. 2, p. 19.
[3] *Spravochnaya Kniga,* p. 386.

sections of Russia, 15,200 Jewish children studied out of a total of 440,681 of school age, or 3.5%.[1]

In 1897 it was reported that the total number of private schools in these fifteen governments amounted to 388 with 15,244 pupils, and that the number of pupils in private and community schools was more than twice as large as the number in the government schools.[2]

The chief influence of the Haskalah on the educational institutions was therefore not in the numbers of children affected, for the great majority of Jewish children attended the Hadarim, but in the tendencies that it introduced into Jewish life. Although not affecting the schools very much, it did affect the individual. The youth of Russia were aroused, and new hopes began to fill their hearts. Whereas Jewish education before the Haskalah had but one aim, that of conservation, this aim, after the Haskalah, was supplemented by that of adjustment to a new Russia. The problem of maintaining itself and at the same time of adjusting itself to what the youth believed were the changing conditions in Russia, bringing better times for the Jews, was the problem of Haskalah education. That Haskalah was rejected by the masses of Jewry is another proof of the antagonizing influence that government associations had upon the movement,

[1] This fact should not be understood to mean that the Jews neglected the Jewish education of their children. On the contrary, it is well known that, though not compulsory (after the days of Kahal autonomy), attendance at a Heder or Talmud Torah was practically universal.

[2] *Spravochnaya Kniga,* p. 643.

as well as an interesting commentary upon the keen powers of observation of Russian Jewry as to the effect that German enlightenment had upon some of its adherents. The recollection of men like Maimon,[1] like whom there must have been hundreds, men who experienced an inner struggle and were ever at war with themselves, as well as the fear that the foundations of the Jewish religion would be undermined, endowed the masses with a wholesome sensitiveness which opposed the tendencies of the Maskilim.[2] It remained for a new movement, which promised to be positive, and which did not carry with it either the associations of the Russian government or the negative attitude to the old, so characteristic of the Haskalah, to breathe a new spirit into the masses of Russian Jewry. This movement was that of Jewish nationalism.

H. THE INFLUENCE OF JEWISH NATIONALISM ON EDUCATION

The response of the government to the attempts on the part of the Russian Jewish youth to become an integral part of Russia, convinced them that there was little hope in Russia. The thought that secularization of culture and general education would lead to emancipation in Russia, as it did in Germany, gradually disappeared and gave way to the conviction that the situation of the Jews in Russia was a hopeless one. The pogroms of the 80's intensified this conviction.

---

[1] See chap. 2, pp. 42-43.

[2] See Kotik, E., *Op. cit.*, v. 2, pp. 267-271. Also Günzburg, M. A., *Debir,* pt. 2, p. 6.

The only hope was in the East and in the return of Jewry to a national home. Thus Jewish nationalism arose in full force among the Jews of Russia.

This change of attitude was reflected educationally in the creation of a new institution known as the Heder Metukkon.[1] The chief aim of the old Heder was religious. The aim of the Haskalah Heder was to combine a Jewish education, regarded chiefly as religious education, with secular culture. Jewish life was to be transformed through the introduction of general culture. To these conceptions Jewish nationalism opposed the idea of transforming Jewish life from within through the culture of the Jewish people itself. The aim of the Heder Metukkon, though recognizing the need and the importance of secular culture, was to give the child an attitude favorable to Jewish nationalism. The changes that were made in the Heder to produce the Heder Metukkon were an outgrowth of this fundamental aim, as well as of the consciousness that the educational institutions must be modernized.

As a result, one of the first fundamentals of the Heder Metukkon was the revival of Hebrew as a spoken language. The old Heder did not teach Hebrew as a language. Those who completed its course knew Hebrew because of their intimate acquaintance with all the sources of Jewish knowledge; those who did not complete the course did not know Hebrew. In the Heder Metukkon, Hebrew was taught as a separate subject, as a spoken language, and as a means to the knowledge of Jewish literature. Hence, the natural

[1] The improved Heder.

method, or the method known as the Ibrit be-Ibrit,[1] was introduced.

A writer of memoirs describes one such Heder as follows: In it the subjects of study were Pentateuch, Prophets, grammar, Hebrew as a spoken language, Jewish history, modern Hebrew literature, and Russian. The teacher of this Heder studied pedagogy, a phenomenon unusual in those days. Another interesting feature was the fact that every hour of study in the school was followed by a ten-minute recess.[2] In this Heder we can see both the aim of Jewish nationalism and a recognition of the need of secular culture reflected in the curriculum.

A detailed account of the curriculum of a Heder Metukkon in Berditchev in 1902 was given to the writer by one of its teachers.[3] The Berditchev Heder was really a system of schools scattered in various parts of the city. The children were graded according to age and knowledge. It contained about nine classes and the course was six or seven years. It had a register of about 350 and was like a modern Hebrew school, with a Board of Directors and a principal. The following is a description of its curriculum: Hebrew was taught by the natural method with the use of pictures and objects. This was done for about three months when the reading of Hebrew, for which the conversational Hebrew was preparatory, began. The textbook used was *Lefi*

---

[1] Hebrew in Hebrew.

[2] Katzovich, I., *Op. cit.*, pp. 248-249, 256-257.

[3] Mr. Zevi Scharfstein, instructor at the Teachers Institute of the Jewish Theological Seminary, New York City. See also "Mesulat Limmud Metukkana," in *Ha-meliz,* yr. 42, no. 26.

Hatof.[1] The hours were from nine to three with one hour for dinner and a ten-minute intermission between one hour and the next. During some of the intermissions, games and songs under the direction of a teacher constituted the program. The writing of Hebrew and the reading of prayers were also taught. In the second class fifteen or twenty minutes were devoted to the reading of prayers. The other subjects were Hebrew, for which the *Bet Sefer Ibri* by Grazovsky was used, writing of Hebrew and grammar, and Pentateuch from an abbreviated text. In the third class, reading of prayers, Pentateuch with the Bible as the text, Jewish history in Hebrew, former Prophets, writing, and in some classes reading of the Torah with the characteristic chant were taught. The fourth class had as its curriculum the same subjects, with the addition of the latter Prophets and more advanced material in modern Hebrew literature. The fifth class began the study of Talmud, and the sixth class continued the same studies.

There was an oral examination by a board of educated people. Diplomas were granted upon graduation when a public examination also took place. Later, when the children began to enter the Russian gymnasium, instruction was shifted to the afternoon and the scheme followed was very similar to that of a modern Talmud Torah in this country, where the child attends public school up to three o'clock and Hebrew school in the latter part of the afternoon.

We may summarize the changes introduced by the Heder Metukkon as follows:

[1] *Lefi Hatof* by David Yellin.

1. The aim became chiefly national.
2. As a result, the revival of the Hebrew language and the teaching of Hebrew as a spoken tongue became an important part of the school curriculum.[1]
3. The curriculum and the method were modernized, with the result that more was accomplished in less time. On the method side new abbreviated textbooks were introduced which, however, resulted in a departure from the original sources of Jewish knowledge. The phonetic method of reading was introduced in connection with the teaching of language, Talmud became a less important subject and usually the child did not get to it at all. History was introduced as a special subject in the curriculum.
4. The physical equipment of the school, its order, and its discipline were a marked improvement upon the old Heder.
5. As in the case of the Haskalah schools, the importance of educating the girls was recognized and Hebrew was taught to them, whereas in the past only Yiddish was known by the women.

In contrast with the Haskalah school we may say that while its aim was that of secularization, the aim of the Heder Metukkon was one of secularization plus nationalization. "Secularization will bring emancipation," was the watchword of Haskalah. Having lost this hope, the Maskilim found consolation in the hope that the Jewish people would return to the land of their fathers to lead a normal life like the other nations of the world.

[1] Rudayev, M. J., "Matarat ha-hadarim ha-metukkanim," in *Ha-zefirah*, v. 29, nos. 182, 184.

I. Summary

A study of the curriculum of the Jewish school shows two tendencies, one of conservation, the other of adjustment. The ancient Jewish curriculum in Palestine was a response to the needs of a people living on its soil. Hence it contained all the knowledge, subjects and skills, that people then needed for living a complete life. With the dispersion of Jewry, the curriculum became a weapon of defense—a means of maintaining the unity of the people in the Diaspora. This fact naturally resulted in a great emphasis upon conservation and made the curriculum consist uniformly, for many centuries, of Bible, Mishnah, and Talmud.

Nevertheless, whenever the Jews came in free contact with another people and with another culture, they responded by a broadening of their school curriculum. This was the case when Hellenism in Alexandria brought Greek philosophy and culture into Jewish life. The same was true when Judaism came in contact with Arabic culture in Spain and with the Renaissance in Italy. In each case the Jewish school underwent important changes as a result of contact with a new environment.

The era of emancipation and the movement for enlightenment, begun in Germany by Moses Mendelssohn, brought to the front the problem of adjusting the curriculum of the Jewish school so as to prepare the Jew for greater interaction with other people. The solution in Germany came through special Jewish schools, at first, and later through a process of assimilation that brought disastrous results. In many cases it was not an adjustment, but a self-effacement. In some cases, the process resulted in a tragic struggle within the individual who had lost the old and could not adjust himself to the new. The transition required was too sudden, and it resulted in individuals at war with themselves.

These two tendencies of conservation and adjustment are also to be seen in Russia and in Poland. The history of the Jews in Russia and Poland and the corresponding educational institutions that they developed show the relation between the environment and the curriculum. Polish Jewish autonomy, which kept the Jews separate from the rest of the population in a distinct estate, made any other than the intensive Jewish curriculum of Bible, Mishnah, and Talmud unnecessary. Whatever Polish was needed was learned by commercial intercourse with the Poles. Russian Jewish life, which kept the Jews apart from the rest of the population by one series of restrictions and oppressions after another, could not but have similar results.

The Jew, who underwent intense physical suffering, turned to his spiritual life and concentrated on that. As a result of this attitude, the Torah and the study of it was the law of life. Life in the street, synagogue, and community could best be understood by the man who knew Torah, and since life was so closely related to teaching, the children were really living their education. The activities of the child were similar to those of the grown-up, with slight exception. The difference in studies was a difference of understanding but not a difference of content. The subject matter was the same.

The study of Talmud, which occupied so much of the time of the Heder and the Yeshibah, was not a means to an end but an end in itself. The love of learning and its pursuit became the compensation for a life of suffering.

The Haskalah, the movement toward enlightenment, which started in Germany and was associated with hopes of possible emancipation, changed the relatively constant curriculum of the Heder and the Talmud Torah, but, on account of its associations with the activities of a hostile government, had little effect on changing the general situation of Russian Jewry or its educational institutions. The Haskalah intensified this negative attitude to the government by making the Russian Jew more conscious of sad reality, and Jewish nationalism followed. It resulted in a new and a modern educational institution, the Heder Metukkon, which no longer attempted to adjust the Jewish child to the Russian environment, with a view to his living in a hostile and oppressive Russia. It rather aimed at imbuing him with a love for a national home of the Jewish people, the home of the Jewish past and the home of the future.

The problem in America is radically different from what it was in Russia and Poland. The public school is not only open to children of all groups but attendance is compulsory. The Jew is free to participate in American life.[1] Here, in the Jewish school, the child should be prepared to participate in American Jewish life and through such participation to contribute to American

[1] For a discussion of the problem in America, see Book Two: *Principles of the Jewish Curriculum in America.*

life. The problem is one of transmitting the important values of the Jewish social heritage and at the same time of effecting an adequate adjustment to the conditions of American life. Spiritual renewal without self-effacement—adequate adjustment without loss of individuality—these should be the watchwords of our educational policy.

TABLE SHOWING CURRICULUM OF HEDER, TALMUD TORAH, AND YESHIBAH BEFORE AND AFTER THE HASKALAH, AND CURRICULUM OF THE HEDER METUKKON

A. BEFORE THE HASKALAH

Elementary Heder Age: 3-5 4-6	Humosh Heder Age: 5-7 6-8	Talmud Heder Age: 7, 8, or 9 to 13	Talmud Torah Age: 4-13	Yeshibah Age: from 13 on
Subjects	*Subjects*	*Subjects*	*Subjects*	*Subjects*
Reading	Humosh	Talmud and Commentaries on Talmud	Reading	Talmud—with more difficult Commentaries and Codes
Blessings	Rashi	Midrash	Humosh and Rashi	Humosh (only in some cases)
Participation in daily prayer	Former Prophets	Humosh and Rashi (only in few hours weekly)	Chanting the Sidrah and Haftarah	
Beginning of Humosh (only in some cases)	Latter Prophets (only in some cases)	Jewish Holidays—Laws of	Talmud (in exceptional cases)	
	Psalms	Laws of Tefillin (before Bar Mitzvah)		
	Hagiographa (only in some cases)			
	Chanting the Sidrah and Haftarah			
	Ethics of the Fathers			
	Jewish Holidays—Laws and Liturgy of (occasionally)			
	Beginning of Talmud (only in some cases)			

B. AFTER THE HASKALAH

Heder	Talmud Torah	Yeshibah	Heder Metukkon
Subjects (translated into Russian, Yiddish, or German)	*Subjects*	*Subjects*	*Subjects*
Prayers	Hebrew—Reading and Writing	Talmud	Reading
Bible	Hebrew Grammar	Commentaries	Prayers
Talmud (less than in old Heder)	Customs and Ceremonies	Codes	Humosh
Hebrew	Bible	Russian	Prophets
Hebrew Grammar	Jewish History	Arithmetic	Grammar
Haskalah Literature	Translation from Russian into Hebrew (only in some cases)	Calligraphy	**Hebrew, as a spoken language**
Jewish History	Russian—Reading and Writing		Talmud
Jewish Catechism (only in some cases)	Penmanship		Jewish History
	Arithmetic		**Modern Hebrew Literature**
	Natural History (only in some cases)		Russian
	Grammar (only in some cases)		
	German (only in some cases)		
	Latin (only in some cases)		
	Patriotism (only in some cases)		
	Vocational Education (only in some cases)		

APPENDIX A

ILLUSTRATIVE HEDER CURRICULA

In the biography of the Baal Shem Tob [1] (1698-1759) the curriculum of a Heder in Cracow is described as consisting of the study of the Bible, its translation, the study of Rashi, the prayers and their order, manners, writing, grammar, and Talmud. If the student is not fit to engage in academic studies, he is sent to study manual work or apprenticed to some master when he reaches the age of fourteen.

Solomon Maimon, 1753-1800, in his autobiography describes the curriculum in his school. It consisted of: (1) The reading of Hebrew. (2) The study of Bible in translation, taught in accordance with the portion of the week. This was translated into Yiddish which Maimon claims was full of errors. All kinds of exegesis are included in the study which prevents the student from understanding the Bible in its simplicity. (3) The Talmud of course forms the main subject of study. (4) Little progress is made with the mastery of the Hebrew language or grammar, both of which are studied only incidentally in the course of the Bible study.

Another Heder of which a detailed description is given is that in Kamenez-Podolsk, [2] in the forties of the nineteenth century. The curriculum described consists of: (1) The alphabet and reading of the prayers. (2) Penta-

---

[1] Kahana, A., *Rabbi Israel Baal Shem Tob.*
[2] Kotik, E., *Op. cit.*, v. 1, pp. 55-61.

teuch. (3) Talmud. (4) Writing, taught by some of the Melammedim. (5) The Prophets, taught only by one teacher. In most cases the teacher did not teach the prophets at all, as it was at times considered heretical to do so.

Lilienthal describes the curriculum in the school at Vilna in the forties of the nineteenth century as follows: "I was told that the children here begin to learn the reading of the prayers and some Humosh; that they visit the school daily from 9 to 1 and from 3 to 6 o'clock; that those learning Humosh have to translate some chapters of the law read the next Sabbath in the Synagogue; that the punishment consists in the use of the rod, and some one of the friends accompanying me remarked that in some of these Hadarim it is customary to give the boys some lashes on Friday afternoon before being dismissed, on account of the mischief which they *will* commit on the Sabbath." [1]

---

[1] Lilienthal, M., "Travels in Russia," in *Op. cit.*, pp. 283-284. See also a humorous description of a teacher who gives whippings for future mischief in Rabinowitz, Shalom (Shalom Alekem), *Jewish Children*, story entitled "Boaz the Teacher."

APPENDIX B

ON THE CURRICULUM OF THE YESHIBAH

"The boy should pay close attention to those portions of Tosafot that dilate on Pilpul and immerse himself in Maharsha and Marshal. Of the later day works, Sifte Kohen is to be studied with the Hoshen Mishpat; however, it is proper to study the Sema, since the Sifte Kohen is merely an explanation of the latter. With the Yoreh Deah the Sifte Kohen is sufficient. One should, however, in this connection look up the Pri Hadosh. The essential thing, however, is Tur Yoreh Deah; the Aharonim one can attend to during the repetition of the Shulhan Aruk. With the Tur Orah Hayim one is to study the Magen Abraham. Of the printed responsa, one is to read first all those of Nachmanides, Joseph di Trani, Elia b. Hayim, R. Asher, Levi b. Habib, R. Moses di Trani, and R. Meir of Rothenberg. Of the earlier authorities there are Solomon b. Adrat, R. Nissim, Maimonides, and the responsa of Joseph Colon, R. Isaac b. Sheshet, Terumat ha-deshen, Maharil, R. Jacob Weil, Terumot, R. Eliezer b. Nathan; of those of our own day, Hawat Yair. For a short cut through the Talmud are recommended Tosafot, with Maharsha, R. Asher, Rif, Ran, Rambam, Tur, Beth Joseph and Shulhan Aruk." [1]

[1] From the will of Rabbi Jonah Landsofer, quoted in Güdemann, M., *Quellenschriften*, pp. 132-134.

APPENDIX C

ON LEON MANDELSTAMM

On August 10th, 1839, the assistant superintendent of education of White Russia wrote to the minister of public instruction requesting special permission for Mandelstamm to enter the university.

"The Jew, Leib Josephovich Mandelstamm, 20 years of age, a resident of Novo-Zhagory in the district of Shavel, Gov. of Wilna, who has received his education at home, wishes to continue his studies at the University of Moscow, and for that purpose has petitioned the director of schools in the Gov. of Wilna to admit him, Mandelstamm, to the local government gymnasium for examination in the subjects of the gymnasium course, and to receive the required certificate which shall enable him to enter the university. But as he has not studied at any of the public educational institutions in the province of White Russia, so, not seeing any basis for complying with his above request, I ordered to notify the above mentioned Jew that he must appeal directly to the authorities of the University of Moscow, on whom the admission to the preliminary entrance examinations depends. In the meantime, the local civil authorities, in view of the existing regulations about the Jews, have met with difficulties about providing him, Mandelstamm, who belongs neither to the first nor to the second guild of merchants, with a passport for the journey to Moscow; and therefore having solemnly resolved to complete his education, and not seeing any other way to accomplish his desire, he again appealed to me with a petition to obtain for him the permission to enter the above named university.

"Having had the occasion during the presence of the said Jew in Wilna to know him closer, I became convinced that he is endowed by nature with good abilities and has a special inclination to learning, which is confirmed also by the fact that with the limited means which were afforded him at the home of his parents, who were not wealthy, he succeeded in learning the Russian, German and French languages, and to become acquainted with all the subjects of the gymnasial course.

"Taking into consideration that such phenomena are unusual among the Jews of this country, and that according to the propositions which have already been made for the establishment of separate schools for the education of Jewish children it is indispensable to have several learned persons from among their own co-religionists to occupy the position of teachers in such schools, I, on my side, would consider it necessary to support the young Mandelstamm in his resolve and to facilitate for him the means to enter the Moscow university.

"Therefore, adding to this as proof of the progress made by Mandelstamm, his own compositions in Russian and modern foreign languages, I take the liberty to represent to Your Excellency to permit that Jew to be subjected to a preliminary examination in the government-gymnasium of Wilna, and to permit him, if he proves himself to possess sufficient knowledge, to repair to Moscow and to enter the university there on the basis of No. 105 of the statute about the Jews which was approved by his Imperial Majesty April 13, 1835." [1]

Uvarov granted this request.

[1] See Wiernik P., "Leon Mandelstamm," in *Jewish Forum*, v. 1, pp. 609-10.

BIBLIOGRAPHICAL LISTS

Bureau of Jewish Education, New York City. List of works on Jewish education. MS. on cards, compiled in 1913.

Columbia University. *Library Bulletin No. 2.* Books on education in the libraries of Columbia University. New York, 1901. History of education: Jews, p. 22.

Dushkin, Alexander M. *Jewish Education in New York City.* New York, 1918. Bibliography, pp. 547-559.

New York Public Library. *List of Works Relating to the History and Condition of the Jews in Various Countries.* New York, 1914. Education, pp. 169-174.

Perezhitoe, v. 1. St. Petersburg, 1909. At the end: Materialy dlya istoricheskoy bibliografii.

> Works in German, French, and Polish arranged in chronological order, 1785-1899.

St. Petersburg. Imperial Public Library. *Catalogue de la Section des Russica ou écrits sur la Russie en langues étrangères.* St. Petersburg, 1873. Now in Jewish room of New York Public Library.

> The titles of books and pamphlets written by Jews or about Jews in Russia in non-Russian languages, listed herein, were compiled by A. Harkavy under the title "Judaica" (21 pp.) at the end of *Evreiskaya Biblioteka,* v. 6. St. Petersburg, 1878.

Strassburger, Baruch. *Geschichte der Erziehung und des Unterrichts bei den Israeliten.* Stuttgart, 1885. Bibliographie der jüdischen Pädagogie in chronologischer Ordnung, pp. 273-310.

> Includes a list of works on Jewish education as well as a list of textbooks on various subjects, both in Hebrew and in German, and a few titles in other languages.

Swift, Fletcher Harper. *Education in Ancient Israel.* Chicago, 1919. Selected Bibliography, pp. 119-125.

Systematic Index of Literature about the Jews in the Russian Language from 1708 to 1889. (Russian.) St. Petersburg, 1893. Section 6, Education. Nos. 3468-4387, pp. 226-270.

BIBLIOGRAPHY

Abrahams, Israel

Jewish Life in the Middle Ages. Philadelphia, 1911.

Especially chap. 19, The Medieval Schools, and chap. 20, The Scope of Education.

Adler, Mordecai

גורל המלמדים Vienna, 1883.

Akiba, Joseph ben Jehiel

לב העיברי Lemberg, 1873.

On the will of R. Moses Sofer (Schreiber).

Anonymous

How Shall We Teach Our Children Hebrew? (In המליץ October 4, 1885.)

Asch, Shalom

א שטעדטעל Warsaw, 1908.

A description of Jewish life in Eastern Europe.

מיט׳ן שטראם Warsaw, 1909.

Reflects the spiritual struggle in the days of Haskalah.

Bader, Gershom

דיא ערשטע אידישע שולען אין גאליציען (In דיא צוקונפט v. 13, no. 2-3, New York, 1908.)

Bernfeld, Simon

Vospitanie. (In *Evreiskaya Entziklopediya,* v. 5, col. 797-812.)

1. In the Bible; 2. In Mishnah and Talmud; 3. In the Middle Ages; 4 In Modern Times; 5. In Most Recent Times.

214

Bernstein, Israel   בנין זקנים וסתירת ילדים (In
השחר v. 7, pp. 473-81, 537-
52, 622-35, 692-701.)
On the influence of Has-
kalah on the old education.

————   העתודים העולים על הצאן (In
השחר v. 6, pp. 366-81, 401-
15,Vienna, 1875.)
On the Heder.

Bialik, Hayim Nahmon   המתמיד (In his שירים Berlin,
1921.)

Borochow, Baer   Education in the West. (In
Evreiskaya Entziklopediya,
v. 13, col. 30-43.)
Containing statistical
tables.

Bramson, Leonty M.   *K istorii nachalnavo obrazovaniya Evreev v Rossii.* St.
Petersburg, 1896.

Deutsch, Gotthard,   Education-Trade Schools. (In
and Jacobs, Joseph   *Jewish Encyclopedia*, v. 5,
p. 48.)

Dubnow, S. M.   Council of Four Lands. (In
Jewish Encyclopedia, v. 4,
pp. 304-308.)

————   Hasidism. (*In Jewish Encyclopedia*, v. 6, pp. 251-256.)

————   *History of the Jews in Russia
and Poland*, 3 v. Philadel-
phia, 1916-20.

————   ועד ארבע הארצות (בספר היובל
לכבוד נחום סאקלאוו War-
saw, 1904.)

Ehrlich, Adolf   *Entwickelungsgeschichte der Israelitischen Gemeindeschule zu Riga.* St. Petersburg, 1894.

Eisenstein, Judah David   Talmud Torah. (In *Jewish Encyclopedia,* v. 12, pp. 37-39.)

————   Yeshibah. (In *Jewish Encyclopedia,* v. 12, pp. 595-600.)

Eliezer ben Judah of Worms   ס' הרוקח Fano, 1505, and later editions.

Evreiskaya Entziklopediya   Talmud Torah. (In v. 14, col. 723-25.)

Frank, Helena   *Yiddish Tales,* translated by Helena Frank. Philadelphia, 1912.
                               Reflects Jewish life in Eastern Europe.

Friedlaender, Israel   *The Jews in Russia and Poland.* New York, 1915.

Fünn, Samuel Joseph   שפה לנאמנים Vilna, 1881.

Gamoran, Emanuel   *Changing Conceptions in Jewish Education,* Book Two. New York, 1924.

Ginzberg, Louis   The Moralist Movement in Russia (In *The Menorah,* v. 36, pp. 237-247.) New York, 1904.

————   *The Primary School.* Philadelphia, 1907.

————   *The Talmud Student.* Baltimore, 1905.

————   *The Rabbinical Student.* New York, 1906.

To reappear in his collection of essays which is to be published by the Jewish Publication Society.

Goldblum, Israel Isser   אײשישאק (In השחר v. 9. Vienna, 1877.)

Struggle for Haskalah in Yeshibah.

Gordon, Judah Loeb   שיחת חולין (In) דיא יונגע יאהרען Warsaw, 1886.)

Poem describing the reaction of the masses to the Crown Schools.

————   כל שירי יהודה (In) קוצו של יוד ליב גורדון v. 4. Vilna, 1898.)

Gornfeld, A.   Russia—The Jew in Russian Literature. (In *Jewish Encyclopedia*, v. 10, pp. 551-554.)

Gottlober, Abraham Baer   על דבר בית ספר הישיבה הבקר אור (In) באדעססא edited by Gottlober, v. 5, pp. 180-82.)

Grossman, Louis   Pedagogics. (In *Jewish Encyclopedia*, v. 9, pp. 570-577.)

Güdemann, Moritz   Education—From Talmudic to Modern Times. (In *Jewish Encyclopedia*, v. 5, pp. 43-48.)

————   *Das Jüdische Unterrichtswesen während der spanisch-arabischen Periode.* Vienna, 1873. *Geschichte des Erizehungswesens und der Cultur der abendländischen Juden während des Mittelalters und der neueren Zeit.*

v. 1: Geschichte des Erziehungswesens und der Cultur der Juden in Frankreich und Deutschland, X-XIV Jahrhunderts. Vienna, 1880.

v. 2: Geschichte des Erziehungswesens und der Cultur der Juden in Italien. Vienna, 1884.

v. 3: Geschichte des Erziehungswesens und der Cultur der Juden in Deutschland während des XIV und XV Jahrhunderts. Vienna, 1888.

The above three volumes have been translated into Hebrew by A. S. Friedberg, under the title of *Ha-torah we-ha-hayim.* Warsaw, 1896.

Güdemann, Moritz   *Quellenschriften zur Geschichte des Unterrichts und der Erziehung bei den deutschen Juden von den ältesten Zeiten bis auf Mendelssohn.* Berlin, 1891.

Günzburg, Mordecai Aaron   דביר   Vilna, 1856-62. 2 v.

————   אביעזר   Vilna, 1863.

Gurland, Jacob   כבוד הבית   Vilna, 1858.

A description of the Vilna rabbinical seminary.

הכרם   Edited by Eleazar Atlas. Warsaw, 1887.

Contains a composite ar-
ticle entitled ארבעה עולמות
comparing the Vilna rab-
binical seminary with the
Volozhin Yeshibah, consisting of:

1. A poem describing the
Heder and the Yeshibah, by
Isaac Rabinowitz;

2. Four letters concerning
the Vilna rabbinical seminary, by Isaac Benjacob to
Isaac Baer Levinsohn;

3. Survey of the Volozhin
Yeshibah, by Micah Joseph
Berdyczewski;

4. Views of the editor.

הלבנון   v. 5, pp. 418, 434, and 450.
Paris, 1868.

Contains a curriculum of
Mantua in 1563.

Hannover, Nathan Nata   יון מצולה   Lemberg, 1850.

An account of persecutions
of 1648-49, containing a description of Yeshibah.

Hessen, Julius   Education of the Jews in Russia up to Alexander II. (In
Evreiskaya Entziklopediya,
v. 13, col. 43-48.)

Horodezky, Samuel Abba   החסידות כמו שהיא (In התקופה
v. 6, pp. 335-346.)

Hurwitz, M. M.   דרך עץ החיים   Cracow, 1895.
                      A description of the Volo-
                      zhin Yeshibah.

Hurwitz, Samuel   פון'ם חדרשען פנקם   Vilna,
                      1908.

Hurwitz, Saul Israel החסידות וההשכלה   (In his
                      מאין לאין   Berlin, 1914.)

Jawitz, Zeeb Wolf   מגדל המאה   (In כנסת ישראל
                      edited by S. P. Rabinowitz,
                      v. 1, pp. 130-46.)
                      Tendencies of Jewish cul-
                      ture in the 19th century.

Jazkan, Samuel Jacob רבנו אליהו מוּוילנא   Warsaw,
                      1900.

Jehudi   החדרים המתקנים   (In המליץ
                      v. 43, nos. 89-90.)

Joseph, Morris   Jewish Education. (In *Ency-
                      clopedia of Religion and
                      Ethics*, edited by James
                      Hastings, v. 5, pp. 194-198.)

Joseph, Samuel   *Jewish Immigration to the
                      United States*, 1881-1910.
                      New York, 1914.

Kahana, Abraham   רבי ישראל בעל שם טוב   Zhito-
                      mir, 1901.

Kandel, Isaac L., and   Jewish Education (In *Cyclo-
  Grossman, Louis   pedia of Education,* edited by
                        Paul Monroe, v. 3, pp. 542-
                        553. New York, 1912.)

Kantor, Judah Loeb   The Talmud Torah. (In *Rus-
                      ski Evrei*, 1880, no. 30.)

Kaplan, Zeeb   קללת אלהים   (In השחר, v. 9,
                      p. 235, 1877.)

On the failure of the rabbinical seminaries of the
Haskalah.

Kaplan, Zeeb   והיו עיניך רואות את מוריך (In
המליץ nos. 4-7, 1883.)

A descriptive story of a
teacher's life.

Katzovich, Israel Isser   זעכציג יאהר לעבען New York,
1919.

Autobiography reflecting
Jewish life and education in
Russia.

Kauffmann, Arkadya Aaron מכתב על דבר החנוך פרחי (In
צפון, edited by E. L. Hur-
witz and S. J. Fünn, v. 2, pp.
43-61. Vilna, 1841.)

Kohler, Kaufman   Education—Biblical and Pre-
Talmudical Data. (In *Jew-
ish Encyclopedia*, v. 5, pp.
42-43.)

Kohler, Max J.   Educational Reforms in Europe and Jewish Emancipa-
tion. (In *Jewish Forum*, v.
2, pp. 704-15, 775-88. New
York, 1919.)

Kotik, Ezekiel   מיינע זכרונות 2 v. Warsaw,
1913-14.

Autobiographical book of
Jewish life and education in
Russia and Poland.

Krauss, Samuel   Joshua b. Gamala. (In *Jewish
Encyclopedia*, v. 7, pp. 289-
290.)

Krupitzky, Z. — Yeshibot in Russia. (In *Evreiskaya Entziklopediya*, v. 8, col. 734-40.)

Levinsohn, Isaac Baer — תעודה בישראל Warsaw, 1901.

Lifshitz, A. M. — החדר (In התקופה edited by David Frischman, v. 7. Warsaw, 1920.)

Lilienblum, Moses Loeb — חטאת נעורים 2 parts. Vienna, 1876.

Lilienthal, Life and Writings — By David Philipson. Especially Travels in Russia, pp. 159-363. New York, 1915.

Linetski, Isaac Joel — דאָס פּוילישע יונגעל Lemberg, 1880.

Lipman, J. G. — Russia—Education. (In *Jewish Encyclopedia*, v. 10, pp. 541-47.)

———— — Russia—Legislation concerning special taxation. (In *Jewish Encyclopedia*, v. 10, pp. 550-551.)

Litwin, A. — יודישע נשמות New York, 1917. 6 v.: v. 1-2, Lithuania; v. 3-4, Poland; v. 5, Galicia; v. 6, Hasidic life.

Luzzato, Samuel David — אגרות שד״ל published by Isaac Shealtiel Graber. Przemysl, 1882.

Maimon, Solomon — *Autobiography*, translated by J. C. Murray. Boston, 1888.

Margoshes, Samuel — *A History of the Curriculum of the Jewish Schools in Germany from the Middle of the*

	17th to the Middle of the 19th Century. MS.
Maybaum, Siegmund	Methodik des jüdischen Religionsunterrichtes. Breslau, 1896.
Meisl, Josef	Geschichte der Juden in Polen und Russland. v. 1-2. Berlin, 1921-22.
————	Haskalah. Geschichte der Aufklärungsbewegung unter den Juden in Russland. Berlin, 1919.
Morgolis, Michael Grigorie-vich	Voprosy evreiskoi zhizni. St. Petersburg, 1889. Chap. 1: Contributions to the History of Education among Russian Jews. Chap. 2: About the Contemporary Jewish Communal Schools.
Mysh, M.	Russia—Legislation. (In Jewish Encyclopedia, v. 10, pp. 548-550.)
Philipson, David	Max Lilienthal, Life and Writings. New York, 1915.
Philo, Judæus	The Senior Student. (In The Jewish Messenger, v. 28, nos. 6-14.)
Raisin, Jacob Salmon	The Haskalah Movement in Russia. Philadelphia, 1914.
Records of Community of Cracow. 1604, 1606, 1615	(In Jahrbuch der Jüdisch-Literarischen Gesellschaft, v. 10-11. Frankfort - a. - M., 1913.)

Reines, Moses   אוצר (In   אכסניות של תורה
    הספרות 1890.)
    On Volozhin Yeshibah.

Ritter, Immanuel Heinrich   *Geschichte der jüdischen Reformation*, 3 parts. Berlin, 1858-1865.

Rosenfeld, Samuel   ר׳ ישראל סלנטר Warsaw, 1911.

Rosenthal, Herman   Kahal. (In *Jewish Encyclopedia*, v. 7, pp. 409-411.)

———   Lilienthal, Max. (In *Jewish Encyclopedia*, v. 8, pp. 86-87.)

———   Russia. (In *Jewish Encyclopedia*, v. 10, pp. 518-534.)

———   Poland. (In *Jewish Encyclopedia*, v. 10, pp. 561-575.)

Rosenthal, Leon   2 תולדות מרבי השכלה בישראל
v. St. Petersburg, 1885-90.

Rosenthal, Vasili   Russia—Artisans in the Pale of Settlement. (In *Jewish Encyclopedia*, v. 10, pp. 534-538.)

———   Russia—Charities. (In *Jewish Encyclopedia*, v. 10, pp. 538-541.)

Rudayev, Moses Joseph   (In   מטרת החדרים המתקנים
הצפירה v. 29, nos. 182-184. Warsaw, 1902.)

Rudermann, Pesah   השקפה כללית על מצב בני ישראל
ברוסיא (In השחר v. 5, pp. 465-476.)
    On the rabbinical seminaries of Vilna and Zhitomir.

Sachs, Abraham Simhah   חרוב'ע וועלטען   New York, 1917.

A description of Jewish life in Russia.

Salidar, Moses   תכן הלמודים בבתי הספר העברים (In הצפירה v. 25, nos. 163-4. Warsaw, 1898.)

Schechter, Solomon   Studies in Judaism, 2 v. Philadelphia, 1909-11.

Especially essays on Hasidism, the study of the Bible, the child in Jewish literature, on the study of the Talmud.

Shayel   Odessa Talmud Torah. (In *Russki Evrei.*, nos. 34-43. St. Petersburg, 1880.

Smolenskin, Perez   גמול ישרים   Vienna, 1876.

————   התועה בדרכי החיים   St. Petersburg, 1891.

S - - -N, Abraham A.   תל שהכל פונים אליו (In השחר v. 8, pp. 112-19, 161-69. Vienna, 1877.)

On the Volozhin Yeshibah.

Society for Promotion of Culture among the Jews of Russia. Founded in 1863. Hebrew title

מפיצי השכלה בישראל בארץ רוסיא

Spravochnaya Kniga po vo-prosam obrazovaniya Evreev. St. Petersburg, 1901.

A guide for teachers in Jewish schools and workers in popular education. For history of this society, see Rosenthal, Leon, *Op. cit.*, and Tscherikover, Ilya, *Op.*

	cit., and Waldstein, A. S., in *Jewish Encyclopedia.*
Stanislavsky, S.	Of the History and Life of One Jewish School. (In *Voskhod,* v. 4, pp. 126-149. St. Petersburg, 1884.)
Steinberg, Judah	בימים ההם Cracow, 1906. A description of militarism in the days of Nicholas.
Strasburger, Baruch	*Geschichte der Erziehung und des Unterrichts bei den Israeliten.* Stuttgart, 1885.
Swift, Fletcher	*Education in Ancient Israel.* Chicago, 1919.
Talmud	בבא בתרא fol. 86; בבא מציעא fol. 21.
Teitelbaum, Mordecai	הרב מלאדי Warsaw, 1910.
Tscherikower, Ilya	A History of the Society for the Promotion of Culture among the Jews of Russia, v. I (Russian). St. Petersburg, 1913.
————	Society for the Promotion of Culture among the Jews of Russia. (In *Evreiskaya Entziklopediya,* v. 13, col. 59-62.)
Vishnitzer, Mark	*Istorya evreiskavo Naroda.* (In his introduction.) Moscow, 1914.
————	Yeshibah. (In *Evreiskaya Entziklopediya,* v. 8, col. 725-34.)

Wáad of Lithuania Records (In *Evreyskaya Starina*, 1909-
1623-1761   1915.)

Warsaw Jewish Community *Z dziejów Gminy Starozakon-
nych w Warszawie w XIX
stuleciw*, v. I, Szkolnictwo.
Warsaw, 1907.

Weissberg, Max   *Die Neuhebraische Aufklär-
ungs-Literatur in Galizien.*
Leipzig and Vienna, 1898.

Wengeroff, Pauline   *Memoiren einer Grossmutter*,
2 v. Berlin, 1910-1913.

Wessely, Naphtali Herz דברי שלום ואמת Berlin, 1781.

Wettstein, F. H.   קדמוניות מפנקסאות ישנים
Cracow, 1892.

Wiernik, Peter   Chapters on Cultural History
of Jews in Russia. (In *Jew-
ish Forum*, August, 1918-
1921.)

————   Haskalah. (In *Jewish Encyclopedia*, v. 6, pp. 256-258.)

————   Heder. (In *Jewish Encyclopedia*, v. 6, pp. 314-315, 1905.)

————   Musarnikes. (In *Jewish Ency-
clopedia*, v. 9, pp. 117-118.)
Translated into Russian
Jewish Encyclopedia.

Woltke, Gr.   Education during the Régime
of Alexander II. (In *Evre-
iskaya Entziklopediya*, v. 13,
cols. 38-58.)

————   Heder and Melammed in Russia and the Kingdom of
Poland. (In *Evreiskaya*

Entziklopediya, v. 15, col. 589-596.)

Wygodsky, L.

Russia—Emigration. (In *Jewish Encyclopedia,* v. 10, pp. 547-548.)

Zarnamardik, Joseph

המליץ In) מסלת למוד מתקנה v. 42, nos. 26-27.)

Zederbaum, Alexander

v. המליץ In) מעשים בכל יום 14, no. 22.)

———

a קהלת In) צער גדול בנים collection of essays and poems edited by Zederbaum. St. Petersburg, 1881.)

Zeven

הבקר אורIn) מכתב מאדעססא edited by Abraham Baer Gottlober, v. 4, pp. 1205-09.)

Zunz, Jehiel Mattathias

עיר הצדק Lemberg, 1874. A history of the Jews in Cracow.

GLOSSARY

Ab—Eleventh month of the Jewish calendar.

Abodah—Religious practice or service.

Aggadah—Narrative portions of the Talmud.

Ahad Ha-Am—Pseudonym of Asher Ginsberg, contemporary Jewish philosopher and founder of spiritual Zionism.

Aharonim—Later authorities on Jewish law (subsequent to codification of the Shulhan Aruk).

Alef Bet—The first two letters of the Hebrew alphabet.

Alfas—Discussions of legal portions of the Talmud by R. Isaac b. Jacob Alfasi, 1013-1103.

Am Ha-arez—An ignoramus.

Aron Kodesh—The Holy Ark in the synagogue, containing the Scrolls of the Law.

Asher, Rabbi—Commentator on Talmud and writer of responsa, born in Germany 14th century.

Bahur (pl. Bahurim)—A young man who studied in the Yeshibah.

Bar Mizvah—The ceremony initiating a boy of thirteen as a member of the Jewish community.

Bar Mosheh—A commentary on the Pentateuch.

Behinot Olam—A didactic poem written by Jedaiah b. Abraham Bedersi, 1270-1340.

Berakot—A tractate of the Talmud.

Bet Hamidrash (pl. Bate Midrash)—Community house for prayer and study.

Bet Joseph—Joseph Karo, Rabbi in Turkey, writer of codes and responsa, 16th century.

Bet Shmüel—Commentary on Eben Ha-Ezer, 1689, by R. Samuel b. Uri Shraga Phoebus.

229

Bilu—The Hebrew initials of "O, House of Jacob, come and let us go!"

Borki Nafshi—Psalm 104.

Colon, Joseph—French Rabbi, writer of responsa, 16th century.

Dayan (pl. Dayanim)—Assistants to the rabbi in the larger communities where the rabbi was too busy to take care of the community himself.

Eben Ha-Ezer—Portion of Shulhan Aruk dealing with laws of women.

Elia b. Hayim—Rabbi in Constantinople, writer of responsa, 16th century.

Eliezer b. Nathan—Writer of codes and responsa, 12th century.

Etrog—A citron over which blessings are recited during Sukkot.

Gaon—Head of Talmudical Academy in Babylonia, also applied to a man of unusual learning.

Grager—A rattle used by the children on Purim.

Gymnasia—Russian schools equivalent to our high schools, and perhaps first two years of college.

Habad—The initials of the three Hebrew words for "Wisdom," "Understanding," and "Knowledge," by which a branch of the Hasidim was designated.

Haber—Degree awarded to learned man in Poland.

Haftarah—The weekly portion of the Prophets read in the synagogue on the Sabbath.

Halakah—The legal portions of the Talmud.

Hallah—Special twists baked for the Sabbath.

Hamishah Asar Be-shebat—Fifteenth day of month of Shebat, or New Year for Trees, also known as Jewish Arbor Day.

Hanukkah Gelt—Money given as a gift to children during the festival of Hanukkah, commemorating the victory of the Maccabees.

Haskalah—The movement for enlightenment.

Havat Yair—A collection of responsa by R. Hayim Yair Bacharach.

Hayim Yair Bacharach—Rabbi in Worms, 1639-1702.

Hayye Adam—Code of R. Abraham b. Jehiel Danzig, 1748-1820.

Hebrah Talmud Torah—Society for promotion of education.

Heder (pl. Hadarim)—Jewish elementary school in Russia and Poland.

Heshwan—Second month of the Jewish calendar.

Hobat Ha-lebabot—Title of ethical work written by Bahya Ben Joseph Ibn Pakudah.

Hosha'not—Special prayers recited on Sukkot.

Hoshen Mishpat—Portion of Shulhan Aruk dealing with civil law.

Hukke Ha-torah—"The Statutes of the Law," a document on education in the Middle Ages.

Humosh—Pentateuch.

Ibri—Term used to designate the reading of mechanical Hebrew.

Ikub Ha-Keriah—Custom of delaying the reading of the law in the synagogue until a wrong committed by one of the congregants has been righted.

Isaac b. Sheshet (Ribash)—Writer of responsa, b. Spain 1326.

Isaiah Horowitz—German Kabbalist, 1555-1630.

Iyyar—Eighth month of the Jewish calendar.

Jacob Emden—German Talmudist, 1697-1776.

Jacob Weil—Rabbi in Germany, writer of responsa and codes 16th century.

Joseph di Trani—Rabbi, writer of responsa, born 1568 in Zefat.

Kadashim—One of the six parts of the Mishnah, dealing with things sanctified for sacrifice.

Kahal—The community organization.

Keburat Hamor—"The Burial of an Ass," title of a book by P. Smolenskin.

Keriat Shema le-enen—Reading the Shema in a house where a baby is born.

Kiddush—Special blessing recited over the wine on Friday evening.

Kopek—Russian penny.

Kuzari—Title of philosophical book by R. Judah Halevi.

Lag Ba-Omer—Jewish scholars' holiday, day on which plague is said to have ceased from amidst the pupils of Rabbi Akiba.

Lamddan (pl. Lamddonim)—Learned man.

Levi b. Habib—Rabbi in Turkey, 16th century, writer of responsa.

Lulab—Palms over which prayers are recited on Sukkot.

Magen Abraham—Commentary on Shulhan Aruk by R. Abraham Abli Gumbiner, b. 1637.

Maharal—R. Judah Löw Ben Bezalel, Austrian Talmudist, 1515-1609.

Maharil—R. Jacob b. Mosheh Halevi Sigali, born in Germany 15th century, Rabbi in Mayence, writer of responsa and codes.

Maharsha—Rabbi Samuel Edels, commentator on Talmud.

Mahzor—Collection of Prayers for the holidays.

Maimonides or Rambam—Philosopher and codifier of Jewish law, born in Spain 1135, d. 1204.

Marshal—Rabbi Solomon Luria, b. 1510, commentator on Talmud.

Mazzol Tob—Congratulations.

Meir of Rothenberg—Rabbi, born in Germany 1215, codifier and writer of responsa.

Melammed (pl. Melammedim)—Name given to teachers in Russia and Poland.

Mezuzah—A small tin case attached to doorpost containing parchment on which is written the Shema.

Midrash (pl. Midrashim)—Homiletical Book.

Mishnah—The law transmitted orally and compiled by Rabbi Judah Ha-Nasi early in the 3rd century.

Mizrah—A special ornamental picture, usually found in the Jewish home, containing the verse, "From the rising to the setting of the sun, may the name of the Lord be praised."

Mo'ed—One of the six portions of the Mishnah, dealing with the holidays.

Moreh Nebukim—The Guide to the Perplexed, by Maimonides.

Morenu—Degree given to learned men in Poland.

Moses d. Trani—Talmudist and exegete, b. Salonica 1505.

Nahmanides or Ramban—Spanish Talmudist and exegete, b. 1194.

Nashim—One of six portions of Mishnah dealing with laws of women.

Nezikin—One of six portions of Mishnah dealing with torts.

Nisan—Seventh month of the Jewish calendar.

Nissim—Rabbi ben Reuben Gerundi, commentator on Jewish law, 1340-1380.

Orah Hayim—Portion of Shulhan Aruk dealing with laws concerning prayers, festivals, etc.

Peot—Earlocks.

Pilpul—Casuistic method in study of Talmud.

Pri Hadosh—Commentary on Shulhan Aruk by Rabbi Hezekiah di Silva, beginning of 18th century.

Purim—Jewish holiday celebrating the saving of the people from threatened destruction in Persia during fifth century.

Ran—Commentary on Alfasi by Rabbi Nissim ben Reuben.

Rif—Rabbi Isaac Alfasi, writer of the Code Alfasi, 13th century.

Rosh—An abstract of legal portions by R. Asher Ben Jehiel, 1250-1328.

Rosh Yeshibah—Head of the Yeshibah.

Schubetze—A long garment worn by the Jews of Poland.

Seder—Name given to ceremonies performed in a Jewish home the first two evenings of Passover.

Sefer Torah (pl. Sifre Torah)—A scroll of the Law.

Sema—Commentary on Hoshen Mishpat by Joshua b. Alexander Ha-Kohen Falk, d. 1614.

Shabuoth—The Feast of Weeks.

Shakh—Commentary on Yoreh Deah by R. Shabbethai b. Meir Ha-Kohen, 1621-1662.

Shalosh Se-udot—The name given to the third meal on the Sabbath.

Shas—Summary name for the entire Talmud.

Shebat—Fifth month of the Jewish calendar.

Shehitah—The ritual method of slaughtering animals.

Shiur—The portion assigned for a given period of study in the Talmud.

Shlakhta—Polish nobility.

Shohet—One who performs the ceremony of Shehitah.

Shulhan Aruk—The code summarizing Talmudic Law and subsequent Jewish customs.

Shurah Grüss—Learning to "send regards" in a letter.

Sidrah—The portion of the law read in the synagogue on the Sabbath.

Sifte Kohen—Commentary on Shulhan Aruk written by Rabbi Shabbetai Kohen—1621-1662.

Simhat Torah—The festival of the "Rejoicing of the Law."

Solomon b. Adrat—Commentator on Talmud and writer of responsa, b. 1235.

Sukkot—Jewish agricultural festival, also associated with Jewish life in the wilderness after the Exodus.

Tallit Katon—Small undergarment with fringes worn by orthodox Jews.

Talmud—The Jewish oral law, developed beginning about 300 B. C. E., finally compiled about 500 C. E.

Talmud Torah—Elementary educational institution for children of the poor in Eastern Europe.

Tammuz—Tenth month of the Jewish calendar.

Tanya—A book written by Rabbi Zalmon, leader of the Lithuanian Hasidim.

Targum—Aramaic translation of the Pentateuch.

Taw—Last letter in the Hebrew alphabet.

Tebet—Fourth month of the Jewish calendar.

Tefillin—Phylacteries worn by Jews in morning prayers.

Terumat Ha-Deshen—Book of responsa written by Rabbi Israel Isserlin, Rabbi in Germany, end of 15th century and beginning of the 16th century.

Terumot—A code written by Rabbi Baruk of Mayence, b. in Worms 12th century.

Tishah Be-Ab—Ninth day of Ab, commemorating destruction of the Temple.

Tishri—First month of the Jewish calendar.

Torah—A very wide term, including the limited meanings of Pentateuch, Law, learning, as well as the broader conceptions of culture and ways of life.

Tosafot—Glosses and comments additional to the commentary of Rashi.

Trendle—A Hanukkah toy somewhat like a top.

Tur—A book of codes written by Rabbi Jacob, son of Rabbi Asher, 15th century.

Turim—General name for the Codes.

Tur Orah Hayim—Portion of Jewish Codes dealing with prayers, festivals, etc.

Tur Yoreh Deah—Portion of Jewish Codes dealing with ritual law.

Wa-ad Arba Ha-Arazot—The Council of Four Lands.

Wayikra—Leviticus.

Wayomer David—Portion of the Daily Service.

Yarmulke—A skull cap.

Yeshibah—The term used to designate the higher educational institutions in Eastern Europe.

Yoreh Deah—Portion of Shulhan Aruk dealing with ritual law.

Zaddik—A leader of the Hasidim, a pious man, who by his faith is regarded as having communion with God.

Zizit—Fringes worn on the four corners of the prayer shawl.

Zohar—The important book of Mystic Lore.

INDEX

BOOK TWO

PRINCIPLES OF THE JEWISH CURRICULUM IN AMERICA

TO MY TEACHER
MORDECAI M. KAPLAN
A PIONEER IN THE
REVALUATION OF JEWISH VALUES

INTRODUCTION

AMERICA is in the midst of a great experiment in democracy. Her well-being depends upon the contributions of all the various groups that live in her midst. It is therefore the moral duty of every immigrant group to transmit to the young what is valuable in its cultural heritage, and thereby to develop the individual and to enrich American life.

This study of the principles of the Jewish curriculum in America is the second in a series of studies on the educational adjustments of the immigrant Jew. American Jewry is in a critical condition. The young find old beliefs and practices incompatible with the present Zeitgeist and are rapidly deserting the ranks. Disintegration follows only too often when those who forsake the Judaism of their fathers substitute nothing of value in its place. The older generation views this process with resignation and despair.

The only solution to this distressing state of affairs is provision for an adequate Jewish education in which the important values of the Jewish group will be transmitted to the young. Such a selection of values must be based on an analysis of the needs of Jewry, from the point of view of group survival as well as from the point of view of group adjustment.

The selection of the important Jewish values is a task as baffling as it is interesting to the Jewish educator. He is on dangerous ground, where prejudices naturally run high and the personal equation is hard to eliminate. The attempt to devise criteria for the selection of Jewish values is, therefore, a very difficult one.

The writer tried to overcome these difficulties by making the analysis which leads up to the criteria as objective as he could; and although the application of the criteria to some specific values no doubt reflects his own outlook on Jewish life, the criteria themselves, he feels, will be serviceable to all groups in Jewry.

The author hopes that the discussion in this volume will stimulate thought and activity on the problem of adjusting the curriculum of the Jewish school to the conditions in America.

E. G.

CONTENTS

vii

PRINCIPLES OF THE
JEWISH CURRICULUM IN AMERICA

PRINCIPLES OF THE JEWISH CURRICULUM IN AMERICA

CHAPTER I

THE ENVIRONMENT OF THE JEW IN AMERICA

THE formulation of an aim of education depends in large measure upon the environment for which it is formulated.[1] In order to determine adequately the aim of Jewish education in America, a knowledge of the new environment of the Jew is necessary. What are the historic antecedents of the Jews in this country? What are the significant changes that have taken place in the life of the Jew who has been transplanted to America? Once these questions are answered we can consider the influence that these changes in social life should exert on the educational system.

A. HISTORICAL BACKGROUND [2]

The Jews came to America in three successive waves of migration. The first began in 1654, with the Span-

[1] It also depends of course upon the capacity, training, and vision of the individual who is formulating the aim and the group for which it is being conceived.

[2] For a more detailed account of the history of the Jews in America, see Bernheimer, C., *The Russian Jew in the United States;* Burgin, H., *Die Geschichte von der jüdischer Arbeiter Bewegung in America, Russland und England;* Dushkin, A. M.,

1

ish-Portuguese group which was numerically small.
Because of subsequent limited immigration,[1] intermarriage, and assimilation, this group is now a dwin-
dling minority of the Jewish population of this country.
The Spanish-Portuguese Jews are economically well
off, and in fact some of them were wealthier when they
came here than the people in whose midst they settled.
They are an orthodox group possessing wealth, dignity,
a certain conservative outlook on life, and religious
fervor.

The second wave of migration was that of the German Jews, which practically began after the Na-
poleonic wars and increased after the events of 1848,
losing its strength in 1870. This group, which is much
larger numerically than the first, consisted of people
who were not so well-to-do as their oriental brothers.
Many of them began as poor pedlars or traders who
scattered all over this country, but by means of
industry, economy, and energy became prominent
business men, financiers, and professional men. The
political liberalism in Germany in the days of 1848

Jewish Education in New York City, part 1, chap. 1-2, and
Appendix J; *The Jewish Communal Register of New York City*,
1918; *Jewish Encyclopedia*, articles, "America," "New York,"
"United States"; Joseph, S., *Jewish Emigration to the United
States;* Kohler, M. J., *"The German Jewish Migration to
America;* Raisin, M. Z., "Hayehudim we-ha-yahadut be-
America," in *Hashiloah*, v. 4-7; *The Two Hundred and
Fiftieth Anniversary of the Settlement of the Jews in the United
States;* Wiernik, P., *History of the Jews in America.*

[1] It is estimated that the total number of Jewish immigrants
to this country in 1818 was only three thousand, and they were
not all Spanish-Portuguese Jews.

prepared them for participation in the civic and political life of their new country.

By now this group constitutes an important factor in American Jewish life. On the whole, its members are economically well-to-do, and they have been largely responsible for the organization of Jewish religious and charitable institutions. In fact, it might be said that their contribution to American Jewish life is to be found in the ideal of philanthropy which they tried to put into practice and the thoroughgoing way in which they proceeded to organize the institutions fulfilling the philanthropic needs of the Jews in this country. They brought with them the movement for religious reform which had started in Germany and thus introduced Reform Judaism in the United States. In connection with their temples they have organized the Jewish Sunday School, which gives Jewish instruction to their children once a week.

The third and the most important Jewish migration to this country began in the 80's of the last century, when the May Laws, which restricted the life of the Jew in Russia socially and economically, combined with the pogroms which followed to drive hundreds of thousands to our shores. This group of immigrants from Eastern Europe is by far the largest numerically of the Jews in this country.[1] But more important even

[1] Estimates of the Jewish population in the United States are 50,000 in 1848, 250,000 in 1880, and 3,300,000 in 1918. Of these 1,562,800 came here from 1881 to 1910, of which 1,476,266 came from Eastern Europe (Joseph S., *Op. cit.*) For sources of other estimates of Jewish population, see Dushkin, A. M., *Op. cit.*, Appendix J.

than their numerical strength are their importance as a new force in the development of Jewish life in America and the possibilities that they offer for the enrichment of American life. This group is very complex, containing within itself many smaller groups. These may be divided, however, into three groups, in accordance with the emphasis they place upon certain aspects of Jewish life.

The first group is one in which religion is the point of emphasis. This group consists of the orthodox, Yiddish-speaking, first-generation immigrants.[1] Their occupations are peddling, shopkeeping, and petty trading, although recently a number of these, too, have become well-to-do. The members of this group try to adhere to the religion of their fathers as much as possible, refusing to make compromises with an environment which militates against strict observance of the faith. Their children, or the second generation, speak English and rarely, if ever, follow in the footsteps of their parents with regard to orthodoxy in religion. This is also true of the members of the first generation who come here at an early age. The educational institution which this group is tending to develop is the Talmud Torah, a week-day, communal, supplementary school.[2]

At one with these in respect to their emphasis on

[1] First generation are considered those who are themselves immigrants. Second generation are those whose parents were immigrants.

[2] By a supplementary school is meant a school which conducts its sessions after public school hours, therefore allowing its children to attend the public school.

the importance of religion is the conservative group, which differs, however, from the former in that its members are ready to make concessions to the environment. In doing so, they neither cling to the extreme authoritarianism of some of the orthodox, nor are they ready to go to the opposite extreme of some of the reform Jews. The conservative Jew tries more nearly to regulate his Jewish life by applying the conception of functionalism,[1] discarding what cannot possibly function in the new environment and maintaining the rest in the spirit of "Traditional Judaism." Like the orthodox Jews, the conservative, too, tend to develop week-day schools or Talmud Torahs closely related to their synagogues, for the education of their children.

A second group that may be distinguished on the basis of its outlook on Jewish life is the Zionist group. As its name implies, the fact of central importance in their attitude is the Jewish people as a distinct nationality, with a racial basis, a common history and literature, common ideals, and a hope that it will be reëstablished in its ancient homeland. Economically these belong to all groups, and from a religious point of view, too, they will be found in all groups, but faith in Zionism as an ideal for the regeneration of the Jewish people is their outstanding characteristic. On the whole they represent an intellectual group. Though they speak English or Yiddish at home, they recognize the importance of Hebrew as the national language of the Jewish people in a rebuilt Palestine. They therefore wish to give emphasis to the study of Hebrew as a living tongue in their Hebrew schools, which are

[1] For a discussion of this conception, see chap. 4.

also week-day schools. The emphasis in these schools, however, is not on religion as in the case of the Talmud Torahs and Congregational and Sunday Schools, but rather on Hebrew culture as the significant element in the national expression of the Jewish people.

The third group may be called the radical group. This group consists mostly of first generation immigrants whose language is Yiddish. They form the large mass of Jewish factory workers and laborers. These immigrants represent the reaction to the restricted, persecuted life of czaristic Russia, as well as to the oppressive labor conditions which they found when they first came to this country.[1] Hence their political-social-economic idealism and their desire for industrial democracy. The Jewish problem appeals to them as a matter of "justice," although they do include a minority of anti-Zionists. These people are developing an intensive social life, through their organization into unions, as well as into literary and dramatic clubs in which they carry on intensive educational activity. With them Yiddish is not merely a language of speech but also a means of raising the cultural state of the masses. The Yiddish press, the Yiddish theatre, and the various publishing houses are to them instruments for improving and developing Jewish culture. Educationally they are developing the Volks-Schule, a weekday supplementary school in which the language of instruction is Yiddish but in which Hebrew also finds its place.

To these groups differentiated by their emphasis on religion, nationalism, or radicalism may be added a

[1] Burgin, H., *Op. cit.*, pp. 106-107.

small number of assimilated gymnasia students and other individuals who drifted away from Jewish things due to a lack of Jewish education.

It should be understood of course that the above classifications are not necessarily mutually exclusive. An orthodox Jew may be a strong Zionist and a radical in economics. A reform Jew may be a Zionist. A conservative Jew may be radical in economics and usually will be Zionist. But taken as a whole it may be said that the Jews may be divided into the above classes, and that each group is trying to develop an educational institution that will meet its particular needs.

B. THE NEW ENVIRONMENT—POLITICAL STATUS

It is clear from the above analysis that the great majority of the Jews in this country are of Eastern European origin, and therefore the influence of the American environment upon them will be best appreciated by a contrast with that of Eastern Europe.

Anyone who is acquainted with both Jewish life in Eastern Europe and conditions of Jewish life in this country will recognize that the transplantation of a human being from Eastern Europe to America represents not merely a physical change but a complete mental revolution in the individual.

For hundreds of years the political status of the Jew in Eastern Europe was a deplorable one. To the evils of autocracy, which all the inhabitants of those countries shared, were added special disabilities for the Jews as Jews. In direct contrast with exclusion from all participation in the political life, the Jew who comes to this country is not only given the opportunity, but is urged and helped, to become a citizen of America. Democracy in government demands not only that all be given the privilege of participating in the organization and direction of the political life but that they also be given the opportunity of an education that will make such participation effective.

The famous dictum in the Declaration of Independence that "All men are created equal" may be untrue to nature, which endows men with different inherited capacities and accordingly brings about some very grave inequalities. But it is significant as an expression of intent on the part of the founders of this country that in political and social life, which man can control, there be relative equality. There are to be no distinctions due to race, creed, or color in the political life. All are to be entitled to protection of person and property, to equality before the law in legal disputes, and above all to freedom from legal restrictions.

By this time such statements sound trite to our ears. But one can see how tremendously full of significance such provisions would be to a people who had been subjected for centuries to all kinds of restriction and oppression. One need only recall the pogroms of 1907 to see what a change took place for the immigrant Jew from Russia and Poland, in respect to his political status, when he came to America. Arriving in a new country, the keynote of which is "Liberty," one to which he had been looking with longing eyes, probably for years before he had been able to emigrate, meant a fundamental change in his life.

C. Economic Conditions

In contrast with special economic restrictions imposed upon him in Eastern Europe, the Jew in this country is relatively free to engage in whatever economic pursuits he wishes. As an individual he may indeed be restricted. At times Anti-Semitism may raise its head to prevent a Jew from entering certain occupations because he is a Jew. But as far as the government is concerned, certainly there are and can be no special economic regulations for any particular group. Advancement in business and professional work depends, as a rule, upon merit or opportunity, not upon creed.

But while this is one of the favorable results of his change of country, it is also true that the Jew from Eastern Europe is suddenly thrown, usually for the first time, into a highly industrialized system in which materialism and keen competition are the order of the day. The power of wealth in this country which at times influences legislation and elects legislators,[1] and which is too often the criterion by which "success" is measured, results in a mad chase for the dollar in the course of which important values may be lost and human beings dehumanized. The United States now includes more men of enormous wealth than the whole of Europe.[2] The result is only too often the worship of wealth and the trampling of the ideal life under foot.

[1] Bryce, James, *Modern Democracies,* v. 2, p. 155.
[2] *Ibid.,* p. 25.

Economic conditions favor a free interaction between Jew and non-Jew, and where the former are in a minority the process of assimilation will be hastened.[1] Where persecution does not help to intensify the group consciousness of a minority, assimilation proceeds rapidly, especially if the majority is not in a low state of culture. In the course of this process, partly a result of the economic life, some significant Jewish values cherished by the Jews in Eastern Europe are completely lost. A strongly competitive society which fosters selfishness instead of service may only too effectually stamp out some of the idealism which Jewish life and literature try to implant.

The need for earning a livelihood in the new country, a need which every immigrant must take into account as soon as possible after his arrival, often compels men, who in Eastern Europe had belonged to an aristocracy of learning, to work in factories or even to become fruit pedlars. Such changes result in mental depression and an undue emphasis on the material aspects of life. That one who was accustomed to spend a considerable part of his time in the study of the Talmud or in reading the Bible and its commentaries should have to adjust himself to the hurly-burly life of this country and become a mere "hand," is one of the tragedies of immigrant life.[2] Yet—what could he do but flee the country in which oppression no longer permitted him to live?

This materialism of our industrial society but too frequently results in the destruction of the traditional

[1] Ruppin, Arthur, *The Jews of Today*, p. 21.
[2] Asch, Shalom, *America*, p. 23.

Jewish respect for learning and culture. It is sad to see that, in spite of the great expenditures for education in this country, and in spite of the many opportunities for a liberal education which this country affords, "love of learning" as an ideal is not as outstanding a characteristic of the masses as it was amidst the Jews in Russia and Poland. The undue weight given to financial success tends to substitute "success" for "Torah," the ideal of the Jewish people for centuries and centuries. Thus we have, on the one hand, freedom from economic restrictions which makes life possible for the Jew. On the other hand, we have all the evils of an industrial competitive system which make the emphasis on a spiritual outlook upon life sadly necessary. Jewish education can supply this outlook which it is difficult to attain in the new environment.

D. EDUCATIONAL CONDITIONS

In a democratic society universal education is necessary, not only because the obligation of citizenship in such a society assumes intelligence and knowledge on the part of the citizen, but also because the multiplicity of stimuli to which an individual must respond and from which he must make his selection, necessitate universal education. For that reason the United States spends vast sums on education and offers unusual opportunities to all. Not only elementary and secondary education, but in many cases higher education, is readily accessible. The number of men who are graduated from the institutions of higher learning in Amer-

ica is far larger in proportion than that in any part of
Continental Europe.[1]

It should be remembered that the Jew had been
subjected to severe educational restrictions in Russia,
restrictions which not only made it practically impossible for him to receive a secular education in the Russian schools but also prevented him from engaging in
secular studies in the Jewish Heder.[2]   This exclusion
of secular subjects from the curriculum of the Heder
tended to intensify his Jewish consciousness, as it
helped to prevent interaction between the Russian Jew
and the rest of the world.

The intense desire for education, which in Russia
and Poland displayed itself in great esteem for the
learned and in the great spread of Jewish scholarship,
as well as in untold sacrifices on the part of those who
defied the environment and stealthily engaged in secular studies, causes the Jew to avail himself freely of
the splendid educational opportunities in this country.
This Jewish love of learning is evidenced by the large
numbers of Jews seeking admission to our colleges and
universities.   In fact so great has their number been
that some of these institutions have in truly Russian [3]
fashion begun to introduce percentage norms for the
admission of Jewish students.

Yet this access to educational facilities has also not
proved an unmixed blessing.   According to one Jewish

[1] In accordance with Viscount Bryce, this number is probably
ten times as large in proportion to population.   See Bryce,
James, *Op. cit.*, v. 2, p. 116.

[2] Book One: *Jewish Education in Russia and Poland*, p. 40.

[3] Before the Revolution.

authority, the jump from ghetto life to the American environment is equivalent to a jump from the 14th to the 20th century. This tends to produce two evils. In the first place, it may result in a neglect of what is of relatively permanent value in the old culture, and as a consequence often cause serious tragedies in the life of the Jewish home where the young jump the gap, while the parents remain where they had been in Eastern Europe. Secondly, a gap of six centuries is one which very few people can jump successfully, and the suddenness of the transition may result in maladjustments of the worst kind. The young quickly learn to negate the old values, and only too often accept nothing new but a superficial veneer of modernism which they call "Americanism." The American educator cannot but look with great concern at such tragedies. He is in duty bound to join hands with the Jewish educator in attempting to solve this problem, through the development of some process of adjustment that will make the transition more gradual and will enable the immigrant to cherish his real values and to contribute them to American life, while he adopts the best of the ideals of America.

E. Social Life

A democratic society demands a process of sharing, a give-and-take relationship among its members. This is to a great extent true of any society where heterogeneous groups, differing in race, religion, and cultural possessions, live together and where relative equality is an ideal which the people strive to attain. Hence, in this country there is interaction going on between

Jew and non-Jew in economic, political, cultural, and social life. The process may not be sufficiently intimate to satisfy those who would like to see America become one great uniformity, where individuals and groups would be lost in the "Great American," but it is sufficiently powerful to break barriers that separated Jews from non-Jews from days immemorial and at times to break bonds that, in the judgment of many, ought to remain unbroken. The faith in equality as an ideal and the tendency to universalize values and to think of them not as possessions of small groups but as world possessions, are all largely responsible for such interaction.

The sharp cleavage that existed between one element of the population in Eastern Europe and another, does not exist in this country. The population might indeed be divided into groups in accordance with wealth possessed but there are no distinct classes recognized. In the ghetto Jewish law regulated Jewish life to a considerable extent, while in this country all civil relations, and even some religious matters, are taken over by the judiciary of the state or nation. This fact is important as it tends to bring all groups together, though at the same time it weakens the hold which the traditional religion had upon the people when it regulated all the affairs of its daily life.

Then again, the churches in Eastern Europe systematically spread hatred against the Jews and prevented the Christians from mingling with them under penalty of the church. In the United States this is not the case. Here and there we may still find a church and an ignorant narrow-minded minister misconceiving the functions of religion and breeding hatred amongst the people, but on the whole the church in this country is coming more and more to serve as a means of developing a spirit of coöperation rather than one of hostility among different groups.

In Russia the pale of settlement produced a ghetto. Nine-tenths of Russian territory was closed to the Jew. In this country the Jew may stay wherever he wishes. Any congregation of immigrants in one section is due to the operation of consciousness of kind or to economic motives, not to government policy. As a result we find Jews scattered throughout the country and in many cases in very small numbers compared with the rest of the population. An assimilative process sets in, often of the self-effacing kind which either destroys the old without substituting the new or so disintegrates individualities as to deprive America of what might have been contributed to it as the valuable heritage of an immigrant group.

Where people were locally segregated from the rest of the population, economically restricted to very few occupations, and culturally limited by the exclusion of secular instruction from the Jewish school, there could be little or no interaction. The outlook on life of Jew and non-Jew was too different. But here, where economically all groups follow the same pursuits, or are free to do so, where they lead a very similar social life, and where they are influenced by the same institutions, such as the press, the theatre, and the public school, there are bound to be a great many shared activities.

Factors such as these tend to bring people together

and break down characteristic ways of life which in the past served to distinguish Jews from non-Jews and functioned as an important means of group survival. When one compares the many influences that operated to make Jewish the environment of the child in Eastern Europe and the absence of these influences in this country, one is overwhelmed at the difficult task that the Jewish educational institutions have to perform.

F. The Influence of Modernism

While a change in the local environment, a new language, new manners, and the adoption of a new culture may of themselves account for the breakdown of important religious and national bonds, the breaking of family ties and the cessation of communal control help in this process. There is, however, another significant factor of which one must take account. That is the influence of modernism. The transplantation of the Jew from the Eastern-European ghetto to this country means for some people a change in outlook on life from medievalism to modernism. It is a fundamental change, a revolutionary change, for the Jewish mind.

Belief, faith, the power of tradition, acceptance of the literal meaning of the Bible, adherence to Talmudic law, all broke down before the advent of a scientific outlook upon life. The experimental method of inquiry in science, the conception of evolution in life and the world, and the implication of all of these for religious beliefs are a part of the spirit of the Modern Age.

At the same time, invention and the increase and improvement in facilities of transportation have brought humanity closer together and have, relatively speaking, eliminated space and time. Human beings thousands of miles apart feel much nearer to each other than ever before, due to the improved facilities for travel and communication. This annihilation of space and resultant feeling of the nearness of people to one another has developed what might be called a tendency to universalization. This tendency emphasizes the similarities of men instead of their differences and is disruptive of particularism. When a sufficiently large number of the members of a group are living a distinct life on their own soil, the process of disintegration may go on outside of the national homeland on the part of some of the members, without destroying group integrity. But when the nation is scattered and its members everywhere a minority, to disrupt their particularism is to endanger their spiritual as well as at times their physical existence.

G. The Results of the New Environment

In Eastern Europe social and economic isolation and political persecution combined to keep the Jews separated from the rest of the population. The old and strong tradition against intermarriage was in full operation. And to intensify the survival value of these two factors was the third—a series of laws which regulated the daily life of the Jews and served as a bond of unity for the entire people. All of these, combined with unquestioned faith in the religion of old and its chief sources, the Bible and the Talmud, were strongly centripetal in Jewish life.

The political freedom and economic and social interaction in this country are therefore in marked contrast to life in Eastern Europe. The effect of a democratic outlook upon life, reinforced by modernism, has brought two results. In the first place, the theoretical foundations of Judaism have come to be questioned. The belief in an anthropomorphic God or in some form of a supernatural being has been shaken, and in many cases no other conception has come to take its place. The new outlook on life that came into being with the spread of Darwinism has largely broken down the faith in the traditional conception of creation and with it the literal authority of the Bible.

Besides the new outlook on life another factor helped to develop a critical attitude. One reason for the preservation of Jewish tradition in the past was that Jewish migration had taken place from countries of a high plane of culture to those on a lower plane of culture. The new immigration reversed the process. The Jews who came from Russia and Poland to the United States came from countries in a low cultural state to one of a higher state.[1] Such a change, too, helps in the breakdown of old beliefs and practices.

Along with the breakdown of theoretical conceptions came the disregard for ceremonial practice. The influences of the religious life at home and in the synagogue in Eastern Europe were in themselves sufficient to give the child a Jewish education without the formal and very intensive education of the Heder. The community life and the control that the "Daat ha-kahal" [2]

[1] Ruppin, A., *Op. cit.*, p. 27.
[2] Daat ha-kahal—The opinion of the community; the desire to have the good will of the community.

exercised were also thoroughly Jewish in their influence.[1]

In this country the Jewish home broke down because the children are often bread-winners. This fact, combined with the comparative rapidity with which the young learn English while their parents do not, results in the development of independence and self-sufficiency on the part of the children and in a breakdown of parental authority.

Parents and children are estranged from each other, and as the children learn in time to look down with contempt at the Yiddish, which they nickname the "jargon," of their parents, they transfer some of this contempt to the religion of their fathers as well.

In the past the synagogue, which had enriched Jewish life, which had functioned as a house of prayer and study, and which had served all kinds of communal undertakings, had been a center of Jewish spiritual life. The thought that spiritual life required group life made the affiliation of all Jews with the synagogue imperative. In this country the synagogue has broken down. Out of the 900,000 adult Jews of New York City who ought to attend the synagogue on the high holy days when almost all are expected, only 415,000 are to be found there, even if we include the many provisional synagogues that are set up only for the three days of Rosh Hashanah and Yom Kippur.[2] The distribution of this attendance by city districts

[1] See Book One: *Jewish Education in Russia and Poland*, chap. 2.

[2] See Kaplan, M. M., On Affiliation with the Synagogue, in the *Jewish Communal Register,* 1917-18.

clearly shows that where the factors of frequent intercourse with non-Jews, improved economic conditions, and in general the environment described above are working in full force there is greater disintegration of Jewish life.   While in Eastern Europe the whole of the Jew's life was Jewish, in this country his Judaism occupies only a supplementary and at times a very small part of his life.   As some one has phrased it, we now have "week-end" Jews and "year-end" Jews.

No exact statistics are available on the observance of the dietary laws in this country.   But it is well known that these laws which in the past served as important forces for maintaining Jewish unity are disregarded in thousands and probably hundreds of thousands of Jewish homes in America.

The observance of the Sabbath and holidays, too, is weak, due to the changed economic conditions.   In Eastern Europe everyone was keenly conscious of the coming of the Sabbath and the Jewish holidays.   The children were duly impressed as the entire community was "Shabesdig." [1]   But with Jewish community life lacking in our non-Jewish environment, whatever of Jewish religious practice remains is but a shadow of what it was in Eastern Europe.   In the new environment some of this Jewish religious practice appears so secular and week-day that the beauty of Jewish religious and communal life is lost.

The process of disintegration reaches its climax in intermarriage.   A study of 100,000 cases of intermarriage in this city shows amongst other facts that intermarriage increases in unusually large proportion as

[1] Sabbath-like.

Jews stay longer in the country. While the ratio of intermarriage of Jews in the first generation is only .64 of 1% it becomes 4.51% for the second generation, an increase of over 700%.[1] In other words, the strong tradition against intermarriage begins to break down as the length of stay of the Jews in a free country increases.

To these facts should be added the all important fact that the Jewish environment in Russia and Poland was outwardly maintained by persecution, political, economic, and social, and inwardly regulated by the sources of the Jewish laws of life, the Bible and the Talmud. The former tended to heighten the Jewish consciousness as all oppression of a minority arouses powerful resistance. The latter meant nothing less than the very significant fact that the Jewish education which the child received, and which consisted mainly of Bible, Mishnah, and Talmud, was related to actual life since these regulated Jewish life.

The intense Jewish consciousness, fostered by persecution which resulted in giving powerful stimulus to the Jewish nationalist movement, became weak in America where, thanks to the ideals of liberty, no such crude stimuli were at work. Whatever Jewish consciousness is to be maintained in this country cannot be the result of negative forces, but must be prompted by a knowledge of the value of maintaining Jewish life. In a democratic society the presence of a minority holding to its traditions in spite of many disintegrating forces must bring about a selective process, in the course of which only those values of the group are

[1] Drachsler, J., *Democracy and Assimilation,* p. 133.

maintained which are of great significance and therefore relatively permanent.

H. SUMMARY

The Jews came to this country in three successive
waves of migration. First came the Spanish Portu-
guese, then the German, and lastly the East European.
Of all of these the third is the largest group in this
country today. The change in the political, social, and
economic conditions of the Jew who came from Eastern Europe to America was in its effect revolutionary.
He found a life diametrically opposed in most significant respects to that which he was compelled to live in
the ghetto.

While the general effect of the freedom of America
was to produce a very desirable interaction among all
the parts of the population, this was accompanied by
the maladjustments which necessarily follow in the
footsteps of a sudden transition on the part of the
immigrant. The new economic conditions resulted in
materialism and brought into clear relief the need for
a Jewish education which would emphasize a spiritual
outlook upon life. At the same time the breakdown
of the Jewish home, the lessened influence of the synagogue, and the cessation of the community control
shifted the entire burden of Jewish education to the
formal educational institutions.

The contact with modernism involved too sudden a
jump from the medieval life of the ghetto. The scientific attitude to life, which resulted in the breakdown
of many theoretical Jewish beliefs and practices, also
brought about a superficial process of Americanization,

which mistakes externalities for the ideals of America, or in a complete breaking of the racial bonds, which leads to intermarriage and to dissolution of Jewish life in America.

Therefore, in formulating our aim of Jewish education in America, we must bear in mind these facts. On the one hand, the aim of education must reckon with a democratic society and a new outlook upon life resulting from modernism. On the other hand, it must provide for the maintenance of what is of vital significance to Jewish group life.

CHAPTER II

THE AIM OF JEWISH EDUCATION IN AMERICA

A. Introductory

THE aim of an undertaking determines the means of its attainment. The aim of education in general and of Jewish education in particular must determine the curriculum of the Jewish school. What is the aim of general education? This question has been asked again and again, and the answers given have differed as widely as the original natures of the authors and the environments in which the aims were formulated. From Plato in Greece of old to our contemporary thinkers, different aims have been assigned to the process of education. While it is hardly possible to say that any one aim has been agreed upon by American educators, one can point to the direction along which American educational theory is progressing. As with the aims that preceded our modern conception, the direction of this aim presents itself as a corollary of a philosophy of life. The philosophy of life implied in American educational theory may be described as democratic. In fact, only on the basis of a democratic aim of education, can we proceed to develop a system of Jewish education in America. It is important, therefore, to point out some of the fundamentals of this

24

democratic philosophy as precedent to the formulation of a desirable aim of education.

B. Some Basic Aims of Democracy

Perhaps nothing can better express the essence of the democratic idea than a contrast between its conception of progress and that which preceded it. The term progress has often been interpreted to mean going ahead along a certain direction, the assumption being that the movement was a "forward" one, proceeding, however, toward a fixed goal. Progress means, from this point of view, the movement of society in the direction of this definite or fixed goal.

Progress for democracy also implies movement in the direction of better states of society. Democracy sets up its ideals, its conception of better states, and it conceives that the movement of society toward better states constitutes progress. Instead of a fixed goal, however, it points only to the direction of progress. This direction is to be found in the path where growth of the individual and of society takes place. Progress is being attained as the individual continues his growth. From this point of view, progress is never absolute because its highest condition can be attained only when provision is made for the fullest continuous growth of each and all. The conditions of society in which this ideal is attained cannot be described in terms of a state of "being" but rather in terms of "becoming." That the direction of progress is along the lines of the continuous growth of the individual and society is one of the first basic principles of the democratic idea.

What is the place of the individual in such a society? He has a privilege and a responsibility. It is his privilege to realize himself. He has the right to carry on those activities that he "purposes"—to further his own ends. For he, himself, is an end. He is not merely a means to some one else's end, not even to the "state." He is an end in himself, and therefore nothing short of the opportunity to grow and develop continuously will meet the ethical demands of the situation.

At the same time this privilege brings with it responsibilities. First is the negative responsibility. As the individual attempts to realize himself he may do so only if he does not interfere with similar attempts on the part of others in the group. In addition to this principle of non-interference, the democratic idea brings with it a positive obligation as well—that of helping other individuals in the group to self-realization. If it is the right of an individual to attain the fullest growth for himself, it is his duty to help others who, as a part of the like process by which they attain the same goal, may require his help.

The obligation to help others arises not merely as an ethical idea due to a conception of the rights of the individual, but as a result of his social nature. For both these reasons the individual is developing best as he learns to share his activities with others in the group. The kind of life based on common interests needed in a society where the individual is free requires an opportunity to give and take, to exchange and share goods both physical and spiritual. This sharing of interests must be continuous and progressive; that is, it should always go on and ever lead to sharing a greater number of interests. The number of interests shared must increase in order that each individual may have the opportunity to engage in a variety of activities, leading to a broadening of the mind necessary in the democratic conception of society. In this way society performs its true function—that of making possible growth of the best in the individual with a view to continuous further growth.[1]

This conception of the function of a democratic society implies the furthering of the unique abilities of every individual. The uniqueness of individuals makes interesting the process of sharing and enriches the sharers. Such uniqueness, in order to be of benefit to others, must at least be permitted to exist. It is the recognition of the worth of such uniqueness as a source of progress in the world that leads to the creation of conditions under which its essential quality can be realized. It would be a most undemocratic society that would extend the rights of growth to an individual without admitting that such a right implies the furthering of that very quality which constitutes him as an individual, different from others in the group. By furthering the unique abilities of every individual the democratic society can attain the kind of progress it seeks—the fullest continuous growth of all the individuals that compose the group.

As a result of this brief statement of the idea of democracy, we may distinguish four criteria by which to judge an educational aim in a democracy:

1. Democracy aims at progress in the direction of the continuous growth of the individual and the group.

[1] Dewey, J., *Democracy and Education,* chap. 7.

2. Democracy demands that each individual have an opportunity for self-realization, provided he does not interfere with similar opportunities of others and that he accept the positive obligation of helping others to attain self-realization.
3. Democracy demands a continuous and progressive sharing of interests amongst the individuals that compose the group.
4. The democratic society makes possible the contribution of each individual to the welfare of mankind in accord with his unique abilities and puts a premium on such variation as is a condition of progress.[1]

How can our aim of education be so stated as to meet all the criteria above mentioned? What view of education will permit us to strive not only for a democratic society within the nation but also for a world constantly growing more democratic?

The answer to this question, it would seem, can best come upon the basis of an analysis of the two basic factors involved in the educational process, the individual and society.

C. The Individual and Society

A false conception of both the nature of the individual and the nature of society has been responsible in large measure for the constant conflict between the two and has resulted in educational theory going astray either in one direction or its opposite. The individual is conceived in terms either of a limited self,

[1] For further discussion of the value of and need for variation in a democratic society see Dewey, J., *Op. cit.*, chap. 22.

and therefore as interested in the pursuit of "selfish" ends,[1] or as isolated from other beings. A good example of the latter is, as Prof. Dewey points out, a philosophy of life that regards "the individual mind as a separate entity complete in each person and isolated from nature and hence from other minds. . . . When the social quality of individualized mental operations is denied, it becomes a problem to find connections which will unite an individual with his fellows. . . . The consciousness of each person is wholly private, a self-inclosed continent intrinsically independent of the ideas, wishes, purposes of everybody else. . . . The problem to which the theory of isolated and independent conscious minds gave rise [is] : given feelings, ideas, desires which have nothing to do with one another, how can actions proceeding from them be controlled in a social or public interest? Given an egoistic consciousness, how can action which has regard for others take place?" [2]

This is an excellent illustration of the fallacy which many people commit in thinking of the individual without considering his true nature. Modern physiological psychology recognizes the social nature of the individual.[3] Psychologically we find that the individual is possessed of many unlearned tendencies that not only lead to association with others but make such association necessary for his own welfare. In other words he is not a definite entity, a mind apart that can

[1] See James, W., *Psychology*, v. 1, chap. 10.

[2] Dewey, J., *Op. cit.*, pp. 346-347.

[3] Thorndike, E. L., *Original Nature of Man*, chaps. 7 and 8. Also Woodworth, R. S., *Dynamic Psychology*, p. 206.

function by itself; the individual demands society for his full realization.

A similar misunderstanding of society is responsible for demands to "subordinate" the individual to the group. Society is conceived of as a distinct entity that has ends of its own as against the ends of the individual. This view, too, is due to lack of sufficient exactness in the use of the term society. When the true nature of society is misunderstood, a series of conflicts must necessarily arise between it and the individual. As a matter of fact, society is a complex term. It is primarily a term used to indicate a number of individuals living together. Maciver says, "Society has no life but the life of its members, no ends that are not their ends, and no fulfillment beyond theirs." [1]

In other words, society cannot be divorced from the idea of the individuals that compose it in such a way as to set one against the other and attribute conflicting ends to them. No society can progress when its individuals deteriorate, and no individual development can take place in a degenerate society. It is hardly possible to speak of the two as distinct from each other, except as a means of emphasizing the thought that when we speak of the individual we are thinking of each of the components of society and that when we speak of society we have in mind this individual, but we also have in view many other individuals.

But the term society can vary as to its content. It may be taken to mean the most inclusive society conceivable—the whole of humanity. When used in this sense it is an instrumentality of thought which enables

[1] Maciver, R. M., *Community*, p. 68.

us to speak of people separated from each other by barriers of time and space, as individuals affected by the conduct of each other. And again, society may be taken to mean any small group of individuals living an associated life. In this sense the school, the synagogue, and the economic group constitute societies.

If we remember that society consists of individuals we will be spared the thought that it can thrive at their expense. The idea that the self-effacement of the individual is to be sought is inconsistent with a conception of the worth of individuality. Individuals who are "self-effaced" lose their individuality. Similarly, a society composed of such individuals is a poor society. Especially is this true in a democratic society. Far from demanding the self-effacement of the individual, the democratic society demands his growth and development in accord with the fullest possibilities of his original nature. The interest of such a society in progress demands the fostering of one of the chief factors of progress—individual variations. The term society as used when we really think of "societies" or specified organizations throws additional light on the relations of the individual to the group. With this conception of society in mind we may think of the individual as belonging to more than one group. We may conceive of his functioning best by being a member of several societies. Thus we do not expect his association to be limited to his family only or to his church only. We can conceive of an individual who efficiently belongs to many societies and whose identification with these gives him new opportunities for self-expression. As Fite points out, "Society grows in consciousness so far as each individual forms personal relations and comes to terms of understanding with the wider range of his fellows. Hence, increase of social consciousness implies an increase in the self-consciousness of the individual concerned. For each new acquaintance means a fresh act of comparison and a distinction in the course of which you give a new character to yourself and thus arrive at an intenser and clearer self-consciousness. At the same time consciousness of mutual relations is intensified and made clear throughout the social group." [1] From this point of view the highest form of self-consciousness on the part of the individual will lead to a greater consciousness of mutual relations or to a higher social consciousness. Individual development is attained through the heightening of social consciousness.

With this conception of the nature of the individual and society we may define the aim of an education compatible with the criteria laid down at the beginning of this chapter. The first and a fundamental criterion of a democratic society we found to be that of making possible the continuous growth of the individual and the group. The term growth must be understood to mean the constant opportunity for the growing entity to accomplish its own ends with the possibility of ever formulating new ends which are within the realm of satisfaction. [2] The essence of the idea of growth would be lost if we were to conceive it as a state in which the individual always undergoes

---

[1] Fite, W., *Individualism,* p. 104.

[2] His ends should always be judged in the light of the criteria set up on pp. 27 ff.

new experiences without at the same time seeing his needs or wants fulfilled. This is what is meant by the individual attaining self-realization. For the individual is endowed with a particular original nature which enables him to do certain things and prevents him from doing others. But this original nature responds differently to different situations. The environment, physical and social, supplies the stimuli which lead to the responses that the individual makes. As a result of this fact any individual may change his responses, depending upon changes in the situaticn. The more varied the stimuli with which he comes in contact the more varied will his responses be. The complex original nature of one individual combined with the infinite possibilities of a changing environment therefore provide for the possibility not only of new responses but also of new ends. In this way the more varied the environment of the individual, the greater the possibility for growth. It is this that makes Prof. Dewey's thought—that growth takes place best in a social medium—so significant. This idea that growth takes place best in a social medium implies both our aim of education and its method, and it is this thought that prompts the writer to say that the aim of education in a democratic society may be best expressed in the term "continuous and progressive socialization." An analysis of the process of socialization and its implications for the individual and society will reveal that it meets the criteria set down for a democratic society and provides for the possibility of a world that is trying constantly to grow more democratic.

D.   THE PROCESS OF SOCIALIZATION

What is socialization? How does the process take place? What part does it play in the educational process? These are the questions that must be answered before it is possible to accept our definition of education as continuous and progressive socialization.

Socialization has been defined as "the participation by the individual in the spirit and purpose, knowledge and methods, decision and action of the group." [1] In order to understand the implications of this idea let us see what is involved in the process whereby an individual is socialized into a simple group. On this basis it will be possible to see what is involved in the socialization of the individual into a highly complex group. How, for example, is the child socialized into the family?

At first certain elemental feelings predominate the consciousness of the child. He is conscious of things at rest and in motion. Later he observes human beings and their seemingly mysterious actions. He learns to imitate these. At the same time he experiences certain sensations such as pain and pleasure. These serve to explain to him the actions of the individuals that he sees moving about. He begins to understand that others feel some of the things he feels and undergo some of his experiences. In short, he becomes conscious of the existence of others outside of himself. [2] This is followed by learning to understand by certain symbols the same things that others understand. He attains

[1] Burgess, E. W., *The Function of Socialization in Social Evolution,* Introduction, p. 2.

[2] Baldwin, J. M., *Social and Ethical Interpretations,* pp. 13-15.

a common knowledge of essential things. This common knowledge increases the extent to which he appreciates the likeness of others to himself. It is the beginning of human "consciousness of kind" based upon a common knowledge. As he gets older he realizes that there are certain relations between the individuals that he sees. He learns of their relations to each other and to him. The terms father, mother, brother, sister become meaningful to him. He realizes that these relations are at times guides to action and lead to one set of activities on the part of the members of the family as against another possible set of activities. He becomes conscious of the need of giving up certain desired ends for the sake of other things that are, generally speaking, more to be desired. By a gradual process he comes to identify his own interests with the interests of the group—that is, the family.

The process is far from being a logical one. It is rather psychological and based upon certain elements of knowledge which gradually bring the individual to identify his interests with those of the group because he attains the habits and attitudes of the group. The individual must be aware of the existence of others like him who experience the same things that he experiences before he can reach the stage of identification with them. He must know their relations and see how the conduct of the various members of the group is affected by the existence of the rest of the group. But once this knowledge is attained, it serves as a basis for giving the individual the emotional attitude of the group, which leads him to regard the success and failure of the group as his.

Professor Dewey expresses this thought when he says. "Setting up conditions which stimulate certain visible and tangible ways of acting is the first step. Making the individual a sharer or partner in the associated activity so that he feels its success as his success, its failure as his failure, is the completing step. As soon as he is possessed by the emotional attitude of the group, he will be alert to recognize the special ends at which it aims and the means employed to secure success. His beliefs and ideas in other words will take a form similar to those of others in the group." [1] This statement helps us to conceive the process of socialization as it takes place in groups more complex than the family. While in the simple group, "certain visible and tangible ways of acting" of themselves come because of the living conditions of the group, in the more complex group these may have to be set up in the school. The individual must be made a sharer in common activities, and in time he will get the emotional attitude of the group.

The entire process of socialization might be divided into five steps: [2]

1. The increasing consciousness on the part of the individual of the other members in the group.
2. A growing knowledge of the relations of these individuals to each other and to himself.
3. A common understanding as to the welfare of the group based on common knowledge, ideas, etc.

[1] Dewey, J., *Op. cit.*, pp. 16-17.
[2] The five steps do not develop in such a way that the second does not begin till the first is completed, etc., but they do represent the process of development as a whole.

4. The gradual attainment of the emotional attitude of the group by the individual.
5. The progressive identification of the individual's own interests with those of the group.

The steps in this process which are relatively easily attained in the case of socialization of the individual into a small group are very difficult to attain in the case of a complex group. The very first step, a consciousness of the existence of others in the group, which is in the case of the family group attained as soon as the child is psychologically able to grasp the idea of *alter*, is very difficult to attain in the case of a complex group, unless one is gifted with a very vivid imagination. The consciousness of others in the large group removed from us in time and space is a basic requirement and one not easily obtainable, if action is to be guided by such a consciousness. How much more complex is the process by which the other steps in socialization may be attained! The individual must make great efforts and must be helped by special agencies before he can reach that high state of a consciousness responsive to the needs and ideals of the large group. It is this very difference between the more primitive forms of association, with the social consciousness which was one of their chief characteristics, and the "great society" of today, with the dangers that seem to threaten it because of a lack of such a social consciousness, that causes the student of social life to wonder what is going to become of the great society.[1]

[1] Wallas, G., *The Great Society*, pp. 6-17.

The only solution to this problem that has thus far been devised is that of a continuous and gradual process whereby the individual first becomes a part of small groups and then of increasingly larger groups till he becomes most highly socialized. Thus one individual first becomes a part of the family. Later he comes to school. The class or the club may be the second group into which he enters. Then he joins various groups that have distinct ends in mind which he values. He joins several such "ideological" societies. These societies may be religious or cultural, political or recreational. Their purpose is apparently of little consequence provided it be not anti-social. Entering each of these or as many of these as it is possible for the individual (limited by original nature and the physical and social environment) to join and to participate in efficiently, helps in his socialization into the next higher group. In this way, one individual not only may, but should, join as many societies as possible. For in a democratic society, as above mentioned, the greater the number of stimuli that a person can react to wisely, the better. The highest point of socialization may be considered reached when the individual has identified himself in the most intensive degree with the highest conceivable society, "The World." It is this thought that prompts Maciver to say, "Society is in us, in each of us, in some degree in all, in the highest degree in the greatest of us." [1] For the greatest have succeeded in responding to so many stimuli, have developed such breadth of vision and such a vivid imagination that individuals, no matter how far re-

[1] Maciver, R. M., *Op. cit.,* p. 70.

moved from them, both in time and space, affect their actions because they are conscious of the existence of these people, their relation to them, and possess a common fund of knowledge and a common emotional attitude resulting in an identification of interests.

Thus to the five steps discerned in the process of socialization we may add another important fact— characteristic of the process as it takes place in the case of a complex group. It is the gradualness with which it takes place. Sound social theory does not expect the individual to join a complex society before he has succeeded in becoming a part of the simplest group—the family. We certainly do not expect him to join his "country" before he has become a member of some simple group such as the ideological societies previously mentioned. This thought should be borne in mind, because it is not only significant for our aim of education but has also some basic implications for method. The process of progressive socialization conceived from this point of view is an opportunity for the constant growth and expansion of the individual. The individual is constantly undergoing new experiences that transform him and make him a bigger individual. In this way his "self" expands and becomes at one with the size of the group into which he has been socialized. His self is as big as the family, as the club, as the community, as the nation, or, in the case of the greatest, as the community of the world. To the extent that socialization provides for the growth of the individual, it meets one of our criteria of democracy which demands the continuous growth of the individual.

Does socialization as an aim of education also meet the demands of the other criteria of democracy? For this purpose it will be necessary to examine briefly the relation between socialization and progress. A careful study of this question by Burgess [1] leads to some conclusions, interesting for our purpose. Bearing in mind that the individual is in large measure the source of progress and that variation is a *sine qua non* for its being, he points out the part that society plays in the process.

To begin with, the creative powers of the individual are the results of his social environment as well as of his original nature. The society in which he lives is a condition of creation. The truth of this will be seen even more emphatically if we remember that to a large extent interaction between individuals and groups often supplies the stimuli that lead to creation. Such interaction would be obviously impossible if the individual were alone on a desert island. It should also be remembered that not only is the new a factor in progress but also the conservation of the old. For progress is very often the derivation of the new on the basis of the old. Were the creations of the past which society conserves lost, the creation of new values would have to start anew. To the extent to which a highly conscious society conserves the old it may be conservative, but along with that very conservatism there is the progressive aspect making new creation possible.

Differently stated, the society that socializes the individual by the process above described utilizes indi-

[1] Burgess, E. W., *Op. cit.,* especially chaps. 1-5.

vidual variations to cause progress. At the same time, if it is a society that puts a premium on the efficient socialization of the individual into many groups it makes possible interaction, the sharing of interests and experiences. To the extent that this society is appreciative of the worth of progress it is quick to take hold of the new and to conserve it for the sake of future progress. That our aim of education as socialization also meets the other criteria of the democratic society follows from the above analysis of socialization which applies only in a democratic state. Only in a democratic society where freedom reigns and "social self-control" takes the place of external social control can an individual be free to enter into all groups (except the anti-social) that he may want to, and, therefore, only in such a society can the process of "self-expansion" as above described continue. Since the process provides for sharing of interests, for expression of individuality, for self-realization, it meets the criteria of democracy. Socialization into certain groups does go on in every society. But in an autocratic society this process is limited to certain groups rather than others and at times is forced upon the individual, because he is prevented from entering any other groups and his social nature demands fulfillment of certain fundamental innate tendencies. Thus, the exclusion of Jews from the economic, political, and cultural life in Russia was a powerful factor for socialization into the Jewish group. For while undoubtedly the intense loyalty of the Jew to his traditions, both because of their intrinsic value and because they served as means of preserving him throughout the centuries, was the chief factor in the socialization of the Jewish child into the ghetto, the closing of all other societies to him intensified and made the process more certain. Such socialization might rightly be called *negative socialization*. It is based upon limited choice.

A democracy aims to socialize the individual by a process which frees and not one which limits. Socialization in this way provides for progress, for growth of the individual and the group, for sharing experiences and interests, and for the utilization of variations which are the cause of progress. The process by which the individual becomes a member of even a simple group such as the family is one in the course of which he learns to give due regard to that part of our criteria of democracy which demands the obligation of the individual to help others in the group to self-realization. Progress is attained through a process of socialization which is continuous and utilizes individual variations. The direction of progress is known to be in the path of greatest socialization—in the discovery of new ends as well as new means. In this way continuous and progressive socialization as an aim of education meets all the criteria that we formulated for a democratic society.

E. Socialization and Education As Life

In the light of the above analysis of the term "socialization," we may now restate our aim of education. In going through the process by which he becomes highly socialized, the individual is going through the process of life. As schoolboy, as member of a family, as member of an economic group, a church or a synagogue, a community, a nation, or the world community, he is truly living. His experiences are unified since he is the individual constantly interacting. He is the common factor. These various relationships are all a part of his life, and each in turn leads to the others in the life process. They are all units—big units of life. If continuous and progressive socialization is a description of the life process, to make it our aim of education is to say that education is life. From this point of view, the thought that if education is life school should mean life activities has great significance both for content and method. The content and method of instruction must in so far as possible be the content and method of life.

Finally, this view of education will apply to any society—not only to America—provided that society aims to be democratic. The ultimate educational aim will be the progressive socialization of the individual into the highest conceivable community—the world. There is sufficient reason in the history of America to justify the thought that an ever-growing, ever-developing concept of Americanism will welcome such an aim and will serve as an example in the fulfillment of this aim.

F. The Place of Jewish Education

Starting with the conception of education as socialization, we may proceed to inquire what place Jewish education takes in this process in a democratic society. The writer does not intend to make this book a justification for Jewish education in America. Recent discussions of Americanization [1] clearly urge that the adequate adjustment of the immigrant in a democracy must reckon with his antecedents. From the point of view of democracy the immigrant must also be considered "an end in himself." He is not here merely to be changed and made into a new mould. As previously discussed, he is entitled to live his own life and not to be compelled to give up his individuality or merely accept conditions for the creation of which he is not responsible. Nor is it true to fact to assume the existence of an American type which the immigrant must strive to approach. The Anglo-Saxon stock is in a numerical minority. Shall the Anglo-Saxon type then be the sole American character? By asking the immigrant to conform to a predetermined American type we not only fail to recognize the uniqueness of individuality, which is an essential of democracy, but we are also asking him to become like a being who does not as yet exist. Such an attitude calls for destroying all old values without proving that there is any harm in maintaining them, when very often preserving these values would result in good to America. "With all our rich heritages, Americanism will develop best through a mutual giving and taking of contributions from both newer and older Americans in the interest of the common weal." [2] Loyalty to America is not developed merely through the negative virtue of disloyalty to one's ethnic group.

[1] See Thompson, F. V., *Schooling of the Immigrant;* Bridges, H. J., *On Becoming an American;* Drachsler, J., *Democracy and Assimilation;* Berkson, I. B., *Americanization Theories.*

[2] Thompson, F. V., *Op. cit.,* Publishers' Note.

America does not desire a dull uniformity. America needs a certain like-mindedness as a basis for its solidarity. Instead of a provincial conception of Americanization which would limit instead of liberate, the free spirits of America would prefer a view consistent with one of the fundamental aims of a democratic society—the liberation of the powers and capacities of the individual for his self-realization. If it is true that this self-realization demands the freedom for the individual to join any society he pleases, he may do so provided such society does not violate the criteria of democracy set down previously.

America is not a crucible wherein all are melted to be turned out a one-shaded product. A democracy cannot demand that those groups who want to continue to live, annihilate themselves in order to become a new American type. Such self-annihilation cannot be demanded except upon clear objective proof of harm if the group life is continued. Furthermore, if a democratic society is to permit the free interaction between individuals and groups, it must permit the existence and preservation of distinctive group values to make interaction significant.

Nor is America a heterogeneous mass of discrete groups who have nothing more in common than the fact that they live in a certain territory. If America means anything as a new experiment in social life, it is the attempt to work out a democratic society in which individuals and groups alike can, unless they be anti-social, develop freely as cultural entities and help create an America of the future. All that can be asked of the members of the group is that they evaluate their own conduct from an ethical point of view and see to it that it has no harmful effect upon other people. The burden of responsibility is, however, upon the government in control to prove objectively that a group is anti-social if it wants to undertake a policy of suppression.

In accord with the "community theory of Americanization," [1] every immigrant group is entitled and should even be encouraged to develop itself culturally and through such cultural development to contribute its share to American life. This thought is expressed in the following quotation. "It (the community theory of Americanization) strives for a culture enriched by the contributions from many cultures and thus multiplies the possibilities of varied experience. It intensifies the idea of duty and responsibility to social life and institutions by adding the ethnic group and all the significant institutions connected with its history to the burden of civilization that each developed citizen must bear. It offers the greatest opportunity for the creation of a full, rich and lofty Personality." [2]

For this reason we assume that Jewish education in America is not only necessary from the point of view of the ethnic group but also from the point of view of a democratic society interested in the enrichment of life. It may be well, however, to see what place Jewish education has in the entire socialization process which has been accepted as the aim of education.

One of the tests of a good educational aim may be the extent to which it views the process as a unified

[1] Berkson, I. B., *Op. cit.,* p. 118.
[2] *Ibid.,* p. 118.

one—as is the process of life. It is this very thought that lends new light to the aim of Jewish education in a democratic world. For if our aim of education is a proper one it will not only be in harmony with the general educational goal but will even help in its attainment. Our general aim of education is continuous and progressive socialization. We found this process a gradual one in which the individual is socialized first into simple groups and later into highly complex groups. This process provides for the individual's being a member of many "groups" and even places a premium upon multiple loyalties provided these are not found to involve any anti-social loyalties.[1] What part does Jewish education play in this process? Obviously, the socialization of the child into the Jewish group. But the Jewish group, too, is a complex one. Hence socialization into it must also be gradual. It must start with the family—the Jewish home. This fact is significant from the point of view of our general aim as well. If it is true that the "development of the socialized person through intimate life in primary groups paves the way for the solution of our social problems," [2] if it is true that the simple groups must first command the loyalties of the individual before he can become an efficient member of a complex group, then entering fully into the life of the Jewish family may be conceived not only as a part of the process by which the child becomes a part of the Jewish people, but an integral part of the process of progressive social-

[1] For criteria with which to test anti-sociality, see chap. 4, pp. 85 ff.

[2] Burgess, E. W., *Op. cit.*, p. 225.

ization up to and including the largest community—
the world.

The danger of failing to socialize the child into the
family has become one of our most serious educational
problems. It is one of the saddest sights in America
to find the chasm created between members of the
same immigrant family—between parents and children.
The immigrant children readily adjust themselves, at
least superficially, to their new environment. They
learn the language of the land; they associate with
their newly-made friends in public school; they join
clubs—they feel themselves a part of the new environment. And yet home with all its possible social influences stands in direct contrast to the public school
because the parents find difficulty in adjusting themselves to their new environment. It might be said that
the solution to this problem is to be found in the
"Americanization" of the parent. But whatever that
term may be interpreted to mean, we ought to realize
the difficulties involved in the case of an adult, especially if he comes from an Eastern European ghetto or
some village in southern Italy, who must adjust himself to a new environment. The process that he must
go through requires at least patience on our part and
time on his part.

And while this process goes on the child rapidly
treads the new path. In a short time the parent,
accustomed to an environment very different from that
of his new home, makes the sad discovery that he does
not understand his child. At times he is not even conscious of this lack of understanding any more than
the child is of his steadily growing away from his father

and mother. But the chasm is there and is a cause of many a tragedy in immigrant life in this country. The negative effects of this breach upon the children can hardly be overestimated. Only the conscious socialization of the child into his family group will overcome this difficulty and will prepare him for entering into the life of larger groups.

The second step in the socialization of the child is that of enabling him to become a part of the religious group (local at first) or community. It is to be expected that wherever original nature can be called upon to assist in the process of socialization, its aid would be enlisted. While it would be difficult to prove the existence of a distinct religious instinct, the universality of the existence of religion in ancient and modern times and the forms which its manifestations take certainly justify the statement that the religious habits and attitudes find their basis in original nature.[1] In primitive groups religion was not only a means of socialization into the group; it was so prominently associated with the entire life of the group as to be almost indistinguishable as a separate factor. So completely was religion identified with the social group that elaborate initiation ceremonies of the ancients inducted the young into the sacred duties that they were to perform as members of the religious community. Tribal consciousness implied tribal religion.

Thus we find that Ellwood, who defines religion as the belief in the reality of the spiritual life and as consisting primarily of an attitude of valuing, emphasizes that these religious values are built up *socially*.

[1] See Coe, G. A., *Education in Religion and Morals,* p. 37.

"They are products, not of one individual mind but of the *collective* mental life of a group." [1] And Ames concludes that "religion is the participation in the ideal values of the social consciousness." [2] This conception of religion is expressed by a Jewish thinker as follows: "Religion is an expression of the collective life of a social group, after it has attained a degree of consciousness which is analogous to the self-consciousness of the individual." [3] It is unfortunate that the current notion of religion is one which dissociates it from life and renders it a realm apart. In the case of the Jewish people we find an instance where the inseparability of religion and nationality has been maintained. So closely are these related that the Jewish educator finds it almost impossible to distinguish between that which functions in Jewish life as religious and that which functions as national—both are so interwoven that any distinctions made are arbitrary and not vital.

From this point of view the importance of socializing the child into the religious group gains new significance. For religious education no longer means merely catechism, or creed, or even beliefs and practices. It means primarily so socializing the child into the religious group that he may be responsive to the factors that maintain it.

The third step in the socialization of the child into

[1] Ellwood, C. A., "Social Functions of Religion," in *American Journal of Sociology,* v. 19, pp. 289-307.

[2] Ames, E. S., *Psychology of Religious Experience,* p. 356.

[3] Kaplan, M. M., "What is Judaism?" in *The Menorah Journal,* v. 1, no. 5, p. 316.

the Jewish group is making him a part of the larger Jewish community—the people. Regarded from the point of view above described, his entering into the religious group might be deemed to fulfill the ethnic aims as well. But as a matter of fact the religious group might be understood by some to designate merely synagogue life. At any rate, it may undoubtedly exclude the participation by the child in certain activities of the Jewish group that might not at present be described best by the word religious. For this reason the term ethnic is here used to mean all those bonds minus what is usually called religious that unite the Jewish people all over the world.

It is interesting to note in this connection that many who would be ready to accept this view of education as socialization would fail to concede the right of socializing the child into the ethnic group. They concede religious education but associate all sorts of imaginary dangers with ethnic group education. Essentially, such an attitude is not merely undemocratic, as has already been pointed out elsewhere, but is also inconsistent. It is inconsistent because if it is true that socialization into the world community is the aim of education [1] and that this can be attained by socialization into many "societies" (provided they be not anti-social), this privilege cannot be extended with consistency to one group and not extended to another. Thus, consistency would demand on the part of such people that they reject either the aim of education as progressive social-

[1] It should be remembered though, that socialization into the world, that is into the largest community, may be of various degrees of intensity.

ization into the world community or the advisability of socializing the child into "America," if they conceive the two as incompatible. The implication certainly is one of a conflict between being loyal to America and loyal to the world. Similarly, an imaginary conflict is seen between loyalty to the Jewish group and loyalty to America. If such conflict exists, consistency would demand either the rejection of American education or the extension of similar rights to ethnic groups unless their anti-sociality can be proven.

The reason why we do not feel compelled to give up American education for the sake of socializing the child into the world is threefold. In the first place, we perceive in America a large group with many and varied shared interests. Secondly, this group not only shows many and varied interests shared by individuals within the group but also much interplay with other groups outside of America. For this reason we do not fear any limitation or narrowing of interests. Thirdly, we conceive for other reasons that America is one of the finest means toward the socialization of the child into the world. The same analysis holds true of the Jewish group in relation to other groups.

Summarizing, therefore, it may be said that if the aim of general education is gradually to socialize the child up to and including the world community, the aim of Jewish education is to socialize the child into the largest Jewish community. Thus, from the point of view of America, Jewish education may be conceived as an integral part of the socialization process which it intends all its children to go through, while from the Jewish point of view this step is in itself a socialization the quality of which is well known and has been tested by centuries.

This thought of the quality of socialization leads one to consider the suggestion of Prof. Dewey that "any education given by a group tends to socialize its members but the quality and value of the socialization depends upon the habits and aims of the group." [1] The implication is twofold. On the one hand, it rules out any anti-social groups. On the other hand, it attaches greater value to that quality of socialization which does not hinder coming in contact with the larger group and which even helps develop that breadth of view and depth of sympathy which should bind all mankind.

It is true that in a democratic society the responsibility rests upon the government to prove a group antisocial, if it wishes to suppress its activities, and therefore this study is not meant to be a defense of Jewish education in America. It might be well though to point out that a study of what some of the Jewish values are—the curriculum of the Jewish school—is a study of the "aims and habits of the group." The aims and the habits of a group must be expressed in the values that the people cherish. The significant thought that one should bear in mind in this connection is that the history of the Jewish people is replete with tendencies to universalization. The synthesizing tendency of the Jewish mind expresses itself in the conception of the unity of God and the unity of man—the basis of internationalism. From the prophets of old to our own days and throughout the development of international-

[1] Dewey, J., *Op. cit.*, pp. 95-96.

ism as a human ideal, the Jew has shown a strong tendency to become a citizen of the world. Holding to a nationalistic idealism, he has nevertheless developed an ideal of internationalism. History too made him live amongst all the nations of the earth, and he became an international being.[1] As a result, the proper socialization of the child into the larger Jewish community really means the socialization of the child into the world.

[1] This fact has been seized upon by Anti-Semites to prove that the Jews have an international organization which unites them; but this is of course lacking in Jewish life.

CHAPTER III

THE PROBLEM OF THE CURRICULUM IN THE JEWISH SCHOOL

A. The Twofold Nature of the Curriculum

If the aim of general education is the continuous and progressive socialization of the child into his ever-widening community, the curriculum of the school should be so developed as to fulfill this aim. The implication of this idea is, in the first place, that just as the word socialization is a description of the life process so the curriculum must be. In the second place, the curriculum being not merely a repetition of the activities of life but rather a selection, it should be an improvement upon the imperfections of the present environment.

The problem of the curriculum of any school is that of so arranging the race experiences that they stimulate children to react properly, to form useful habits and attain useful knowledge in the process. The starting point should be the life surrounding the child, which to a great extent includes in its daily activities most of the experiences of the race, expressed or implied. In this way education becomes a reflection of life.

When a situation in life is unsatisfactory, when certain relationships exist in actuality which are not considered ultimately desirable, it becomes the duty of the school to supplant these by substituting in its "miniature community," a better life—in this way improving upon the imperfections of the environment. By creating the situations that stimulate wise reactions on the part of the child, the school not only serves to guide the child in later life by enabling him to live in the present but also provides for progress by causing situations in school to improve upon undesirable features of the present social order.

B. Theory and Practice

These two thoughts, that the school curriculum should be a reflection of life and that the school should improve life and idealize it, are being accepted more and more widely in our educational theory. But while theoretically accepted in many quarters, this view is far from being carried out in practice. In fact, so tremendous is the gap between educational theory and practice that very often undeserved reflections are cast upon a well deserving educational theory which has really never been applied.

This failure to make practice reflect theory is not always due to wilful neglect or to a distrust of the new. The task of freeing oneself concretely from an educational procedure that has been in vogue for centuries is a difficult one and requires at times the readiness of the revolutionary for making changes. Besides, keen analytical ability is required to discover what the implications are of the idea that the curriculum should be a reflection of life.

The curriculum-maker must analyze the environment carefully, must find out what the experiences of the child are, what knowledge, habits, and attitudes he unconsciously attains in the course of these experiences, and what knowledge, habits, and attitudes are implied in some of the activities of that environment which the child must first attain. His analytical ability must then protect him further against bringing those things into his curriculum which will merely tend to perpetuate the evils of the present. These difficulties may perhaps be so apparent as to require little emphasis were it not for the fact that their implications for the curriculum of the Jewish school are particularly far-reaching.

C. The Unchanged Curriculum

The problem of the curriculum of the Jewish school is much more aggravated by the position in which the Jewish people finds itself—a people living in every land as a minority group, with a strong desire for life, trying to maintain itself under adverse conditions. The curriculum of the Jewish school is at present primarily a literary curriculum consisting of the study of the Bible, modern Hebrew literature, the Talmud, the prayer book, etc. If in the teaching process in the Jewish school the curriculum is to utilize the interest of the child, it will have to be less of a literary curriculum, for it is very difficult with such a course of study to utilize the interests of the child to any great extent. When to the literary curriculum an antiquated method is added, the failure of our schools to appeal to the young is obviously accounted for. As Prof. Dewey points out, "It is a development of experience and into experience that is really wanted. And this is impossi-

ble save as just that educative medium is provided
which will enable the powers and interests that have
been selected as valuable to function. They must
operate and how they operate will depend almost
entirely upon the stimuli which surround them, and
the material upon which they exercise themselves." [1]
If the material upon which the interests of children
must exercise themselves is only literary and unrelated
to actual life, it becomes impossible to attain the development along Jewish lines that is really wanted.

Why is it that the material in the curriculum of the
Jewish school has been, relatively speaking, unchanged
for generations? Why is it that the Jewish people,
so skilled in adaptability, has maintained considerable
uniformity in the school curriculum throughout the
ages?

In the first place, the history of the Jewish people
throws significant light on the subject. Ever since
70 C.E., when the second temple was destroyed and
the people were driven into exile, the Jew has been a
man without a country. He was scattered amidst all
the people of the earth. The soil as a basis for national
unity having been lost, the culture of the people had
to serve instead as a binding force for the Jews all over
the world. The Jews in Babylonia, in Spain, and in
Germany had to be bound to each other by some concrete ties if they were to preserve their individuality
among the nations. It was to be expected that education would be called upon to perform this function.
Where the function of a school system is not merely
to transmit the social heritage to future generations

[1] Dewey, J., *The Child and the Curriculum*, p. 24.

but to provide for "spiritual renewal" whereupon depends the very existence of the people, the tendency will be for the curriculum to be fixed and static. Otherwise that precious unity which means the very life of the group is threatened.

Another reason, which is also historical, may be found in the conditions under which the Jew lived in the lands of the Diaspora. In the Middle Ages throughout Europe, and to this day in Eastern Europe, the Jew was not treated as an equal by the state. Persecutions and discrimination were for many years the rule rather than the exception. Political, economic, and social restrictions operated to exclude the Jew from the society of others in the larger group. The result was the creation of the ghetto. Since the Jew was excluded from mixing in the life of his neighbors, he lived a life of his own within ghetto walls. There all his needs had to be fulfilled. There he could find solace from the horrors of an unfriendly world that gave him no rest.

Educationally, too, the exclusion of Jewish students from general schools and universities operated to make their own schools, their own studies, the only source from which to quench their spiritual thirst. In the words of the national Hebrew poet, Bialik, "they forgot their suffering in the study of a page of the Talmud." In this way ghetto life and educational restrictions acted to make the curriculum of the Jewish school static and unchanging. For had the Jew mingled with his neighbors, had other educational institutions been open to him, had there been freedom and a give-and-take relationship between him and his neighbors, it would have been necessary for the Jewish school and its curriculum to undergo considerable modification.[1] The student of education, who knows well how close is the relation between the political, social, and economic conditions of a people and their educational institutions, will therefore be little surprised that political persecution and economic and social discrimination resulted in a curriculum unchanged for years.

But undoubtedly one of the most significant causes in maintaining an unchanged curriculum is to be found in its very nature. The curriculum—valuable race experiences—contains certain elements that are so fundamental that they may be considered, relatively speaking, permanent, in addition to other elements that are subject to change. It would follow that the more general, the more inclusive, the values to be transmitted to future generations, the more permanent the curriculum. Thus the people who produced the ideals of the Bible would be expected to maintain the study of the Bible as one of the main items in their course of study. The interpretation of certain ideas and ideals may change from time to time and may have to be adjusted to changed conditions, but amidst the changes certain elements remain as fundamentals and these should constitute the basis of the curriculum. These three reasons—the need of maintaining the unity of a people without a land, the ghetto life, and the actual desire to maintain certain values—have resulted in an unchanged literary curriculum in the Jewish school.

[1] See Book One: *Jewish Education in Russia and Poland,* chap. 1.

D. The Need of Adjusting the Curriculum

The literary curriculum of the Jewish school was transplanted from Eastern Europe to America. The new environment quickly brought about a consciousness of necessary changes. Thus the Russian Jew who for years had been excluded from the educational institutions of his native land found himself free to send his child to public school—an opportunity that he eagerly seized and widely used. At the same time provision had to be made for the Jewish education of his children. Efforts have been made to transplant some of the educational institutions of Eastern Europe, the Heder, the Yeshibah, the Eastern-European Talmud Torah. All these attempts have failed. The new conditions required new means. Thus after a process of trial and error, supplementary Jewish schools have been established which permit the Jewish child to attend public school, to mix freely with other children of various nationalities, and yet provide for his Jewish education after school hours. This is a concrete illustration of an adjustment made by the Russian Jew to the American environment. A free public school ready to receive children of all groups made a supplementary Jewish school necessary and thus became an important factor in moulding the educational policy of the Jews in America.

But the problem is much more difficult in the case of the curriculum. What to teach in the school cannot be readily decided by administrative considerations. To transfer an Eastern European curriculum to the Jewish school in America could not but result in ineffectiveness. For how could a course of study suitable to one environment be effective in an environment totally different? The Eastern-European curriculum, planned for a whole day of Jewish instruction, has to be condensed into one or two hours a day at most. A change must take place. The curriculum, too, must be adjusted. How shall this adjustment take place?

It is easier to say that the curriculum of the Jewish school should be vitalized, than to carry the theory implied in this thought into practice. From a certain point of view, the idea that the curriculum should be synonymous with life ought to find no difficulty of acceptance in the Jewish school. This thought is really descriptive of what took place during centuries of exile and persecution. The entire life of the Jew was to be found in the inner, enclosed, compulsorily limited life of study. The curriculum of the Jewish school was the life of the Jewish group perhaps to a greater extent than in any other school system. But the very conditions under which such close relationship existed between the school and life revealed its limitations. The school was life in the absence of freedom to live outside of school. In lands of freedom where happily this condition does not exist, the idea that the Hebrew school should be a reflection of life must be given different interpretation. The Jewish school should reflect Jewish life wholly—not in its limitations.

But it is possible to embody such a conception in all its implications only in that country where the Jews will live as a majority people having a free opportunity to develop and foster Jewish culture, and where the peculiar abilities of the Jewish people will find expression without being hampered by an environment that acts as a centrifugal force upon Jewish life. In America or any other free country it is neither possible, nor in the opinion of the writer, desirable, to have that kind of a distinctive Jewish school system that will take upon itself the complete responsibility for the education of the child.[1] Since the life reflected is not primarily Jewish, the school that can best perform the function of a reflector is the American public school. Only in Palestine where a thoroughly Jewish environment would surround the child could the school be said to reflect Jewish life in its entirety. In the Diaspora, too, Jewish life may be reflected in the school but, since it is relatively limited in its scope by a non-Jewish environment, the idea that the school will be a reflection of life can have at best but a limited application in the Jewish school.

For, if the "subject matter of education consists of meanings which supply content to existing social life,"[2] what can be done in the case of a school whose base—the social life of which it is the product—is limited in scope? Here, if anywhere, the danger is great that the curriculum-maker will copy the imperfections of the environment and that the idea that the curriculum should be a reflection of life will become a source of error instead of a source of truth.

E. METHOD OF THIS STUDY

Thus the difficulty of making a curriculum for the Jewish school in America can hardly be overestimated.

---

[1] As the parochial school system would attempt.

[2] Dewey, J., *Democracy and Education,* p. 226.

There are, however, basic principles upon which it is possible to proceed. In the first place, since the curriculum of Eastern Europe is the one that has been brought over into this country, an attempt to determine the curriculum of the Jewish school in America might well be preceded by a recognition of the fact that the curriculum of Eastern Europe was an expression of the conditions of that environment.[1] An analysis showing how the environment changed should result in a new curriculum. A study was therefore made of the origin and development of the curriculum in Russia and Poland, showing how the educational forces that were potent in Eastern Europe worked for the maintenance of Jewish group life in an environment where ghetto life was forced upon the Jew.

Secondly, a conception of the curriculum as a reflection of the present requires that it be evolved with the present environment in mind. This means that the course of study in the Jewish school must be considerably affected by the conditions of the land in which the child lives. Hence the curriculum of the Jewish school should in some measure, at least, vary with the lands of the Diaspora. For the needs of the children and the conditions under which these needs have to be fulfilled will vary with the local environment of the child.[2] Those forms of activity have to be chosen which are most suitable to the condition of the child. Hence the curriculum must not only be affected by the conditions of the land in which the Jew

[1] See Book One: *Jewish Education in Russia and Poland*.

[2] Bonser, F. G., *The Elementary School Curriculum*, pp. 70-71.

finds himself but must also change in certain respects, if the conditions in that land change.

At the same time provision has to be made whereby the curriculum will not lose those relatively permanent values which should be the fundamentals in any curriculum. Thus, while the emphasis upon the present will save us from an "idealized past" which is so divorced from the present that it serves as a "solace of the spirit," as was really the case under ghetto conditions, a thorough knowledge by the teacher of the race experiences will enable him to give the child the necessary guidance. Certain habits and attitudes are easily attained by an unconscious educational process. The school should be ready through its knowledge of the present to select what is vital in the past, to reinforce the habits and attitudes unconsciously attained by the child, and to utilize them as a basis for further education. On the other hand, the further education must contain in it those fundamental Jewish values which are essential to Jewish life. The teacher must therefore know these if he is to be successful in his task. "Save as the teacher knows, knows wisely and thoroughly, the race experience which is embodied in that thing we call the curriculum, the teacher knows neither what the present power, capacity or attitude is, nor yet how it is to be asserted, exercised and realized." [1] And we may add for the curriculum of the Jewish school that unless he knows the fundamental Jewish values he neither knows what to transmit that will preserve a group life that is and should be free to

[1] Dewey, J., *The Child and the Curriculum*, p. 40.

interact with other groups, nor the method by which to transmit it to future generations.

This need of formulating some essentials of a curriculum is much more urgent in the Jewish school than are the attempts to devise minimum essentials in the public school. For the attempt to devise minimum essentials in the public school is not a question of the life and death of a group. It is true that a great deal of benefit can result to the American school from such studies. Time will be saved and children will come to their activities outside of school better prepared to live as intelligent citizens. These attempts make such study sufficiently worthy of our effort.

In the case of the Jews in America, the problem is much more serious. Assuming that the maintenance of the Jewish group is of value both to the Jew and to America, a system of education is essential to accomplish this aim. It so happens, however, that the rapidity with which Jewish immigration to this country took place created an abnormal situation with regard to facilities for Jewish education. Ordinarily a group settles, and as its needs develop, it develops means of fulfilling them. Under normal conditions an intelligent group can so regulate its life that fulfillment will keep pace with need.

Jewish immigration to this country was, however, rapid and intermittent. The Jews came in three successive waves of immigration and each time they came in tremendous numbers. The result was that their educational needs multiplied too rapidly for their ability to fulfill them. German Jewry has, for a number of reasons that need not here be mentioned, specialized in fulfilling the philanthropic needs of the community. Jewish education has in the meantime been neglected. At present there are about 300,000 Jewish children in New York City of school age of whom only 25% are receiving Jewish instruction.[1] The lack of facilities, both physical and in personnel, is so great that it will take a long time for the Jewish community to provide all the children in this city with an intensive [2] Jewish education. It may be that in the smaller communities outside of New York City where the number of children is not as great, facilities can be provided. But certainly the problem in New York City, which has 1,500,000 Jews or one-half of the Jewry of the country, deserves special attention.

The meager facilities for intensive Jewish education have therefore made it necessary for the Jewish community to devise a new means of education, which, though not intensive, will nevertheless serve as a means of affiliating the young with their people. Such a scheme may be called extensive education (*vs.* intensive). Instead of giving classroom instruction, it would aim to provide great numbers of children with mass instruction in the auditorium of some of the big Hebrew school buildings. This is an attempt to provide for the thousands of children who are outside of our Jewish schools at present. The curriculum that such a system of extension education will need must necessarily consist of the very essentials of content that will serve to

[1] Dushkin, A. M., *Jewish Education in New York City,* part II, chaps. 1 and 2.

[2] By an intensive education is meant classroom education at least two days a week after public school hours, besides Sunday.

make the child feel itself a part of a people. What are these essentials that will attach the young to the old and prepare a generation of Jewry to live in America? From this point of view an analysis of some fundamental Jewish values is paramount in the making of a curriculum for the Jewish school, and such an analysis requires the development of criteria of values.

Any attempt to formulate criteria for the development of a curriculum for the Jewish school in America must, however, reckon with our aim of education—the continuous and progressive socialization of the child into the Jewish group in harmony with the conditions of the new environment.

CHAPTER IV

CRITERIA FOR THE CURRICULUM OF THE JEWISH SCHOOL

A. CRITERIA IN GENERAL EDUCATION

THE problem of the curriculum in general education has of late been regarded as that of finding adequate criteria for determining what is essential in the continuous growth of the individual in accordance with his original nature and the laws of learning. The need for finding criteria for selection became more insistent as various new subjects began to clamor for admittance into the school and as democracy appeared to fail in educating citizens to be ready for the many stimuli and opportunities for choice in modern life.

Starting out with the conception that education is life and that growth consists in the process of ever forming and executing new ends in life, the curriculum-maker usually proceeds to analyze the needs of life and to use these as criteria for the making of his curriculum.

The needs of life vary in different environments and with the conception of the breadth or narrowness of life which in turn depends on the philosophy of the individual. Hence in a democratic society the criteria will be different from those in an autocratic society. A democratic society where social control is dependent not on force but on social responsibility will give emphasis to social responsibility as a criterion. Thus we find that Dewey and Bonser set up the social criteria, and their analysis of life which gives rise to their criteria is affected both by their democratic philosophy and by the local environment of America. Hence their criteria are the result of an aim which is not limited to country but is human and world-wide, and is modified by the conditions of the local environment. In the same way, our analysis of the aim of education as a process of continuous socialization with the largest group as the end, together with our analysis of the environment of the Jew in America, will lead to the criteria for the curriculum of the Jewish school in this country.[1]

B. PERMANENCE AND CHANGE

Before proceeding, however, to the development of the criteria resulting from the new environment and our aim of education, the reader should note the important fact that the very idea of establishing criteria for the making of a curriculum of the Jewish school in America implies the possibility of change. A criterion is a measuring rod, a point of view, from which we derive a conception of relative values. In the past some of these values may have formed a part of the curriculum without having been subjected to any test

[1] Prof. Dewey mentions efficiency, sociability, æsthetic taste, trained intellectual method, and conscientiousness, pointing out, however, that they ought to be regarded as points of view from which to survey the field of subject matter and method (*Democracy and Education,* pp. 285-286). Prof. Bonser's classification consists of health, practical efficiency, citizenship, and recreation (*The Elementary School Curriculum,* pp. 13-14).

whatever. The authoritarian cannot accept even the idea of trying to find new criteria since, finding them, change might follow. To him the permanent and fixed elements are important, and he is inclined to decry all effort at change as evil. The derivation of new criteria, therefore, should be regarded as an adjustment arising from a modern outlook upon life, which sees how change is a fundamental fact in life and recognizes that variation has been in large measure a source of progress.

In a democratic society that is supposed to be dynamic—that is supposed to provide for constant opportunity for change—where social structure is flexible, plastic, and ever subject to improvement, the curriculum must be constantly reinterpreted in terms of new ideas and ideals arising from new needs. Hence the imperative need for adjustment of immigrant peoples, their ideas and ideals, to America.

But the authoritarian may question the advisability of such flexibility. If a society is to permit change all the time, how can it insure the necessary amount of order or "social stability?" Especially in these days, when change seems to be the order of events, people might fear the "social instability" of dynamic societies. In the same way the Jewish authoritarian may take the attitude that to subject the curriculum of the Jewish school to new criteria is to threaten the elaborate structure of the Jewish heritage handed down to us through centuries of labor and martyrdom.

It should be remembered, however, that a dynamic society is one in which there is constant interaction not only between people but also between ideas and ideals. A new ideal cannot be accepted until it has, so to speak, been permitted to interact with the old. If, after open-minded consideration has been given to the new idea in comparison with an alternative, the new is accepted, it cannot be maintained that the old structure is threatened by the mere flexibility of a dynamic state of affairs. The old is given the opportunity of interacting with the new and is rejected only when it becomes incompatible with life.

Thus it is well to examine a new idea to see whether it is a deductive generalization or a result of the observation of the needs of life operating in a modern world. One of the ways by which to judge the validity of criteria for the curriculum of the Jewish school is to see whether they arise from the needs of the Jewish people living in a modern world or whether they are creatures of the imagination divorced from such needs.

It may be further urged that such a flexible outlook upon life threatens all ethical foundations since it permits change without establishing a fixed goal. This lack of fixed goals is admitted by writers on democracy, but they take care to emphasize that amidst the flexibility of society the direction of progress is known and followed. It is to be sought along the lines of the continuous growth of the individual and the group. What tends to further growth, to increase the possibilities of growth, should be encouraged. Anything which tends to hinder this process of growth should be discouraged. By supplying society with the direction of progress democracy supplies the necessary stability for desirable change.

In the dynamic society, too, there are some values that are relatively permanent. A good example is this very attitude to change. Children should be taught that change is a fundamental fact of life and that while it may lead to degeneration as well as to progress it is nevertheless a condition of progress. They should be taught that, if society has sufficient foresight, change may be controlled so that it proceeds in a desirable direction. Therefore a critical attitude is essential. New proposals will have to be subjected to critical examination in the light of the old, but it should be borne in mind that the new may be pregnant with progress. So the dynamic society may have other values that might be conceived of as relatively permanent. The difference is that in a static society (in the extreme) all values are transmitted as *the truth,* subject to no change, whereas from the dynamic point of view these values, or most of them, are *relatively* permanent and the attitude to change permits many of them to be considered in the light of alternatives possibly to be rejected in favor of greater values.

The authoritarian may object that the transmission of this dynamic attitude to the young is indoctrination. It is, in the sense in which all education of the young is in some way indoctrination. But it is an alternative to another indoctrination worse in kind and degree. For the indoctrination of a person with a dynamic attitude to life infuses within him a serum which, theoretically, at least, may turn against dynamism [1] itself. For if change is the condition of progress, even this attitude of readiness to change ought to be subject to change.

[1] Dynamism in this discussion is used as a noun derived from the adjective "dynamic," as this is used in discussions on static and dynamic societies.

To this the logician may answer that the inculcation
of dynamism may lead one to be critical of everything
except the attitude of dynamism itself. But history,
as Prof. Robinson has pointed out, favors the attitude
of the dynamist.[1] History proves that the critical
attitude, the attitude favorable to change, has resulted
in progress. And this is the value which we dare not
neglect in a democratic society.

There is one other consideration which psychology
should teach the authoritarian; that is, that the social
order and all its established values are ultimately the
product of original nature. "The native impulses and
cravings of man have to be tamed and enlightened by
the customs, arts and sciences of civilized life, but every
item of these arts and sciences was first created by
forces within man's own nature. . . . The most elaborate and artificial moral training which a social group
prescribes is still ultimately an expression of man's
nature." [2] And if it is true that the lives of those who
pursue the cause of truth and justice are "proof that
human nature itself can change itself for the better,"
to give up the ideal of dynamism means to rely only
on all that previous original nature has wrought and
to preclude the possibility of utilizing the advantages
of improved original natures. Dynamism gives us the
great opportunity for progress through the "ultimate
source of all values."

If the Jewish people live in a dynamic society they
cannot afford to neglect this attitude to change.
Fortunately it is hardly necessary to preach this

[1] Robinson, J. H., *The New History,* chap. 8.
[2] Thorndike, E. L., *Original Nature of Man,* p. 311.

thought to a Jew. Only a living and changing religion has enabled the Jewish people to maintain itself throughout the ages. Holding to what was relatively permanent, they knew the secret of adequate adaptation which enabled them to accept what was valuable in other cultures and transform it into a means of furthering group life. The study of the changes in the curriculum of the Jewish school whenever Jewry came in contact with new culture is proof of this fact.[1]

It is but necessary to apply this principle of change and adaptation to conditions today just as it has been applied by Jewish thinkers in days past. Prophetic Judaism, perhaps the finest expression of Jewish idealism, and probably the most permanent, was replaced by Rabbinic Judaism at a time when historical conditions made a new method of life necessary for the Jew in order to maintain his identity. In the meantime, Rabbinic Judaism, which had as its basic principle the idea of adjustment to new conditions, and which has served as a means to an end—the preservation of the people—has become incompatible with the changes that have come into Jewish life today. The "fence around the law," which was an adjustment for the lack of a normal basis of life, has been perpetuated by years of persecution and social and economic cleavage from the rest of the world. Although it is true that every means becomes at some time an end, it is also true that it ceases to be even a means when it fails to function in the realization of what is a relatively more permanent end. Thus, if Rabbinic Judaism in its present

[1] See Book One: *Jewish Education in Russia and Poland,* chap. 1.

form cannot avail to preserve Jewish life in America and even permits a process of disintegration to go on, there is need for a new adjustment.

C. THE MEANING OF ADJUSTMENT

Biologically, adjustment means the condition by which an organism maintains itself in a new situation without giving up its individuality. Adjustment is not disappearance or self-effacement. Self-effacement, in fact, is the opposite of adjustment, it is the failure to adjust. For only when individuality is maintained is it possible to say that one has adjusted himself. To disappear is to remove the need for adjustment. The dead are dead and require no further adjustment.

Adjustment also implies reckoning with those new conditions of the situation which require change. The change must not, however, affect the essential individuality of the being, or the being would become untrue to self. In the same way the adjustment of a group means the maintenance of group life, group individuality, but in harmony with the new conditions of the situation confronting the group. Thus the adjustment of the immigrant groups in America must not be a self-effacement. For then individuality would disappear. The disappearance of the individuality of the group would mean not only the destruction of self but also a loss to America and ultimately to mankind, to whom the existence of all individualities should be considered as potential contributions, when these are not anti-social and especially when they are possessed of a creative vitality. Compromises are indeed made in life, but these must not affect essentials of individuality. The essentials are necessary for life and cannot be given up.

Hence, in the judgment of the writer, the so-called "assimilated" Jew was not adjusted but maladjusted. He had lost his own Jewish values and had only too often substituted nothing in their place. Although his forefathers had been persecuted for maintaining their Jewish values, he gave up his Jewish values in order that he might be sufficiently "like" the people in whose midst he lived. His individuality was gradually lost and he did not usually attain the position for which he paid so heavily. While the ghetto maintained Jewish life in all its warmth and enthusiasm but became too narrow, emancipated Jewish life became too superficial and lacked depth of being or resulted in maladjusted men and women.

But the Jew has shown great assimilative powers of a different kind throughout the ages, the kind of assimilation that maintains what is worth while in one's own individuality, though yielding to changes growing out of new needs of life. The Jew established many contacts and maintained his identity. This responsiveness to life is well illustrated by contact with Hellenism, by the work of Maimonides, and by the kind of education given to Jewish children in the Middle Ages during the days of freedom in contrast with that of the days of oppression.

So the Jewish curriculum, if it is to be adjusted, must reckon with the changed environment of the Jew in the modern world and yet maintain certain ideas or values that may be considered relatively permanent. Adjustment may require the rejection of some unessentials and surely requires the reinterpretation of essentials from age to age and the realization of these values through the particular avenues of approach suitable to the new environment. Hence, our criteria for the curriculum of the Jewish school in America should lead to the selection of what is essential and relatively permanent in Jewish life.

D. THE IMPLICATION OF OUR AIM OF EDUCATION

I. GROUP PRESERVATION

Since the new environment of the Jew affected the formulation of our aim of education, a proper analysis of this aim and the conditions that produced it should lead to the development of criteria for the Jewish curriculum. The aim formulated was that of continuous socialization. Since socialization into the ethnic group was found to be a part of this process, this socialization implies the preservation of the group.

Group preservation in the opinion of the large majority of the Jewish people has several significant implications. In the first place, it means the establishment of the Jewish people in their own historical land, where as a people they can live a normal life, like all the nations of the earth. The need for the Jewish people to live in Palestine arises, not only from an emotional desire to reëstablish them in their ancient home, but also from a sociological analysis of the Jewish problem. It is the application of a well accepted sociological law, that a small Jewish minority living in a non-Jewish environment cannot possibly continue the process of creating values. The general life is not an expression of any minority group. To conceive of the Jewish people as a living people, potentially creative, means to provide the conditions favorable for such creative work. Only in an environment which is an expression of the life of a group can the characteristic values of the group be developed.

Secondly, group preservation means the preservation of Jewish culture in the Diaspora as a means of keeping alive the Jewish consciousness for the great task of reëstablishing the people on its ancient soil, as well as for the sake of the intrinsic values of Jewish culture. In America, as well as in other lands, it means the transmission of what is valuable in the Jewish social heritage and what will serve as a means of survival to the group. Since the preservation of Jewish culture means the maintenance of the Jewish home, without which Jewish cultural or religious life in any Diaspora land would be out of the question, it means the continuation of biological perpetuation through the refusal to intermarry.

The writer is well aware of the opposition by many enlightened and liberal men and women to such a method of preservation. This opposition is, however, in large measure, due to a misunderstanding of the aim of this Jewish prohibition. The Jewish refusal to intermarry arose from a desire to maintain the integrity of the group and not from a mere desire for separatism. In its very earliest form, in the Bible, this reason is evident. "When the Lord thy God shall bring thee into the land whither thou goest to possess it, and shall cast out many nations before thee . . . thou shalt make no covenant with them . . . neither shalt thou make marriages with them: thy daughter thou shalt not give unto his son, nor his daughter shalt thou take unto thy son.   For he will turn away thy son from following Me, that they may serve other gods; so will the anger of the Lord be kindled against you, and He will destroy thee quickly." [1]   This is another way of saying that the extinction of the people would follow intermarriage, a fact which sociologists will admit of any minority group.   The best proof that this was the real cause of the prohibition against intermarriage and not a mere desire for separatism is the fact that there were times when Jewry admitted many proselytes, the condition being acceptance of the faith. In other words, when the marriage contracted was secured against being disruptive of group life it was permitted.   If this fact is borne in mind, a good deal of the animus accompanying the opposition to this custom will disappear.

But the prohibition against intermarriage is even more significant if one remembers the condition under which the Jewish people have lived since the destruction of the temple.   The common physical basis, the land, a distinct form of government, a common spoken tongue, and a common, constantly developing culture, which serve to unite all others, are lacking in the case of the Jewish people.   They have no land and no government, and while they have one language for prayer, they have at least as many languages for speaking and reading as the lands in which they are dispersed.   They have a common culture but no favorable opportunity to enable it to develop constantly.   Hence, religion

[1] Deuteronomy, 7: 1-4.

has been one of the most powerful bonds of unity. The refusal to intermarry, a religious precept, was regarded as perhaps the most important means to the all important end—the life of the group. Anyone who bears this fact in mind and remembers that the Jewish people is the only people on earth and in history that has succeeded in maintaining itself by artificial means under adverse conditions for two thousand years, cannot but look with a sympathetic attitude upon the Jew who makes untold sacrifices as an individual in order to maintain the life of the group, at times even suppressing a most powerful instinct lest it lead to the disintegration of group life.

As has already been pointed out,[1] intermarriage, even amongst the Jews, is rapidly increasing with the breaking down of artificial barriers and with the increase of social intercourse among all men regardless of race and creed. It is possible that with the reëstablishment of the Jewish homeland it will increase further. When the perpetuation of Jewish life in Palestine is assured, those who now consciously inhibit because of a desire to maintain the group will no longer feel the need for restriction, since they will know that the stream of Jewish life will go on even if it should decrease in distinctness in the lands of the Diaspora.

This conception of group preservation must, however, be affected by two fundamental influences on the life of the Jew in America, the influence of modernism and the influence of a democratic outlook upon life. How these two facts will affect our criteria we shall

[1] See chap 1.

see later. But one fact is clear so far, and that is that
in the process of socialization the life of the ethnic
group must be preserved.

How is the group to be preserved? It is commonly
accepted that the aims, ideals, habits, and attitudes
of the group are the means of its survival, since these
are transmitted from generation to generation through
the educative process. For purposes of this discussion
all of these may be grouped under the general classification of values. There are two kinds of Jewish values.
One may be called humanistic [1] values in the sense
that they are generally human and if accepted by all
people would result in a better state of society. A
good example of this type of value is the Jewish ethical
value. Some Jewish ethical values may have greatly
pervaded the consciousness of the Jewish people, but
they are universal in their applicability. They apply
to the human race as a whole. The second type of
Jewish value is one that has served peculiarly as a
means of preserving the group. Values of the second
type may therefore be called survival values. An
illustration of the humanistic value would be the conception of justice. An illustration of the survival value
would be the Passover Seder.[2]

It should be understood that these are not necessarily mutually exclusive. In fact, it may well be that
all humanistic values are great factors for the survival

[1] The word humanistic will in this study be understood to
mean "of value to humanity as a whole" or of humane tendency
and not in the sense of "humanities."

[2] The name given to the order of ceremonies followed in the
celebration of the first two evenings of Passover.

of the group, especially today. The honoring of father and mother which is a humanistic value no doubt has resulted, in the case of obedient children, in the preservation of many Jewish values which the same children would have otherwise disregarded. It is true that, since the human has a strong appeal to the young today, any humanistic value which has historically been a part of the Jewish people, and which has been reflected in its literature and cherished by the members of the group, serves as a means of survival. But there are some humanistic values that in Jewish life have been so closely associated with group life that they are of peculiar survival value. There are others that are not universal, not general, but nevertheless are values of the group and have functioned as a means of preserving it. In other words we may classify all Jewish values into these two general classes: (1) humanistic values; (2) survival values.

When we examine the survival values we find that they are not all of the same type. Amongst these can be distinguished three kinds. Some values that have been found to be of great survival value have also been found to be humanistic in character. A good illustration of such a value is the Jewish Sabbath. The Jewish Sabbath may no doubt be considered to have been one of the most important survival values. At the same time, the fundamental ideas of the Sabbath are universal and of value to the whole of humanity. Such a value might be classified as humanistic under the general heading of survival. It is therefore hyphenate, *survival-humanistic*.

There is, however, another kind of Jewish value that

may be general but is not on the same plane as the former. An illustration of such a value would be the singing of special liturgical songs (Zemirot) on Friday evening or the beautiful ceremony of kindling the Sabbath lights. In the sense that an appreciation of these might conceivably be cultivated by a non-Jew if he be interested they might be considered general. But no one will claim that they have the same humanistic value as the conception of justice or the Sabbath. They are in a peculiar sense possessions of the people that observe them. They are appreciated particularly after one has associated with the group. They are survival values, but their essential aspect is not humanistic but rather cultural and æsthetic. These might therefore be classified as *cultural-æsthetic* values.

The third kind of survival value neither possesses the humanistic aspects of the first nor the cultural-æsthetic aspects of the second. Yet the values of this third type are also survival values. They have functioned greatly in the preservation of the life of the group. But their value is not intrinsic as in the case of the first two. Their value is *merely* survival. Some of these, however, are very important for survival because they are deeply rooted social habits in Jewish life. They have their roots in the far past, in the cradle days of the group. They are almost universally observed. Above all, the violation of such a value by a member of the group places him, at least in the minds of the rest of the group, as an outsider, as one who has broken the bonds. Of course, not all the values in this class are to an equal degree deeply rooted. A good illustration of this class, which may be called the *deeply-*

rooted, is the refusal to intermarry or the observance of the Dietary Laws.

Thus Jewish values may be classified into two general classes: (1) humanistic values; (2) survival values. The second class, which includes ceremonial values, may then be further subdivided into three classes: (a) humanistic (e.g., the Sabbath); (b) cultural-æsthetic (e.g., Zemirot and kindling of Sabbath lights); (c) deeply-rooted (e.g., refusal to intermarry).

II. ADJUSTMENT TO MODERNISM

Another implication of our aim of education as a continuous process of socialization is the widening of the interests of the individual. In accordance with this conception, socialization into the ethnic group must be in harmony with socialization into the largest conceivable group—the world.

It has already been pointed out that with the breakdown of the ghetto and the coming of the Jews to America, many Jews of the ghetto have been brought in contact with the world of today and what we might call the present Zeitgeist. Adjustment to this Zeitgeist is essential. It might, however, be maintained that the present Zeitgeist, as expressed in this country, shows many unfavorable features which ought to be rejected, or, at any rate, disregarded. There is a good deal of truth in such an assertion. For this reason the writer will point out what he considers to be some of the essential features of the present Zeitgeist to which Jewish life must adjust itself.

Modern life has succeeded in relatively eliminating space and time. The railroad, the steamship, the airplane, the telegraph, and the newspaper have accomplished wonders in this respect. The many inventions of modern man have brought men together. The diffusion of the power to read has resulted in a sharing of the cultures and customs of men by people removed from each other in space. The rise of democracy throughout the world has increased and intensified the desire to share activities with others. The result has been that the thinking man today has become more than ever a citizen of the world.[1]

An intelligent individual permits his actions to be affected in some measure by this sense of social responsibility which is, or should be, world-wide. In the same way the intelligent group must question the results of its own actions in terms of such social responsiveness. This might be called the criterion of universalization. Does this act which the group is about to do, this idea which the group has accepted, tend to bring men nearer together or does it tend to separate them? If it tends to separate them, is it the kind of separation that has value to the group and does no harm to any other group, or is it the kind of separation that has no intrinsic value and only increases the barriers that separate men? Thus the criterion of universalization may be applied in several ways, positively and negatively. Positively, it would lead to an emphasis on certain Jewish values in the curriculum which tend to bring men nearer to each other. This

[1] One might disagree with this statement in view of the animosities displayed by men of all nations in the Great War. The writer, however, considers these aberrations due to artificial stimulation by those interested in the actual conduct of the war.

is the case when a value is universally applicable, and, if accepted by all people, would result in the enhancement of life. Negatively, this criterion serves to exclude any value which cannot be at least theoretically universalized. If the question, "Would this value, if accepted by all people, tend to interfere with life?" is answered in the negative, the value may be said to pass the criterion of universalization. This criterion may serve therefore to include some values which, when theoretically universalized, will not be found to be of significance to humanity at large but will not be anti-social and will have meaning in the life of the group itself.

Another more outstanding characteristic of the present Zeitgeist is the scientific outlook upon life which man has adopted. The appearance of Darwin's *Origin of Species* was an important event because it changed the whole of modern philosophy. The conception of the "superiority of the fixed and the final," which dominated philosophy for two thousand years, gave way to the idea that beings come, develop, and pass away.[1] This bringing to the front of the idea of evolution revolutionized the thinking of man and affected religion tremendously. Belief in tradition, the authority of the Bible, and religion in general were shaken by the questioning attitude that necessarily accompanied the experimental method of enquiry which science adopted.

The difficulties that the scientific outlook brought become more evident when we note the changed ideas of cause and effect that man developed. Before the

[1] Dewey, J., *Influence of Darwin upon Philosophy*, pp. 4-19.

scientific age man did not necessarily conceive of cause and effect as immediately related in action. Belief made causes that were very remote account for the events of life. No direct connection had to be shown between cause and effect. The cause was not observed, nor did it have to be verified. Belief took the place of verification. That is why rain could be "produced" by certain invocations to the spirits. The cause for rain was remote, and man saw no difficulty in assigning such remote causes to effects observed. But the coming of science and experimentation changed this conception altogether. Effects observed, the individual seeks to find their cause right near them. He seeks to verify the cause and causes effects. In this way he questions whatever he sees and tries to find a satisfactory answer. This spirit of enquiry has also been transferred into the field of religion where the historical method is employed. One can readily see how the literal truth of certain Biblical accounts was shaken by such an attitude to cause and effect and undermined by the sceptical and critical attitude which accompanies experimental enquiry.

The problem of the Jew, therefore, is how to live in a modern world, accepting such a scientific outlook on life and at the same time maintaining what is valuable in Jewish life. The task of harmonization is not a simple one, nor can it be accomplished by disregarding this outlook on life which pervades all modern thought and action. Jewish values have to be tested by the criteria of universalization and a scientific outlook upon life before they can be said to be compatible with the present Zeitgeist.

III. ADJUSTMENT TO AMERICA

Perhaps one of the most important evidences of the spirit of modernism is the growth of democracy. So important a manifestation of modernism is the democratic outlook upon life that it deserves special consideration and emphasis, although logically it might be considered a phase of modernism.

The curriculum of the Jewish school must be adapted to the conditions of life in this country. Theoretically this means harmonizing Jewish values with a democratic outlook upon life. Practically it means the adaptation of these to the social and economic conditions amidst which the Jews live in this country.

Our aim of education is a democratic one. The curriculum must not go counter to what have been found to be some of the essential characteristics of the democratic philosophy of life.[1] On the contrary, it should even further the possibility of the realization of democracy's highest ideals. The anthropocentric conception of the universe emphasized by the Jewish religion is quite in harmony with the human aims of democracy.[2] The sanction for action may have been conceived in times past to come from a different source. But the general motives are equally human.

Positively, then, there is no difficulty about the aim since in both cases the aim is human. Negatively, the curriculum must not violate such fundamentals of democracy as the sharing of interests and the development of give-and-take relationships between

[1] Chap. 2, p. 27.
[2] Berkson, I. B., *Theories of Americanization*, pp. 19-21.

people. It should permit sufficient intellectual freedom for the child to be influenced by other ideas than
those of the ethnic group. Taking the attitude that
the democratic society must provide for the continuous growth of the individual and the group, the curriculum in our schools should not hinder the possibility
of coming in contact with other groups. On the contrary, it should be a concrete expression of the consciousness that the individual and the group can realize
themselves best only in social relationships. It should
make it possible for the individual to react to the many
varied stimuli of modern life and develop within him
the recognition of the value of mutual interests to
society. It should permit continuous adjustment, so
necessary to a condition of freedom and interaction
between peoples. In doing so it will pass the criterion
of democracy.

Adjustment to America also means the adjustment
of the curriculum to the changed and changing conditions of the social and economic life of the Jew in
America. Here is where we should note another result
of modernism, the great change that has taken place
in economic life. The development of industry on a
large scale has resulted in making the life of the workers
one of routine. The worker is no longer free to arrange
his time as in the days of home industry and appren-
ticeship. He must become a part of the big machine
and adjust himself to it to a considerable extent. Ob-
jectionable as this state of affairs may be, we must
reckon with it as a factor which affects traditional
Jewishness and makes the observance of some customs
in this country very difficult. Wherever a value, how-

ever, is of deep meaning to the life of the group, the strong will of the group will preserve it in spite of the difficulties in the way due to economic or other social facts. If a value is not felt to be very vital to the group, it gradually falls into disuse.

In this connection accepting dynamism is of great help. The dynamist conceives of the Jewish people not as a fixed entity but as a changing, constantly developing organism. Anyone who really considers the Jewish people a *living* organism must see them *living* and *changing*. Life means change. In the case of a people it may mean the rejection or the change of old values and the creation of new values. Jewish life is in itself in some measure a criterion for the selection of values. Certain values deemed by the race invaluable are continued in the life of the group at all costs. Others deemed less valuable from the point of view of survival are dropped with the first difficulty that new conditions bring to a man who otherwise would maintain them. Present practice, in the case of customs and habits, present belief, in the case of ideas, ideals, and attitudes, are to some extent criteria of value. It may be true that when taken alone such criteria would be inadequate, since present practice might be, and in a good many cases is, undesirable. But taken with other criteria, present practice helps us judge the relative worth of values. For want of a better word we might call this criterion the criterion of functionalism.[1]

The criterion serves not only to call attention to the

[1] Referring to the extent to which a value still functions in the life of the people.

extent of present usage, but, by emphasizing the Jewish people as a living, changing being, causes the curriculum-maker to observe carefully present-day Jewish
life in order to fulfill in his curriculum present-day
Jewish needs. It shifts the center of gravity of the
Jewish curriculum from the past, where it has been
for centuries, to the present and the future.

Our criteria, therefore, are:

1. *From the point of view of the ethnic group*
   a. Humanistic values (not highly survival)
   b. Survival values
      (1) Humanistic
      (2) Cultural-æsthetic
      (3) Deeply-rooted
2. *From the point of view of the present Zeitgeist*
   a. Universalization
   b. A scientific outlook on life
3. *From the point of view of the American environment*
   a. A democratic outlook on life
   b. Functionalism

E. COMPARATIVE VALUES

How will the above criteria be used? In the first
place, it is important to note that the criteria have
two aspects. Some are meant primarily to insure the
inclusion of the relatively permanent elements of the
Jewish curriculum. Others serve to emphasize those
elements which will lead to a broadening of sympathies
furthering the process of socialization. These are their
positive aspects. Negatively, they will serve to exclude
from the curriculum anything that will hinder in
marked degree the process of continuous socialization.

It should be remembered that the values of a people, its aims, ideals, habits, and attitudes, are not things that can be measured with the same quantitative exactness with which one counts heads. It would be futile to pretend that these criteria will therefore be exact, mathematical standards of measurement for Jewish values. This fact should not, however, prevent us from making use of them as expressions of tendencies of interpretation of Jewish life. Following as they do a certain aim of education, they are indicative of a new spirit in the field of Jewish education in America. Above all else, they should not be considered absolute. They are meant to be helpful and suggestive to the Jewish curriculum-maker and may serve to introduce the process of reason and apply it to the field of the Jewish curriculum.

With this limitation in mind, one may note that the criteria derived from the point of view of the ethnic group really constitute a classification which serves as a criterion at the same time. If Jewish values are divided into essentially humanistic and survival, this is a classification of values. But it is a classification that in itself serves as a measuring rod. Every Jewish value that is described as essentially humanistic need not be subjected to any other test. If it is humanistic it possesses intrinsic worth and is surely in harmony with socialization into the largest conceivable group, since the very word humanistic implies universal— applicable to all.

But within the group of survival values we have a sub-classification, the humanistic (survival), the cultural-æsthetic, and the deeply-rooted. This classifica-

tion, too, serves to determine the relative worth of
values. It is self-evident that a value which has functioned greatly in the preservation of the group and is
also generally humanistic is of greater worth than one
that is only deeply rooted. In the same way there
may be some values that are strongly survival, strongly
humanistic, have cultural-æsthetic aspects, and are
deeply rooted. Those would be considered the most
important whereas a value to which only one of those
characteristics apply would be of less importance in
the curriculum. What has no intrinsic value but is
just a means to an end is in most cases of still less
importance.

Within the group of survival values, the other
criteria arising from the need of adjusting the curriculum to a new world-outlook and to the environment in
America have to be applied. A value which is significant from the point of view of survival should be
tested by the criteria of universalization, scientific outlook on life, democracy, and functionalism before its
position on the scale of Jewish values can be determined.

It may happen that conflicts will arise between
criteria. A value may be significant from the point of
view of survival and may at the same time be undemocratic. In that case the question of degree will
be an important factor. If a value that is highly important from the point of view of the preservation of
the group is undemocratic only to a slight extent,
democracy should, in the judgment of the writer, yield
to group preservation. Besides, the realization of the
aspirations of a people that has been deprived of its

rights is in itself a very important democratic aim.
If, on the other hand, a value is found to be highly
undemocratic and only in a small degree helpful to
survival, it should yield to democracy. If a value is
equally important from the point of view of survival
and equally undemocratic, and evidence of its harm to
democracy is as available as evidence of its importance
for survival, it must be rejected, as incompatible with
a democratic society. It is just in such conflicts of
criteria that the curriculum-maker will have to remember that neither the values nor the criteria can claim
mathematical exactness. The balance of reason has
to be introduced and careful consideration has to be
given to all the elements in the situation.

In this connection it is important to remember that
the Jews in America are living in a period of transition.
The parents are products of the Old World and the
children rapidly becoming products of the New. While
some values will be clearly recognized by all as supreme,
others, not so significant, may have to be maintained
during days of transition, when rejecting them might
cause tragedies in the home life of thousands of
families. Some of these transitional values need
not enter the curriculum as values to be maintained
by the children but as factors to be known by them,
facts in the life history of their parents, ideals toward
which, for the good of the entire community, they
should be sympathetic. After the period of transition
is over, certain values which have no intrinsic worth
will lose their psychological worth and will disappear
from the curriculum, except occasionally as links with
the past. But until that time comes, the Jewish edu-

cator must handle these values with the consciousness that in tampering with them he is touching some of the tenderest spots in the hearts of thousands of men and women and perhaps affecting the spirit of peace in thousands of Jewish homes.

Such a careful use of these criteria will help one to remember some of the ways in which even the very finest expressions of the present Zeitgeist have to be modified and refined. Thus, while no one will deny the great value of our scientific outlook on life, many will look with concern at the direction to which this increase of scientific activity has led modern man. The influence has been altogether too technical and mechanical and not sufficiently human. Hence the destructive uses to which science has been lately put. Scientific activity has to be regulated and controlled by humanness. This is just one illustration where one criterion will serve to limit another and where the very humanizing influence of a Jewish education has an important function to perform for humanity.

F. THE APPLICATION OF THE CRITERIA BY ALL GROUPS

It has been previously pointed out that the Jews in America consist of several groups,[1] each of whom emphasizes a different aspect of Jewish life. From this fact it naturally follows that one curriculum for all groups in Jewry would be an impossibility. All groups have, however, this one important fact in common, that they are interested in the survival of the Jewish people and their adequate adjustment to American life. They may, however, differ in their conception of

[1] See chap. 1.

what survival and adjustment mean and what method to pursue. Since they all agree on the importance of survival and adjustment, the previous analysis of types of values making for group survival and the criteria for adequate adjustment might be used by all these groups in the development of curricula for their schools.

There are indeed some, and they may be found in various groups of Jewry, who will reject all criteria. They are the authoritarians amidst every group, who believe that what was and is must always be and that the very thought of subjecting any value to criteria necessarily rejects the authoritarianism which they hold dear. Those people will continue to regulate themselves and the curricula of their schools by whatever sources of authority they recognize. Those who are interested in the preservation of Jewish life and also in some standards of measurement by which they can decide what is important will find the criteria previously developed helpful in the making of their curricula.

The emphasis which each group gives to certain aspects of Jewish life will lead to varying interpretations of the values subjected to our criteria, and therefore to different curricula for each group. The resulting curricula which they will develop after they apply the criteria will, however, be considerably different from their present curricula. An illustration will make both of these statements clear. There are many orthodox Jews who are very strict in their observance of the Jewish law but who do not expect a similar attitude on the part of their children. Such

Jews would no doubt be glad to adopt some standard of measurement by which to determine which Jewish values are important for transmission in the Jewish school. At present they have no criteria whatever. It is well known that most orthodox Jews insist on the importance of the ability to read the Hebrew prayers (Ibri) fluently. But the only object of reading the Hebrew prayers fluently is to be able to pray and to participate in public worship. As soon, however, as the orthodox Jew will apply the criterion of functionalism to his curriculum, he will realize that in order that the ability to read Hebrew fluently should function in the life of the child he must be trained to participate in the synagogue. The synagogue must begin to function. Or if he finds, as he probably will, that the synagogue functions only to a very limited extent, he will use his criterion of functionalism to select other Jewish values that will function more than "Ibri," and he will give them preference in his curriculum.

At the same time it could be readily seen that the orthodox Jew will apply his criteria differently from the reform Jew. In teaching Jewish history, for example, the orthodox Jew will no doubt give greater emphasis to the development of Rabbinic Judaism than the reform Jew. The application of the criterion of functionalism will in his case lead to such emphasis as would probably not be the case with the reform Jew. Similarly it might be shown that the reform Jew who has been born in this country will not teach his children to speak Yiddish because it does not function for his group. At the same time the national radical Jew

will certainly teach Yiddish to his children because it
does function in the environment of his group.

The reform Jew will not, however, have the same
curriculum that he now has if he will apply the criterion
of functionalism. For example it is a well known fact
that many elementary Sunday Schools give formal
direct and verbal instruction in religion and ethics.
Functionalism will tell them that such instruction is
bound to be ineffective. The curriculum will therefore have to be changed so as to teach only those elements of religion and ethics which can be taught
through child activity, through situations that arise
in home and school. Certain other elements which
might be recognized to be of importance will be post-
poned to some future time when the mental development of the child will permit more formal instruction.
In short, although the particular analysis of the meaning of survival [1] and the subsequent application of the
criteria to some of the values [2] represent the author's
outlook on Jewish life, the criteria in themselves may
be used by all groups in Jewry as scientific instruments
with which to develop a more balanced curriculum for
their schools.

G. The General Nature of the Criteria

Although these criteria were developed in connection
with an attempt to adjust the curriculum of the *Jewish*
school to American life, they will be found, in the
judgment of the writer, to be generally applicable.
Any immigrant group that wants to maintain its cul-

[1] See p. 78.
[2] See chap. 5.

ture and at the same time adjust itself adequately to American life and to a world outlook upon life will probably find the classification of its group values to be similar, and may find the analysis of the American environment to which they have to adjust themselves applicable. The same applies to the analysis of the important elements of modernism. If every group in America were ready to subject its values to criteria of compatibility with the progressively larger groups, even to the largest, there would be little to be said against multiple cultural loyalty.

It is quite pathetic to see how many are ready to permit all kinds of religious denominations to continue educational activity without question or objection. They call these "religious" activities, and since America permits religious freedom they cannot very well question these. They fail, however, to see the reason for permitting any group that frankly considers some of its values ethnic or cultural, and does not designate them "religious," to continue its educational activities. There is no inherent reason why a value that is ethnic or cultural should be considered incompatible with a democratic view of life, any more than a principle or a practice in religion.

H. Summary

Our aim of education, as continuous and progressive socialization, implies (1) enabling the child to participate intelligently and effectively in the life of the ethnic group, which means group preservation, and (2) the adjustment of group values to American life and to the present Zeitgeist. The means of group preservation are its important survival values as well as its humanistic values, which, because of historical association with group life, also become important from the point of view of survival.

The survival values have to be subjected to the criteria arising from the needs of American life and the need of adjusting the curriculum to the present Zeitgeist. These are the criteria of universalization, a scientific outlook on life, a democratic outlook on life, and functionalism. The use of these criteria will give an order of comparative values.

CHAPTER V

TYPICAL JEWISH VALUES

An attempt to discuss a fairly complete list of Jewish values would require several volumes. For purposes of this discussion it will be necessary, however, to point out the general value of a Jewish education and to discuss a few specific values, with the view of illustrating the classifications and criteria of values developed in the previous chapters.

The term values has till recently been associated and even now is associated with the word eternal. Each value had to be related to a transcendental "Reality" in order to be considered really valuable. The point of reference for a value was to be found in the Absolute Reality. Recently, however, values have no longer been regarded as eternal or as general or as related to transcendentalism. A value is valuable because it performs a specific function. It is valuable as it serves a certain purpose. The point of reference is to be found in human life.

In the same way we may say that the value of a Jewish education is the preservation of the Jewish people itself. We want the Jewish people to live a life worth while, one which will be satisfying to itself and which will enhance the life of others. It is for this reason that Jewish values in this discussion are judged by their specific functions in Jewish life and in the life of the larger community. All the humanistic Jewish values are of intrinsic worth and therefore can contribute to the life of Jew and non-Jew alike. All the Jewish cultural-æsthetic values are of intrinsic worth and therefore beautify Jewish life and, conceivably, if experienced by non-Jews with the necessary apperceptive mass, would beautify their life as well. Both kinds may be termed intrinsic values.

Some Jewish values, however, may have no intrinsic worth. They may serve only as a means of preserving the life of the people and therefore be instrumental to the preservation of the intrinsic values. These may be called instrumental values. All values that were described in the previous chapter as survival values, and which are neither humanistic nor cultural-æsthetic, would be considered instrumental values. Such values would not be considered of importance in the curriculum unless deeply rooted in Jewish life, in which case removing them would result in considerable harm, since with their breakdown many other values would follow.

Before discussing some typical Jewish values as illustrative of the intrinsic and the instrumental values, the humanistic and the survival values, it may be well to point out some of the general advantages of a Jewish education.

A. The General Value of a Jewish Education

Some of the general values of loyalty to the Jewish group from the point of view of democracy have been pointed out in a previous study.[1] It was there shown

[1] Berkson, I. B., *Americanization Theories,* chap. 4.

how sincerity of outlook, one's sense of right, and one's courage are tested and strengthened by membership in a minority ethnic group. The writer wishes to emphasize what seems to him to be *the* important value of a Jewish education from the functional point of view above presented. It is to be found in the very simple idea that upon Jewish education depends the preservation of the Jewish group. The saving of the life of the Jewish people is the important functional value of a Jewish education. Incidentally, it may be pointed out that a list of Jewish values gathered from Jewish life and literature which would form the content of this education shows a distinct emphasis on human ideals.[1]

From its earliest days a tendency has pervaded Jewish life to shape the destinies of man in accord with the highest human ideals. It was this tendency that led the Biblical writer to say that man was created in God's image. It was this that led Israel to interpret all its historic experiences in terms of a spiritual deity whose attributes were Justice and Mercy and who cared for them and made of them "a great nation." Again it was this spiritual tendency that produced the prophetic idea of a God of the world who guided the destinies of all nations by the laws of Justice and Truth.

When the Jewish people conceived of themselves as a chosen people they thought in terms of a spiritual nationality. This fact explains the secret of their existence for two thousand years under the most adverse circumstances. They understood the value of

[1] See Appendix.

substituting spiritual weapons when the political and territorial 'broke down. They shifted the center of Jewish life from the outer to the inner life and maintained themselves by guarding their cultural possessions and striving for the spiritual ideals contained in their literature.

B. JUDAISM AS LIFE

The success of the Jewish people in maintaining itself might therefore be attributed to its conception of the "Chosen People." This idea, much-maligned, loses its derogatory associations if it is understood, as in Jewish literature and thought it has been understood, in spiritual terms. The prophets of old conceived of the Jewish people as "chosen" to exemplify in its life the ideals of Justice and Righteousness which they held to be the essence of their religion. It was a grave responsibility that they placed upon their people —more of a responsibility than a privilege. In the same way the intelligent nationalist Jew today conceives of the return to Palestine of the Jewish people as an opportunity, not essentially political, or territorial, although these might to some extent be means to ends, but cultural—an opportunity to live once more a normal life that will permit Jewish culture and Jewish human-idealism to develop anew. He sees in Judaism the culture of a people living and functioning, changing itself and changing its products, possible of development and improvement, and potentially, eternally creative. He believes that the Jewish contributions to civilization in the past warrant his faith in the possibility of future contributions. The fact that so many of the humanistic Jewish values were created under conditions of normal life when the people lived on their soil leads him to believe that those favorable conditions should be restored.

In the same way, the thinking Jew does not find in his religion a mere abstraction to be indulged in as an intellectual pleasure on Sabbaths and holidays, but his very life. His religion pervades his life and thus eliminates the dualism from which those suffer whose religion is merely an affair of the church or the synagogue. The unity of God means in his practical life the elimination of the dualism of good and evil and the association with God of the highest ideals in life, which in turn must affect his daily conduct. The dualism between the ideal and the real is overcome by making the ideal real and by raising the real to the ideal. This conception of religion has been well characterized by Prof. Friedlaender in his description of Polish Jewry.

"The central feature of this Polish Judaism is the same as of Talmudic Judaism: it is the all embracing influence of religion—religion in that indissoluble combination of the concrete and abstract, of the ideal and real, or of theory and practice, which has been characteristic of Jewish genius from the time of the prophets down to this day. It is, to use the ancient rabbinical terms which are without equivalents in modern phraseology, Torah and Abodah. On the one hand, it is Abodah, religious cult or service, i.e., the practice of the law, the regulation, under the authority of religion, of the highest as well as the lowest functions of life, that ceremonial Judaism which does not claim to bring heaven down upon earth, but has certainly succeeded in lifting the earth a little nearer to heaven, by transforming the physical acts of life into spiritual values. It is on the other hand, Torah, the study of the Law, the theory of faith, or that Deah-eth-Adonai, that Knowledge of the Lord which in Biblical phraseology is the nearest approach to what in modern parlance we term religion." [1]

It is due to this close identification of religion with life that the separation between nationality and religion introduced by some Jewish theoreticians is meaningless. Jewish religion is so much an outgrowth of the living Jewish people as to make the classification of Jewish values into religious and national rarely possible. Only an erroneous conception of religion, which makes it play an insignificant part in man's life, and that at stated hours and during certain periods of the year, can make such artificial distinctions.

Judaism implies not only an outlook on life but also a way of life. It is therefore a mistake to think that a series of principles can constitute it. It has been a living, evolving set of habits and attitudes, customs and ceremonies, skills and appreciations, language and literature. All of these apply to social life. Hence it is not necessary to find certain distinguishing features in order to develop a Jewish curriculum. It is sufficient that the Jewish people has in the course of its existence developed ways of life the aim of which is to elevate mankind and make it happier. This then may be considered another important value of a Jewish education—the truth it would implant that theory

[1] Friedlaender, I., *The Jews in Russia and Poland,* pp. 159-160.

is valueless in religion unless it is translated into practice. Idealism must be made real.

One can readily appreciate what a difficult task it is to select from a complex Jewish social heritage of four thousand years the essentials of the curriculum. But unless a consistent effort is made to do so, the Jewish school in America, which has little time at its disposal and many difficulties to overcome, is doomed.

In attempting to classify Jewish values the writer used the following procedure. First, he gathered as inclusive a list of Jewish values as he could get. For this purpose he made use of the Bible, the "Taryag Mizvot," [1] the Shulhan Aruk,[2] and his own knowledge of what values are current in Jewish life today. Since the Bible represents the early literary product of the Jewish people, and the summaries of Talmudic discussion represent later Jewish life, both of these sources plus the additions from observation of modern life constitute a list of practically all important Jewish values. To make sure, further, that no significant idea or ceremony was excluded this was checked up by a reading of the Aggadah.[3] To avoid unnecessary labor, all those values were eliminated which no longer function today, even for the most orthodox Jews. Such are most of the laws of purity and sacrifice, or laws that are dependent upon Jewish life in Palestine. The remaining list was then classified into humanistic values and

[1] A list of 613 commandments for the Jew to observe.

[2] A summary of Jewish civil and ritual law.

[3] Bialik, H. N., and Rabinizki, I. H., *Sefer Ha-aggadah.* A compilation of the non-legal portions of the Talmud and books of "Midrash," topically classified.

survival values. The survival values were further
subdivided into three categories—humanistic, cultural-
æsthetic, and deeply-rooted—according to the defini-
tions previously discussed. A discussion of all of these
human values in Jewish life and the subjection of all
of the survival values to our criteria, arising from the
need of adjusting them to modernism and to democracy, would require several volumes. It will be sufficient to note, however, that most of the values are
humanistic [1] and that amongst the survival values
there are very few that are not of intrinsic worth (i.e.,
neither humanistic nor cultural-æsthetic).

The rest of this chapter will therefore be devoted to
a discussion of some typical humanistic Jewish values
and of some typical survival values, to show how our
criteria may apply.

C. Love of Learning

Love of learning will serve as one typical illustration
of a Jewish value that is humanistic, because it is
so outstanding both in Jewish literature and Jewish
life as to be practically universally admitted. Perhaps no better proof need be given than the remarkable fact that the chief landmarks of Jewish history
are the results of learning. Among the outstanding
landmarks of Jewish history are the completion of the
Biblical Canon, the compilation of the Mishnah, the
sealing of the Talmud, Maimonides' Guide to the Perplexed, Mendelssohn's translation of the Bible, and the
Haskalah.

[1] See Appendix.

In early Biblical days, the Israelites were commanded to teach the Torah [1] to the young. Every festival was an occasion for the instruction of the young. [2] Joshua was commanded to meditate in the Torah day and night. The parents' most sacred duty was to teach the child Torah. The Priests and the Levites taught the people on every occasion of temple services, and the prophets interpreted their past experiences in terms of human idealism.

But even more emphatic are the sentiments concerning learning found in the Mishnah and the Talmud and Midrashic literature. The world depends upon three things, of which one is the pursuit of learning. [3] The Torah is compared to light. [4] "The study of Torah is more important than the building of the Temple." [5] Among a list of important commandments which a Jew should keep, taken from Mishnah and included in the daily prayers, are the duty of honoring father and mother, doing acts of charity, and making peace between people, but the statement concludes with this sentence, "The study of the Torah outweighs all of these." [6] No better proof can be given of the unusually high esteem in which learning was held than the Rabbinic statement that God is engaged in teaching the little children, [7] and that "when the little children

[1] Deuteronomy, 6: 7.
[2] Exodus, 12: 26.
[3] *Ethics of the Fathers*, chap. 1.
[4] *Talmud*—Tractate Megillah, p. 15.
[5] *Ibid.*, p. 16.
[6] *Mishnah*—Peah, chap. 1.
[7] *Talmud*—Tractate Abodah Zarah, p. 3.

engaged in study were driven into exile, the Divine presence, too, was exiled with them." [1]

Study for its own sake was considered a great "mizvah." Man is enjoined to study, not for the sake of being considered wise or for the sake of gaining respect from others nor for the sake of making a living but for the sheer love and joy of study.[2] It was further considered a good deed and a sign of great religious piety to study for the sake of teaching others. "He who learns in order to teach, to him will the means be vouchsafed, both to learn and to teach," [3] and the assumption is that that is the finest possible reward. Teachers were held in high esteem, at times being respected even more than parents. The same esteem was given to all the learned, and the rabbis enjoin the people to give special honor to him from whom they learned even "one letter." [4] Rabbi Yohanon comments on the word "builders" as follows: "These are the learned who are engaged in world building all their days." [5]

That this love of learning was not merely expressed in Jewish literature but actually affected the events of life is indicated by the widespread education amongst the Jews during the Talmudic period. As early as 70 B.C.E. Simon ben Shetach introduced compulsory education for adolescents, and in 64 C.E. Joshua ben Gamala instituted a similar measure for children of

---

[1] *Midrash*—Ekhah Rabbah.
[2] *Talmud*—Tractate Nedarim, p. 62.
[3] *Ethics of the Fathers,* chap. 4.
[4] *Ibid.,* chap. 6.
[5] *Talmud*—Tractate Sabbath, p. 113.

six and seven. Academies developed rapidly in Palestine and Babylonia. To these, students flocked in thousands. So widespread was the ideal of learning amongst the Babylonian Jews that they "applied the term 'Am Ha-Arez' to one who, though he had mastered the Bible and the Mishnah, had not penetrated more profoundly into Jewish lore." [1]

The same love of learning is reflected in the "Hukke Ha-torah" of the 13th century and is sacredly transmitted as one of the chief commands to the children in the last wills of medieval Jews.[2] It was the same love of learning that produced the great intellectual activity of the Jews in Spain and resulted in a curriculum embracing practically the entire field of knowledge of the world at that time.

In more recent days this love of learning displayed itself in the general diffusion of learning amongst the Jews of Russia and Poland,[3] and often made learning the basis for selecting a husband for the finest Jewish daughters.

It was the same veneration of learning and the learned that made the Russian Jewish cradle songs express the hope that the little baby would grow up to be a Rabbi or a Lamddan for, "Torah is the best Sehorah." [4] It was the same ideal of learning that sent the child to Heder at the early age of three and gave him an intensive Jewish education till he grew old

[1] Ginzberg, L., *The Jewish Primary School,* p. 9.

[2] See Güdemann, M., *Quellenschriften.*

[3] See Book One: *Jewish Education in Russia and Poland.* chap. 3.

[4] Sehorah—goods, wares, merchandise.

enough to continue to study by himself in the "Bet Hamidrash." [1]

It was the same ideal that resulted in the rush to the general schools for a secular education, when these were thrown open and where they were not associated with governmental oppression or attempts at conversion. And it is the same ideal that brings so many Jewish children to the high schools and so many Jewish young men and women to the colleges of this country and the world over wherever opportunities for learning exist. [2]

This Jewish value is described by a non-Jewish writer in the following words: "Learning was for two thousand years the sole claim to distinction recognized by Israel. 'The scholar,' says the Talmud, 'takes precedence over the King.' Israel remained faithful to this precept throughout all her humiliations. Whenever in Christian or Moslem lands, a hostile hand closed her schools, the Rabbis crossed the seas to reopen their academies in a distant country. Like the legendary Wandering Jew, the flickering torch of Jewish scholarship thus passed from East to West, from North to South, changing every two or three hundred years from one country to another. Whenever a royal edict commanded them to leave, within three months, the country in which their fathers had been buried and

[1] The community house of study.

[2] It is also interesting to note that out of 107 Nobel prizes awarded, 9 were awarded to Jews, or almost 1000% more than they are entitled to by percentage of the world population, and over 500% more if comparison is made between the Jewish population and the general population in the countries from which Nobel prize winners came.

their sons had been born, the treasure which the Jews were most anxious to carry away with them was their books. Among all the autos-da-fé which the daughter of Zion has had to witness, none has cost her such bitter tears as those flames which, during the Middle Ages, greedily consumed the scrolls of the Talmud." [1]

There is no doubt in the minds of those who are at all familiar with Jewish life and literature that love of learning for learning's sake, the spread of learning amongst the masses, and respect for the learned are Jewish ideals cherished to a marked degree by the Jewish people, and that these ideals have been transmitted and are being transmitted to the young through a Jewish education. That these are ideals of human, of universal, value is beyond question.

D.   The Jewish Conception of Charity [2]

Another humanistic value that one might select as characteristic of Jewish life and literature and as a typical value of a Jewish education is the attitude to and the practice of charity. The English word charity really fails to convey the central thought of the word Zedakah used in the Hebrew, a word which might be rendered in English as righteousness. A Jew does not give charity. He practices righteousness. This is significant in that it takes away the usual associations of doing a favor to the recipient. Zedakah is not merely a voluntary matter depending on the kindness of one's

---

[1] Leroy Beaulieu, A., *Israel among the Nations.*

[2] See Bogen, B., *Jewish Philanthropy;* article, "Charity," in *Jewish Encyclopedia;* and for wills of Jews during Middle Ages, Güdemann, M., *Hatorah we-ha-hayim.*

heart, a deed which one who is not kind may abstain from doing. A Jew *must* give Zedakah. It is his duty to be righteous, and righteousness must express itself not only negatively, in not doing wrong, but in the kind of social responsibility which makes the poverty of one's neighbor a sacred duty for consideration by every Israelite. In Hebrew, Zedakah may be further associated with the use of various forms of the root of the word in other connections. Thus Zeddek [1] is declared to be the foundation of God's throne.[2] God himself is righteous. God will deliver him from evil who does righteousness.[3] There are many such references throughout the various books of the Bible all of which tend to emphasize the main thought, the duty, not only the appeal to emotions, but the intellectual duty to do acts of Zedakah.

This duty is emphasized in the many books of the Bible. The Israelites are commanded to help the poor man in accordance with his needs.[4] The Ammonites and Moabites are never to come into the community of Israel because they failed to meet the Israelites with bread and water when the latter escaped from the bondage of Egypt.[5] In taking off the produce of the fields, all fallen sheaves or forgotten sheaves, as well as those growing at the corners of the field, must be left for the poor and the stranger.[6] Most interesting

---

[1] Righteousness.
[2] Psalms, 89:15, 97:2; also Deuteronomy, 24:13.
[3] Psalms, 41:2.
[4] Deuteronomy, 15:7-11.
[5] *Ibid.*, 23:5.
[6] Leviticus, 19:10; also Deuteronomy, 24:10 ff.

is the fact that the injunction applies to the stranger
as well. Such a warm appeal as is made for the
stranger in the Pentateuch, representative of the outlook of a people during ancient days when all strangers
were looked upon with suspicion, can still be a source
of instruction to many "Americanization" workers
today.[1]

That Zedakah is a duty and not a matter of choice
to the individual is the result of the idea that the
goods of the world belong to all alike since they are all
God's. The land belongs to God. "And the land shall
not be sold in perpetuity, for the land is Mine; for ye
are strangers and settlers with Me." [2] The Levites, the
strangers, the fatherless, and the widow must all be
considered. They must be given a "tenth" of one's
possessions. It is their *right* to receive that, not a
special kindness on the part of the giver. The reward
for Zedakah is large. Long life, riches, happiness are
the lot of him who fulfills his duty. The many expressions of the Bible on the subject may perhaps be
best represented by the following quotation from the
great prophet of the exile, Deutero-Isaiah. The
prophet proceeds to point out what is an acceptable
day to the Lord, in the following words:

> Is it not to deal thy bread to the hungry
> And that thou bring the poor that are cast out to
> thy house?
> When thou seest the naked that thou cover him,
> And that thou hide not thyself from thine own flesh?
> Then shall thy light break forth as the morning

[1] Exodus, 22:20.
[2] Leviticus, 25:23.

And thy *righteousness* shall go before thee,
The Glory of the Lord shall be thy rearward.
Then shalt thou call, and the Lord will answer;
Thou shalt cry; and He will say: "Here I am."

   .   .   .   .   .

And if thou draw out thy soul to the hungry,
And satisfy the afflicted soul;
Then shall thy light rise in darkness,
And thy gloom be as the noon day.[1]

Similar to the ideal of learning, the ideal of charity finds ample expression in rabbinic literature. "Give him (the poor man) of His (God's) for thou and what is thine are His",[2] reëchoes the same thought previously quoted from Leviticus. He who refuses to give Zedakah is like a worshipper of idols. "A man who gives even a small coin to a poor man is visited by the Divine presence." [3] The duty of giving Zedakah extends even to those who are themselves the recipients of it." [4]

Zedakah is its own reward. "More than the master does for the poor man, the poor man does for the master," in giving him an opportunity to do Zedakah.[5] The reward of life for deeds of Zedakah is well illustrated by the following rabbinic legend concerning a pious man who constantly practiced this virtue. "Once he (the pious man) was sailing on a ship. A wind came and sank the ship in the sea. Rabbi Akiba who

[1] Isaiah, 58:7-10.
[2] *Ethics of the Fathers,* chap. 3.
[3] *Talmud*—Tractate Baba Batra, p. 10.
[4] *Talmud*—Tractate Gitin, p. 7.
[5] *Waikra Rabbah,* chap. 34.

saw this came to Bet Din [1] to testify that the widow
might remarry. By the time the Rabbi was to give his
testimony before the Bet Din the man himself appeared. Said Rabbi Akiba, 'Weren't you drowned in
the sea?' 'Yes' answered the other. 'And who
brought you up from the sea?' 'Zedakah that I practiced brought me up from the sea,' was the reply.
'How do you know?' asked the Rabbi. Answered the
man, 'As I went down to the depths of the sea, I
heard a great noise coming from the waves. They
were saying to each other, "Come, let us raise up this
man from the sea. He has practiced Zedakah all his
life!" ' " [2]

These expressions are indicative of the high regard
for this value, which is also substantiated by the facts
concerning the organization of charity. In Mishnaic
times each community had a special treasury for
weekly meals to the poor and another fund for immediate relief. The collection of funds was in the hands
of trustworthy men who had power to compel people to
give, even to the extent of seizing their property.[3]
The money collected and the food and clothing bought
for immediate relief were distributed to poor, Jews and
non-Jews alike.[4] The men in charge of these funds
were considered so reliable that he whose parents were
amongst the Zedakah trustees was raised to the priest-
hood without further investigation into the family,[5]

[1] Court.
[2] *Abot Di Rabbi Nathan,* chap. 3.
[3] See article on "Charity" in *Jewish Encyclopedia.*
[4] *Talmud*—Tractate Git.,p. 61.
[5] *Talmud*—Tractate Kid.,p. 76.

although to avoid all suspicion the collectors of alms
were not permitted to separate from each other during
the entire time of collection.

Significant also is the manner in which it was deemed
advisable to distribute charity. In spite of the fact
that to give was a matter of righteousness and duty,
the spirit was emphasized. He who gives even a small
coin to the poor is blessed sixfold, but he who speaks
to them and makes them feel happy is blessed eleven-
fold.[1] It was considered especially worthy to give so
that the giver did not know who was the recipient and
vice versa. Giving thus secretly is declared to elevate
one even above Moses.[2] Consideration for the feelings
of the recipient resulted in the injunction to offer
money as a loan to him who would otherwise hesitate
to accept, no matter how needy.

Furthermore, the Biblical phrase, "in accordance
with his need" was interpreted to mean in accordance
with his accustomed way of fulfilling his needs.   A
man who had been rich and had servants was to be
supplied, if possible, with those as well, a provision
which would certainly look extravagant were not the
aim consideration for the rich man who became poor.
The sage Hillel is quoted with approval in the Talmud
as running three miles, acting as servant to a rich man
who became poor and to whom Hillel gave charity.
Hillel's poverty prevented him from supplying this
rich man with a servant, and he felt that he would not
have done his duty till he offered himself as servant.

---

[1] *Talmud*—Tractate Baba Batra, p. 40.
[2] *Ibid.*, p. 9.
[3] *Talmud*—Tractate Ket, p. 67.

Charity embraced many activities, helping orphans, helping the poor, redeeming the captive, assisting the sick, burying the dead, and providing for hospitality to poor travelers. Abraham is stated to have built road houses where food was placed for all wayfarers. In Jerusalem it was customary to spread a tablecloth in front of the door of one's house to indicate that the poor might enter and partake of food.

Closely associated with the idea of Zedakah was that of Gemilut Hasadim, the doing of kindness, which was at times used interchangeably with certain types of Zedakah. More often it referred to such help given to a man in need as enabled him to become economically independent again. Giving a loan to enable one to re-engage in business activity and "come to himself" again is an illustration of Gemilut Hasadim.

This attitude to and practice of charity continued in the Middle Ages. Provisions for the poor through organized community efforts were made in the many cities where Jews dwelt. Rabbi Eliezer ben Isaac of Worms (1050) in his will commands his children: "Show reverence to the poor man, give him a gift secretly and not in the presence of others. Give him food and drink in thy house." [1] Maharam Minz in the middle of the 15th century describes the provisions for charity in his community, as follows: "All, both old and young should contribute to the Kuppah." [2] A similar attitude of the people to charity is reflected in many of the wills of the Jews in the Middle Ages.

[1] See Güdemann, M., *Hatorah we-ha-hayim,* part 3, p. 144. See also v. 2, pp. 179 and 213.

[2] *Ibid.,* part 1, p. 96: Kuppah—charity box.

That this attitude is still a living factor amongst Jewry of today may be seen from the philanthropic activity of the Jews in America, for the relief of Jewry in Eastern Europe, as well as from the organized work of the various federations of Jewish philanthropic institutions in the larger cities like New York, Chicago, Boston, etc. The Joint Distribution Committee of America allotted in the last eight years about $50,000,-000 for relief of Jewry in Eastern Europe. The Federation for the Support of Jewish Philanthropic Institutions in New York City, which may be taken as an illustration, spends yearly a sum of more than $3,000,-000 for the maintenance of ninety-one institutions affiliated with it. These include all kinds of institutions—medical, correctional, vocational, religious, educational—and there are many more institutions doing philanthropic work throughout the city which are not affiliated with the Federation.

Like the ideal of love of learning, Zedakah has been reflected in the literature of the Jewish people throughout the ages, and these expressions in literature were actually reflections of life-activities in which charity played an important part. An adequate Jewish education would result in a cultivation among other virtues of the virtue of charity amongst the Jews of the future.

E. PALESTINE

Just as love of learning and Zedakah may be considered typical of humanistic Jewish values so Palestine, the Sabbath, and the Dietary Laws may be considered typical of Jewish survival values. Palestine has been selected both because of its importance for the future of Jewish life as well as because of the unusual attention which it now receives, not only in Jewry, but also in the rest of the world.

To begin with, Palestine is a survival value which is deeply rooted in Jewish life. The promise of God to Abraham that he would become the father of the chosen people is at once associated with the promise of the land that he would inherit. From the very beginning the destiny of the Jewish people and the idealism of which it conceived itself the bearer were bound up with "The Land." To dwell in happiness in the land was declared the reward of a good life, while exile was considered the just punishment for idolatry and iniquity.

The love of the land has been a characteristic of Israel throughout the ages from the first day of exile. The daily prayers reiterating the hope that Zion will be rebuilt have been a part of every Jewish prayer book until the 19th century, and continue to hold a significant place in the prayers of the vast majority of Jews today. Even on festive occasions the Jew did not permit himself to forget his desolate homeland. The ceremony of breaking a glass at a wedding is meant to remind the Jew of the destruction of his holy temple. The hope of return was kept awake in the hearts of all Jews through their belief in the Messiah who was to deliver the children of Israel scattered in the four corners of the earth and bring them back to the Holy Land. That this hope for return was not merely fanciful but real is evidenced from the readiness with which some of the Jews followed the false Messiahs that arose throughout the years after the destruction of the second temple.

To bear these facts in mind is to realize how deeply rooted in Jewish life is the love for Palestine and the hope of the return. Few will doubt that Palestine has served as an important and effective bond of unity for scattered Israel.

With the breakdown of the ghetto the importance of Palestine as a survival value has increased. Once in contact with the currents of general life and culture, the Jew lost many of the bonds of unity which had previously held the people together. The process of assimilation through intermarriage increased. The maintenance of Jewish life and a Jewish educational system in Diaspora lands can at best but supplement the forces of the non-Jewish environment and the general educational institutions in the country in which the Jews live. Especially is this true in a democratic state where interaction among the various elements of the population freely takes place.

Though hopeful that Jewish life will continue to develop even in the Diaspora and that America will become an important center for Jewry, we should clearly face the fact that the free development of a people in accordance with its past and in accordance with its characteristic genius cannot take place in a land where this people is a minority, however welcome. We cannot go counter to sociological law in this respect. For a full and free development of Judaism— of Jewish civilization—Palestine offers the only opportunity. Hence its importance as a survival value.

Palestine is, however, a survival value which has

important humanistic aspects. In the first place it is apparent that as a land of refuge for the oppressed at a time when America seems to close its doors to immigrants, Palestine serves an important humane end. However, the writer sees in Palestine a humanistic value of still greater significance. The Jewish people has been a creative people. One of its essential contributions has been a culture embodying high ideals of life. Palestine offers the possibility of developing new culture and new values. It offers the Jewish people a favorable environment for creative activity, and such creative activity is the means by which a people makes its contributions to mankind, resulting in the development of cultural, æsthetic, or religious values of universal significance. The creation of distinctive values is not only the *right* of a people but its *duty* to mankind. It cannot fulfill its duty adequately in the Diaspora. Israel can serve humanity best by the creation of distinctive values. Israel does not "wish to become the salt of the earth, which, after being dissolved in the whirlpool of nations, is bound to lose its saltiness." [1]

It has been pointed out that modern Jewry, which has distinguished itself in many activities, has done little in the field of religion which was so outstanding an expression of Israel in the past. Is it not possible that Jewish genius may once more express itself by developing religious culture, if given the environmental freedom needed for adequate self-expression as a people?

Certainly there is nothing in helping to reëstablish

[1] Friedlaender, I., *Past and Present,* p. 447.

the Jewish people in Palestine that is inconsistent with the criteria of universalization or a scientific outlook on life. From the point of view of democracy, too, there can be little doubt that helping a persecuted people to attain a right given to every other people on earth will further one of the fundamental aims of democracy.

To the above analysis we may add that Palestine has recently become a more highly functional value than ever before. It is no longer a mere distant hope. It also presents an immediate task which has attracted attention, not only of the whole of Jewry, but of the whole world. Through the League of Nations the nations of the world have acknowledged the rights of the Jewish people. Our own government has expressed its approval of the Balfour Declaration. Under the circumstances the transmission of Palestine as a value in the Jewish school is one of the best means of relating the school to Jewish life.

It is well to avoid a confusion of thought too often brought about by the suggestion that there is here involved a question of dual political allegiance. The Jews in America will live in America and will give their undivided political allegiance to America. Together with other American citizens they will no doubt participate in what is worth while in American life. In addition they will bring to American life their experience as a people with a rich past. If Jewish life in Palestine develops new cultural values—and the Jews in the Diaspora lands can but give a helping hand in such development—the influence of the Jewish center in Palestine will make the cultural contributions of the Jews in America richer. There is no reason from the

democratic point of view for fearing the enrichment of
life that comes from the addition of another culture.
That America does not in fact fear such an attitude
toward the rebuilding of Palestine is seen from the
support given on several occasions by the American
Government to the Balfour Declaration and to the
mandate issued by the League of Nations to Great
Britain.

Jewish life will continue to develop in the Diaspora
and contribute its share to general culture. But these
contributions will necessarily be limited, due to a non-
Jewish environment. The settlement of a large number of the Jewish people in Palestine, which will
enable Jewish individuality to perpetuate itself, offers
to remove these environmental limitations and therefore presents an important survival value with universal aspects. It offers the possibility of developing new
religious, cultural, and æsthetic values—a new contribution of the Jewish people to civilization.

F.   THE SABBATH [1]

Like Palestine, the Sabbath and the Dietary Laws
will serve to illustrate some Jewish survival values.
The Sabbath has been chosen because it offers the
combination of a survival value rich in content, containing some humanistic, as well as some cultural-
æsthetic, aspects, and because it is at the same time an
institution deeply rooted in Jewish life. It will also

[1] See Joseph, Morris, *Judaism as Creed and Life;* Greenstone,
J., *The Jewish Religion;* Schechter, *Studies in Judaism, First
Series,* Essay on "The Law and Recent Criticism;" Webster, H.,
Rest Days.

help to illustrate the way in which our classification of
values and criteria will apply, if we consider side by
side with the Sabbath, the Dietary Laws, a value also
deeply rooted but possessing none of the humanistic
and cultural-æsthetic beauty of the former.

It is highly unfortunate that lack of knowledge
should have brought about so great a misunderstanding
of the Sabbath as exists today.   There is a widespread
impression that the Sabbath is a day of austerity filled
with manifold restrictions which make of it a burden
to those who observe it.   That Judaism did not intend
such a result is seen from a mere perusal of the literature enjoining Sabbath observance, as well as from an
analysis of what constitute its main features.   There
is no doubt that the rabbinic idea of making a "fence
about the law" resulted in multiplying prohibitions
with regard to the Sabbath, but the main ideas of the
Sabbath certainly intended no such effect.

The Biblical injunction concerning the Sabbath
clearly provides that it should be a day of rest from
physical labor.   The idea that man should rest after
a working week of six days is a humanistic idea.   That
this was the intent of the original provision is further
seen from the very humane clause attached to it that
"the man servant, maid servant, the stranger and even
the ox and the ass," should "rest as well as thou." [1]   To
give prestige to the sanction of this day of rest is added
the reason that even God rested on the seventh day,
while the humaneness of the provision is associated
with the redemption from Egyptian bondage.   Even
the angels were commanded to rest on the Sabbath,

[1] Exodus, 20: 8-11; Deuteronomy, 5: 12-15.

and legend records that the restless river, the mythical Sambation, which throws up stones all week, comes to rest on the holy Sabbath.

Closely associated with this idea of rest is the conception of the Sabbath as a day of joy, which is emphasized in rabbinic literature and clearly seen from the nature of the many pleasant duties which a Jew is asked to perform for the sake of the Sabbath. Special preparations for the Sabbath, intended to make it particularly joyous, are begun on Friday afternoon. The house is given a special cleaning in honor of the Sabbath. Special "Hallot" [1] and all kinds of cakes are baked. Dainty Sabbath dishes are cooked. The table, decked with a snow-white cloth, is beautifully set, the bottle of sparkling red wine with which the Sabbath is to be "sanctified" prominently adding color and beauty to the appearance of the room. The ceremonies of the lighting of the candles and the reciting of the special Sabbath blessing usher in "Bride" Sabbath or "Queen" Sabbath, as she is lovingly named by the rabbis. In some homes it is customary for the parents or grandparents to bless the children. The father who comes home from the synagogue with his "Gut Shabbos" [2] greeting adds to the joy and Sabbath spirit in the home by the singing of "Shalom Alekem," a pretty, imaginative Sabbath selection welcoming the angels of peace and rest. To this beautiful home scene the good angel, in company with the angel of evil who peeps in through the windows of every Jewish home on Friday night, gives his blessing to the family and

[1] Sabbath bread.
[2] A good Sabbath.

the angel of evil perforce must say "Amen!" [1] The
reciting of the "Kiddush" over the wine and the participation by all the members of the family in this
ceremony add joy to the Sabbath and impress the
young with the beauty of Jewish life. The Sabbath
meal with its characteristic dishes is then enjoyed.
Between the various courses special Sabbath selections
or "Zemirot," as they are called, are sung by the entire
family. Where possible several families get together
after the meal to continue Sabbath festivity. All come
in festive Sabbath attire. Singing and quiet games
continue till late at night.

Special prohibitions are mentioned by the rabbis
and actually observed today *against sadness* on the
Sabbath. It is considered a duty to eat "three meals"
during the day of rest. The description of this joyous
spirit of Friday evening applies equally to the following day. Many a rabbinic legend tells of rewards to
those who celebrate the Sabbath with joy while one
describes the giving of the Sabbath to Israel in the
following words:

"The Holy One, Blessed be He, said to Moses,
'Moses, I have a good gift in my treasure house. Sabbath is its name, and I want to give it to Israel. Go
and bring them the good news!' " [2]

Not a small part of the Sabbath joy may be attributed to the spiritual activity in which the Jew engaged
on that day. Busy during week days with earning
a livelihood, he had the opportunity on the Sabbath
to study, to read, to enjoy the kind of rest which is

---

[1] *Talmud*—Tractate Sabbath, p. 119.

[2] *Ibid.*, p. 10.

found in the change of activity from the pursuits of a business week to those of learning and intellectual discussion. The Sabbath was a day of rest, a day of joy, but also a day for prayer and instruction. The welcoming of the Sabbath is marked by special services in the synagogue. The Reading of the Torah, one portion each week, serves as the basis for study and discussion during the day. In the late afternoon various groups of Jews are to be seen studying Ethics of the Fathers, Mishnah, or Talmud, in accordance with their interest. The third meal of the Sabbath completes the program of the day with more "Zemirot," while the evening prayers, with the reciting of "Habdalah," the special prayer for distinguishing the week day from the Sabbath, symbolize with their accompaniment of spices, the departure of the "additional soul" with which every Jew is endowed when the Sabbath comes.[1]

Those who are acquainted with Jewish life and literature will agree that these are the three essential features of the Sabbath—rest, joy, spiritual activity. These three ideas and the practices that grow out of them are humanistic. Economic conditions may make impossible the observance of all of them in the *same way* in which they were observed in the past. But the consideration of the question of function does not show that present day life militates against these which are the important aspects of the Sabbath. It may be that the rest can be only partial. It may be the spiritual activity will center less about prayer and more about

[1] See Heine, H., "Princess Sabbath," in Friedlander's *Standard Book of Jewish Verse*, p. 253.

study and discussion and surely some of the Sabbath joy can be maintained.

What then are the reasons for the impression that the Sabbath is incompatible with present-day life? The writer firmly believes that they are to be found not in the essentials but in the unessential aspects of the Sabbath, the many detailed restrictions that were an outgrowth of the idea of making a "fence about the law." These prohibitions do not militate against democracy. They are the kind of personal acts that have relatively little effect on the lives of others. They can be conceivably universalized for the most part and so most of them pass the criterion of universalization. Though in some cases the original reason for their existence no longer functions their observance cannot necessarily be considered incompatible with a scientific attitude to life. But they fail to pass the criterion of functionalism. Social and economic conditions make their observance today very difficult, almost impossible.

It should be pointed out that the general principle underlying most of the prohibitions is, that work which is done on the Sabbath to save work which might be done another day is forbidden. This conception is quite consistent with the main idea of the Sabbath as a day of rest. But as the years passed many of these prohibitions ceased to function in the same way as they did in the past. As an illustration one might take the prohibition against riding on the Sabbath. This prohibition is one which was intended to insure Sabbath rest. But it is well known how impossible it is to observe this injunction today and in this country or in any large city. All the conditions of social and economic life militate against it, and to such a large extent that most of the Jews in New York City probably disregard the prohibition. Here is where the criterion of functionalism, combined with a rational, balanced application to the question under consideration, will be of help. The first will point to the unusual difficulties in the way of observing this prohibition in this country. The second will show that it is not one of the essentials of Sabbath observance. In fact it could well be shown how for some Jews whose business compels them to work on Sunday and who also heed this prohibition, the Sabbath is made a day of burdens. Instead of giving them an opportunity to spend the day socially with their friends or relatives whom they might have to travel to see, they are compelled to stay at home and are deprived of the Sabbath joy they might get. It may be that this prohibition, in their case, tends to negate the Sabbath spirit and destroy it by emphasis on the letter.

The writer does not arrogate to himself the right to make decisions on questions of Jewish traditional practice. But he believes that he is justified in pointing out how his criteria of values tend to operate. If used with good judgment and with a historical sense they will actually serve as a guide to the intelligent teacher or curriculum maker. They will lead to emphasis on essentials and will gradually weed out the unessentials in the Jewish curriculum.

It may, however, be contended that, wherever the immigrant parents cherish certain values and the children develop a point of view that will show some of these values to be of little significance, the chasm between parents and children will widen. Such a contention is justified. The answer is twofold. In the first place, it is better that the child should develop this attitude under the guidance of an intelligent Jewish teacher, rather than (as he does now) under the pressure of social and economic conditions of the environment that may at times militate against some things that are of great value. Secondly, under the guidance of the Jewish teacher the child will learn the reason why his parents necessarily have a different attitude to some observances from that which he has. Considerations of history will give him a sympathetic attitude to his parents, and will protect him from the disrespect which is too often shown by those children who have rapidly made their adjustments to the environment without guidance.

The above analysis of the Sabbath serves to illustrate a survival value that is essentially humanistic. Ahad-Ha-am has correctly pointed out that more than Israel has kept the Sabbath, the Sabbath has kept Israel. This certainly is a tribute to the great value that the Sabbath has for maintaining the group life. It would be a mistake, though, not to see the humanistic value of this institution in its three main aspects of rest, joy, and spiritual activity. At the same time, the ceremony of kindling of Sabbath lights and the singing of "Zemirot" may serve to illustrate the type of the cultural-æsthetic value which has intrinsic worth and is not inconsistent with our other criteria. The sheer beauty of these customs can hardly be conveyed to one who has not practiced them. The following poem may serve as an illustration of what the scene of the Jewish mother "blessing the Sabbath candles" has meant to the young.

Kindling the Sabbath Light [1]

From memory's spring flows a vision tonight,
My mother is kindling and blessing the light;

.   .   .   .

She murmurs devoutly, "Almighty, be blessed,
For sending Thy angel of joy and of rest.

"And may as the candles of Sabbath divine
The eyes of my son in Thy Law ever shine."

Of childhood, fair childhood, the years are long fled;
Youth's candles are quenched, and my mother is dead.

And yet ev'ry Friday, when twilight arrives,
The face of my mother within me revives;

A prayer on her lips, "O Almighty, be blessed,
For sending us Sabbath, the angel of rest."

And some hidden feeling I cannot control
A Sabbath light kindles deep, deep in my soul.

G.   The Dietary Laws [2]

The Dietary Laws may be considered another illustration of a survival value, but of a different type.

---

[1] By P. M. Raskin.   Quoted in *Book of Jewish Thoughts,* compiled by J. Hertz, p. 189.

[2] See Morris, Joseph, *Judaism as Creed and Life;* Greenstone, J., *The Jewish Religion,* and "Dietary Laws," in *Jewish Encyclopedia,* v. 4, cols. 596-598.

They will serve to illustrate the survival value which is neither humanistic nor cultural-æsthetic. It can be classified only as deeply rooted.[1] It is possible that some Jews will resent the statement that the Dietary Laws have no intrinsic value. They are right in that some aspects of them may be considered to have intrinsic worth. Opinions as to the function and value of the Dietary Laws are divided, but in classifying the Dietary Laws as a value that is merely deeply rooted, the writer is considering not any aspects of them but the *general intent* of the *original Biblical provisions* that gave them authority in Jewish life and the way in which they *functioned* in the Jewish past and function in Jewish life today.

There is some justice in the contention that the Dietary Laws have the psychological value of developing self-control on the part of the individual who observes them. It does develop one's self-control to have to resist daily, at times under difficult circumstances, the temptation of breaking them. There is no doubt also that some of these laws are humanitarian, at least in their intent. The provision against the mixing of meat and milk is based on what is interpreted as a humanitarian provision in the Bible, "Thou shalt not seethe a kid in its mother's milk," while the "Shehitah," the Jewish way of slaughtering animals for food, is intended to avoid as much cruelty to the animal as possible. Certainly the provision against eating "part of the living" animal, which is included amongst the

[1] It will be interesting to note that in the entire list of about 800 Jewish values only 5 were classified as not intrinsic—merely deeply rooted.

seven Noachian Laws given to the whole of mankind, is a humanitarian law. With the advent of the scientific tendency these laws have also been studied from the point of view of health. The provision against eating from beasts that died a natural death and the provision for removing the superfluous blood from meat have a hygienic basis. "Although there are still those who make much ado about sapping the strength of the meat through the custom of 'salting,' the preponderance of scientific evidence from modern hygienic, physiological and pathological work points in unmistakable terms to the superior wholesomeness of Kosher meat. Kosher meat, that is, meat which has been freed from its superfluous blood, is undoubtedly possessed of greater keeping qualities than any form of raw meat." [1] These various aspects of the Dietary Laws certainly are of intrinsic value.

Nevertheless, the essential purpose of these laws and their main intent in Jewish life was different. This main idea is expressed in Leviticus immediately after the injunction to separate the clean animals from the unclean. "And ye shall be holy unto Me, for I, the Lord, am holy, and I have set you apart from the people, and ye shall be Mine." [2] The real significance of this sentence as the reason for observing the Dietary Laws can be understood only if the meaning of the Hebrew word, "Kadosh," translated into the English, "Holy," is understood. On the one hand, it implied the distinguishing of the people, separating them from

[1] Macht, David I., "The Carrier of Life," in *The Menorah Journal,* v. 5, no. 2, p. 119.

[2] Leviticus, 20:26.

others.   On the other hand, there were associated with this word all the ethical laws in the Book of Holiness where the formula is repeated that the Israelites should observe all these laws, for "I, the Lord your God, am Holy."

The object of the Dietary Laws from this point of view is that of means.   They are to serve as a means to an end, the preservation of the Jewish people by means of these practices for the sake of the great humanistic values that have been transmitted to them.   To this Biblical reason we may add the historical fact that the Dietary Laws, which necessarily reminded the Jew three times daily of his Jewishness and its implications, performed an important function in the preservation of the group.   That millions of Jews scattered all over the world daily subjected themselves to these laws could not but add strength to the unity of the people, which they sadly needed throughout the ages and in all lands where they were a persecuted minority.   It was this close relationship between religion and life which saved the people from doing wrong on week days to atone for it on holidays and enabled them to remember the Jewish precept of the Rabbis, that "Practice is a fundamental."   Though the observance of the Dietary Laws is on the wane, they are still observed by millions of Jews throughout the world to this day.

These laws therefore are essentially a means to an end.   In the course of the ages the end has invested the means with sanctity.   They have become deeply rooted in Jewish life.   They have a tradition going back to Biblical days.   They were maintained throughout the ages and are maintained in Jewish life today to a considerable extent. For these reasons they may be classified under the heading of instrumental values that are deeply rooted.

These laws should, however, be considered from the point of view of our own criteria. Theoretically they certainly could be universalized. Unless only those are selected which have intrinsic value, they would not necessarily enhance the life of a non-Jew who might conceivably accept them, but neither would they bring negative results. To the extent that some of them have good intrinsic reasons for existence they will be found compatible with a scientific outlook upon life, and the same will be true of the others provided that they be conceived of as the observing of a certain tradition as a means to an end and not as mere taboos.

From the point of view of democracy the Dietary Laws might, however, be questioned. It should be remembered, though, that democracy permits a person to eat what he pleases. Such minor matters have little or no effect on others and democracy is not much concerned with them. But to the extent that these laws limit the possibility of coming into intimate relationships with non-Jews they might be considered undemocratic. They are a barrier in some respects to the free intercourse between Jew and non-Jew, but certainly no more than vegetarianism.

Here is where another criterion has to be taken into consideration. It should be pointed out that these laws *still* perform the function of serving as a bond of unity amongst the Jewish people. As long as the Jewish people are not established in Palestine, every bond of unity that is abolished tends to disrupt Jewish life in

the Diaspora.   In other words the Dietary Laws have
a high functional value.   Reason would demand,
therefore, that we ask ourselves this question: Are
the Dietary Laws to a greater degree undemocratic
than they are functional, that is, helpful to survival of
the Jewish group?   This question must be answered in
the negative.   The amount of democracy in terms of
quantity that would be violated by the observance of
these laws is small in comparison with the harm to the
unity of the people, at a time when every effort should
be saved for the rebuilding of its ancient Jewish home.

For the above reasons the writer believes that the
Dietary Laws constitute one of those values which,
though not intrinsic, except in some minor respects, are
deeply rooted and do not affect our criteria sufficiently
to be excluded.   It should be noted at the same time,
that we have a standard of comparative values and we
can with little difficulty conclude on the basis of the
previous analysis that the Sabbath is by far a more
important Jewish value than the Dietary Laws.

CHAPTER VI

THE RECONSTRUCTION OF THE CURRICULUM

IF the preceding analysis of the problem of Jewish education is sound, the curriculum of the Hebrew school should consist of a list of Jewish values like the ones gathered and classified by the writer from Jewish sources and from observation of present-day Jewish life.[1] Such a list of values may be further subdivided into skills, habits, customs, ceremonies, activities, knowledge, attitudes, and appreciations, and these should be organized around activities in which the children in the Hebrew school will engage. Some of these values will demand a place in the curriculum, since they arise from the felt needs of a child living in a Jewish home influenced by the Jewish community. Some needs that would be fulfilled by the attainment of certain Jewish values would not be felt unless stimulated by the school. The stimulation, so that a need becomes a felt need, is as much a function of the school as the fulfillment of needs that are already felt. These skills, knowledge, and attitudes will result in developing on the part of the individual the outlook of the group which will make him responsive to its needs.

A curriculum of values instead of subjects would, however, involve the complete transformation of the

[1] See classified list of values in Appendix.

present Jewish school. Since the writer believes that evolution and not revolution is the method in educational progress, he cannot advocate such a sudden change. Besides, such a transformation, to be effective, would require years of work on the curriculum. The transition from a curriculum of subjects to a curriculum of values subjected to criteria must be a gradual one, just as in the public school the transition from subjects to activities must be a gradual one.[1] Some subjects should be chosen, which can be more readily organized on the basis of values and adequately tested by our criteria, as the first step in the process of transforming the Jewish school. This transformation will then be gradually applied to the other subjects in the Hebrew school curriculum. The best subject for the purpose of starting the changes in the present curriculum is that of Jewish customs and ceremonies. Our criteria can be readily applied, for by its very nature the subject allows for considerable activity on the part of the children. Jewish customs and ceremonies constitute a section of present-day life of Jewry and functions amongst a large number of Jews. Once applied to one subject, other subjects will follow, especially as our teachers become interested in the problem of the curriculum.

A. THE APPLICATION OF OUR CRITERIA TO THE TRADITIONAL SUBJECTS OF THE JEWISH SCHOOL

The criteria presented not only point to a curriculum of values but also affect vitally the content and

[1] See Bonser, F. G., *The Elementary School Curriculum*, pp. 105 ff.

method of the traditional Hebrew school subjects.
They cannot be used mathematically, but they can be
used as indicative of certain new tendencies in Jewish
education. These new tendencies will form the attitude
of the curriculum-maker, and this attitude will in turn
result in a selective process within the various subjects
of study in the Jewish school. The next part of this
chapter will be devoted to a discussion of how these
subjects will be affected by the new attitude.

I.   THE TEACHING OF HEBREW

No one can doubt the great cultural value of the Hebrew language. To know the Hebrew language is to
have access to the idealism of the Jewish people in its
most original forms of expression. That such a knowledge is of great survival value will be seen from the
tenacity with which the Jewish people clung to it
throughout the ages, both in prayer and in study.
When to this fact is added the new phenomenon of the
resurrection of Hebrew as a living, spoken tongue (not
as it had been for a long time merely the language of
prayer), one can appreciate its value for creating an
important bond of unity between the Jews and Palestine and through Palestine with the scattered people
all over the world. Certainly a knowledge of Hebrew
is not incompatible with universalization or democracy
or a scientific outlook on life.

But one should recognize that there are several aims
in the teaching of Hebrew, and whether the course of
study pursued by the child will function will depend
upon the harmonization of aim with execution. If the
aim is formulated, as that of enabling the child to speak

Hebrew and to read the Bible and modern Hebrew literature intelligently, it should be recognized that this aim can be attained only by a course of study extending over several years for seven to eight hours weekly (or a minimum of five). Where children cannot stay for a sufficient number of years or cannot attend a sufficient number of hours during the week, the teaching of Hebrew for the length of their stay is wasted. It fails to function, since the knowledge attained in that limited time is not sufficient to enable them to use what they have learned and it will be soon forgotten. It is much better to realize that under the circumstances Hebrew cannot function as the medium of integrating the child into the Jewish group. Some other medium must be found. The school should in such cases formulate as the aim of its course in Hebrew, participation in the synagogue service. The preparation for this is not so difficult and can be accomplished in less time.[1] This study should enable the children to become intelligent participators in the synagogue service. This knowledge of prayers, combined with a knowledge of certain words and phrases in Hebrew which are of particular social value in Jewish life, will be all that the children will attain in so short a time. But if they attain this knowledge they will be better off than if they pursue a course in language and literature without reaching the point where that knowledge can function in their life. The criterion of functionalism demands that the curriculum-maker formulate different aims in the

[1] Gamoran, E., *The Problem of Jewish Extension Education* (MS.). Landesmann, Alter F., *A Curriculum for Jewish Religious Schools*.

teaching of Hebrew to meet the particular conditions in his school.

It is also well to remember that a child who is graduated from the Hebrew school rarely attains more than the ability to read the narrative portions of the Bible. Unless he continues his studies after elementary school age, Hebrew may not function even in his life. When we remember that at present the average school in New York City requires about three hundred beginners to graduate a class of nine in six years, the problem is even more serious. Under the circumstances, we might well seek to discover the reasons for such conditions; whether the social conditions alone are responsible or whether our method is at fault is a question well worth investigation.

It therefore becomes imperative to remember the limitations of the Hebrew curriculum. It reaches at present an unusually small number of children. In the attempt to make all children go through the same course of instruction in Hebrew, other subjects are omitted which might function in the life of the child and might be mastered with less effort. Our Talmud Torahs and Hebrew schools are doing little more than preparing a small group of young men and women to enter upon courses leading to teaching in the Jewish schools. They fail to produce intelligent, cultured Jews to any considerable extent. The children leave the schools knowing neither Hebrew nor some other subjects [1] that they might learn more easily than Hebrew, if these were included in the curriculum and if

[1] For some of the subjects that might well be included, see pp. 155 ff.

the child were given the opportunity to pursue these in the early days of his stay at the school. Bearing in mind these limitations will help us to see the importance of certain other subjects suggested subsequently in this chapter.

II.   THE TEACHING OF HISTORY [1]

Perhaps no subject except that of customs and ceremonies will be as much affected by our criteria as will Jewish history. The emphasis on what is worth while for the survival of the group points to the importance of formulating as one of our aims in the teaching of history, the developing and maintaining of a Jewish consciousness. The individual is socialized into the group when he relives the significant experiences of his group through history. This will lead to the selection of the great personalities in Jewish history and the achievements of the Jewish people for our history curriculum. The criterion of functionalism points to the selection of those facts of the Jewish past which will make the Jewish present intelligible. Those portions of Jewish history that deal with the adjustments made by the people when in the past new situations confronted them will gain importance. The struggle between Hellenism and Hebraism in the days of the Maccabees, the period of the Jews in Alexandria and Philo, the cultural state of Jews in Spain and Italy will gain new meaning and will serve as excellent illustrations of the idea that is written on the pages of

[1] See Honor, L. L., "The Teaching of Jewish History," in *The Jewish Teacher*, v. 1, nos. 2, 3, 4, and v. 2, no. 1.

Jewish history, the constant reconstruction of life without its destruction. Mere dates and names will be excluded from the Jewish school. Only that will enter which is vital either because it is important for the development of a Jewish consciousness or because it is helpful to an understanding of the present.

At the same time, the remaining criteria that emphasize adjustments to a new world will lead to other selections in Jewish history. The criterion of universalization will call for emphasis on those parts of Jewish history which point out the human aspirations of the people.

For example, the desire on the part of the free spirits in Israel to bring the whole of mankind nearer to each other and to establish peace between the nations of the earth deserves special attention. In this connection, the curriculum-maker and the teacher, too, should remember that the aims of universalization are fulfilled only when the value of these ideals to human life is pointed out and when the historical attitude is utilized as a means of holding these up as worthy ideals today. The ends of universalization might be negated if, instead of emphasizing the intrinsic value of the ideals, it were implied that the Jewish people were the only people that cherished these ideals. History might degenerate to propaganda and universalism to chauvinism. It is important, not only to emphasize the universal ideals of the Prophets, but also to point out how the people fell short of these ideals. In this way the Jewish people will be presented as a people having its shortcomings, but also having its seers who denounced these and who pictured before the masses their high ideals, urging them to realize these ideals in life.

The present method of teaching history in the Jewish school fails to accomplish these aims. As a rule no selection is made on the basis of adequate criteria or of any criteria. The teacher is usually assigned to teach a period in history and is left to decide for himself what to teach and how to teach it. Very few schools have even an outline for the teaching of Jewish history which shows an analysis of the field with some aim in mind. Criteria are not used for the selection of subject matter. History is factual, consisting of lists of events, names, and dates to be remembered.

Similar difficulties exist with regard to textbooks. The textbooks on Jewish history represent the same undiscriminating tendency. They tell stories and preach a moral that easily escapes the children, and they fail to make even an important event, an event significant to the understanding of the present, concrete and real. In the one case, the result is that the history taught does not function because it is too didactic; in the other, because it is not sufficiently concrete to impress the child. The criteria of survival and universalization are disregarded, since no criteria are used in planning the curriculum or in writing the textbook. The teaching of history in most of our schools will continue to be useless and non-functional until adequate criteria are applied to the selection of facts and ideas within the subject and until these are reflected in the textbooks and the methods employed.

III. THE TEACHING OF BIBLE [1]

One of the most important subjects of instruction in the Jewish school is and should continue to be the Bible. Its value as a means for the survival of the Jewish group has been recognized by constant study under most adverse circumstances. Its cultural-æsthetic value as literature has been explained by a host of writers. After all, there are, from the point of view of literature alone, few collections that combine such literary values as the beautiful legendary simplicity of the narrative in Genesis, the sincere, sweeping exhortations of Deuteronomy, the impassioned, forceful writings of the Prophets, and the lyrical beauty of the Psalms.

But instruction in the Bible becomes even more significant when we examine it in the light of our criteria. That one should approach the Bible with a scientific outlook on life is the best way of protecting one from the common mistake of reading into the Bible the latest discoveries of science. To remember this fact is to learn to read the Bible in the light of the time it was produced. While such an attitude may prevent one from accepting the Bible literally, it will serve to point out more forcefully the ideals of the people that wrote their experiences in terms of a certain point of view, which found expression in the spiritual interpretation of their experiences.

The criteria of democracy and universalization lead to an emphasis upon the human values of the Bible

[1] The writer is much indebted to his teacher, Prof. M. M. Kaplan, who is doing pioneer work in the interpretation of the Bible from a Jewish and modern point of view.

which are recorded on almost every page. The conception that society is bound by certain laws, laws of justice and mercy, is one of the main underlying ideas in the Pentateuch. It is noteworthy that the Jewish conception emphasized justice, not only to the poor who might most often be the subjects of abuse, but also to the rich against whom prejudice might lead to injustice. Similarly characteristic from a human point of view are the land laws, the underlying idea of which is that the "land is Mine" [1] and therefore cannot be sold into perpetuity. The human ideals of the Pentateuch are reënforced in the other books of the Bible. Examples could be multiplied from the Prophets and the Hagiographa. Who will doubt that the teaching of these ideals from the point of view of universalization could become a source of good will amongst all men?

The chief difficulty in connection with most of the teaching of the Bible in our present elementary schools is the failure to pay attention to content. The Pentateuch is usually studied in Hebrew, and in the desire to deal with difficulties of language the teacher is too often forgetful of the beauty of the content. This is further aggravated by the fact that the most intensive schools usually fail to cover more than the Pentateuch in Hebrew. The rest of the Bible, which was not studied in Hebrew, is not studied at all. From the point of view of universalization a great opportunity is lost. It is high time that all the Hebrew schools institute a course in the Bible in English, even for those who study a small part of it in Hebrew, so that an

[1] Leviticus, 25 : 23.

opportunity be given for emphasizing the humane ideals of Biblical teachings. It is wrong that the desire to teach the Bible in Hebrew should lead to the neglect of the Bible altogether.

There are two other difficulties in connection with the teaching of the Bible at present arising from the disregard of the criterion of a scientific outlook on life. The writer firmly believes that one of the chief causes for the breaking away from religion on the part of the youth is the attempt to teach the Bible literally. A break between parents and children could be avoided if the Bible were taught as a vast literature developed by the Jewish people in the course of centuries, instead of teaching the young the literalness of Biblical narratives and thus exposing what is closely associated with their religion to the onslaughts of a new outlook on life. Such an attitude, combined with a sympathetic understanding of their parents' outlook, would result in avoiding many a tragedy in the Jewish home.

Closely associated with this attitude would be the development of an appreciation of the Bible from a cultural-æsthetic point of view. The Bible is being *studied* in the Jewish school, but not sufficiently *appreciated*. The selection and study of beautiful portions from a literary point of view would serve to develop an appreciation of the cultural-æsthetic beauty of the Bible.

The criterion of functionalism would emphasize those Biblical ideals which can function in our life today. By selecting these and teaching them, the child would not only be enriched culturally; he would be humanized. That after all is the chief aim of all education.

IV. THE TEACHING OF LITURGY

The teaching of liturgy in the Hebrew school has always been a serious problem. On the one hand, few will doubt that from the point of view of both language and content, liturgy cannot be highly recommended as a subject of instruction for young children. On the other hand, the content is so intimately related with the synagogue that to leave the child uninformed in that respect is to close the synagogue to him.

The solution to the problem of teaching liturgy is to be found in following two principles arising out of the criterion of functionalism. First, liturgy should be taught in a manner to enable the child to relate his knowledge either to prayers used in the home or to attendance at the synagogue on the Sabbath (where the synagogue functions for the group). This would not necessarily imply learning to translate the prayers but would imply a general knowledge of the order of service, the ability to read the prayers in Hebrew, the ability to be able to find the place where the leader of the congregation is reading, an understanding of the most important responses, and a familiarity with the meaning of some of the most important prayers used at home or in the synagogue.

Secondly, in view of the fact that synagogue attendance on the Sabbath is not very large, due to economic conditions which prevent the parents from attending, even such preparation will not often function. For this reason the school should, in the case where the synagogue still functions in desire though not in actuality, introduce a Sabbath service for children. Such a Sabbath service would not only serve as an attractive extra-curricular activity in the school but would also be the core about which the teaching of liturgy in the classroom would be organized. Those prayers would be taught which would be used at the Sabbath service. The order of prayers on Sabbath and holidays would then be learned as a means of enabling the child to take part intelligently in the children's Sabbath service. By choosing appropriate traditional melodies for most of the important prayers, singing could be correlated with liturgy and with the Sabbath service. Telling an interesting Jewish story, or occasionally giving a simple little talk on a problem arising out of some situation in the school, will serve to make this service both instructive and entertaining. This service will also furnish an illustration of how the activities and values which are now called "extra-curricular" could form more and more the curriculum of the Jewish school.

V. THE TEACHING OF SINGING

Singing is one of the few items in the traditional curriculum that offers activity to the children. The difficulty in the teaching of this subject, however, was that it was rarely related to life. Children were taught songs that they never used outside of school. In this respect, too, our curriculum must change. Jewish music should be functional. If the particular group for whom the curriculum is made is strongly affiliated with the synagogue, liturgical songs should find a prominent place in the curriculum. If the synagogue does not function much in the life of the group and the nationalist movement does, Hebrew nationalist songs and Yiddish folk songs may be introduced. In each case these should be taught in relation to their use outside of school. Wherever possible the teaching of the liturgy of the home or the liturgy of the synagogue should be correlated with singing. In many cases it will be desirable to effect such correlation between the teaching of Hebrew or Yiddish and singing. The general underlying principle should be that those songs should be taught which are sung outside of school, and which will therefore enable the child to participate in singing in the home, in the synagogue, in the club, or at the community gathering.

At the same time, it is well to note that experience in the teaching of singing in the last few years shows that here, if anywhere, supply creates demand. The intrinsic beauty of the songs led to singing. People who had rarely before sung any Jewish songs began to sing them in their clubs, on hikes, at family gatherings, etc. This is an illustration of how intrinsic values can be made to function when their appeal is strong. There can be no doubt that the lives of the young men and women who sing beautiful Hebrew and Yiddish songs together with their American folk songs have been culturally enriched. It is therefore of great importance to bear these two ideas in mind in connection with the teaching of singing—teaching those songs that are related to the home, the synagogue, the club, and the local community, and teaching those songs which, from a cultural-æsthetic point of view, are beautiful and appealing so that they will be sung outside of school.

VI. THE TEACHING OF TALMUD

Few will doubt that a knowledge of the Talmud enables one to have ready access to a great part of Jewish literature. At the same time, that close relationship between the study of the Talmud in Heder and life outside of Heder does not exist in this country. If life were regulated, as it was in Russia and Poland to a great extent, by Talmudic law, Talmud would have a functional value and we could say that it passes the criterion of functionalism. But we all know that life in this country is little affected by a study and knowledge of the law developed in the Talmud. There is no doubt that men are and can be affected by the humane tendencies of Jewish law, or by the poetic beauty of the Aggadah, in the Talmud. And yet the limited time at the disposal of the child will hardly permit us to make Talmud a subject of study in the elementary schools. Those who are preparing themselves to do special work in the Jewish community should be given an opportunity to study the Talmud. Where the desire for an intensive education is sufficiently great, so that it continues beyond the elementary stages, the child may study the Talmud in the Jewish secondary school. But in the elementary Jewish school the best that can be expected, and only of those who pursue an intensive course for at least six years, is to get a glimpse into the Aggadah. Where the study of the Halakah can be pursued, the aim should be to give the child a sufficient number of selections so that he can get a concrete idea of the Talmud. Though the laws of the Talmud may not function in his life, the word Talmud usually does, but to the child it is a mystery. This mystery should be unravelled and the word Talmud made to mean something concrete and definite. Those portions should be selected which deal with either questions of ritual law still in vogue (functionalism) or which are representative of the humane tendency of Jewish law (universalization and democracy).

That these suggestions for the teaching of Talmud are practical is indicated by their acceptance (without the preceding analysis) in most of the Jewish schools today. The Hebrew elementary schools no longer pretend to teach the Talmud to any great extent. Where it is taught at all, it is rather preparatory to more intensive courses to be pursued by the students in the Jewish secondary school.

B. THE IMPLICATIONS OF OUR CRITERIA FOR ADDITIONAL SUBJECTS

It would be a mistake to think, however, that our criteria can be immediately applied only to the extent of affecting the traditional subjects. On the contrary, while the criteria of universalization and a scientific attitude will affect largely the spirit and in some cases the method by which the subjects of the school are being taught, the need of adjustment to the conditions in America implies a fundamental change in the arrangement of the subjects within the curriculum. These two criteria will lead to the introduction of new material into the school curriculum. The following paragraphs are meant to be suggestive of some possible changes that might result.

The emphasis of the curriculum must be on the *affiliation* of the Jewish child with the *institutions* at present functioning in Jewish life. These are (in various degrees according to the different groups in Jewry) the home, the local community institution (synagogue, Y. M. H. A., Jewish center), the larger community, and the entire Jewish people. The aim of the school should be to enable the child to function as an efficient member of the home, the synagogue, the Y. M. H. A., the Jewish center, and the community, and the curriculum of the school should contain those subjects and wherever possible those activities that will enable the child to participate intelligently in the life of these institutions.

It is also important that his stay in the school develop on the part of the child the ability to be critical of the present forms of these institutions. In reflecting the activities of home, club, synagogue, and community, the school must improve upon them and eliminate some of the shortcomings from which these institutions suffer. For example, if the synagogue is not organized so as to interest the people, the miniature synagogue in school, if that is the local institution into which the child is to be socialized, must be made interesting and meaningful to the child. The object is for the child to attain what is best in the present form of our heritage and to strive to improve upon it.

While some of the present subjects in the Hebrew school curriculum tend to socialize the child into the institutions of Jewish life, such socialization is accidental rather than purposed. And there is a great difference between teaching a subject like customs and ceremonies as such and teaching it with the definite purpose of enabling the child to participate intelligently in Jewish home life. With this purpose in mind, the child can be given an opportunity to plan Jewish activities and to execute them intelligently in a manner which will lead to home practice. When this main purpose is disregarded the course in customs and ceremonies is little more than a pale description of what is done by Jews.

Not only will there be a difference in the manner in which a subject is taught but also in the kind of subjects taught. As an illustration of the additions which will be made to the curriculum as a result of this approach, one may take Yiddish—a subject of instruction for children of homes in which Yiddish is spoken. It is well known that if the parents at home speak Yiddish and read the Yiddish papers, the failure on the part of the children to read the language and to appreciate its literature is one of the causes of the chasm between parent and child. This chasm could be bridged by teaching Yiddish to children of homes where the language is spoken. It will take much less time and effort to teach Yiddish to a child who hears and occasionally speaks the language at home than it will to teach the same child to read Hebrew literature and to speak Hebrew, which he does not hear in the home. To center one's attention on the home as the aim means to introduce Yiddish as a course of instruction for all children of Yiddish-speaking neighborhoods.[1] In two years the children can learn enough Yiddish to solve the home problem and the remaining years of Hebrew school can

[1] See also pp. 151 ff. on teaching of liturgy and singing.

be devoted to the study of Hebrew or other subjects.[1]

The affiliation of the child with the synagogue will lead to similar emphasis in teaching for those groups for whom the synagogue functions. Just as in the case of the home, customs and ceremonies will be related to participation in synagogue service. Liturgy will be related either to the synagogue of the parents or, what is more desirable, to the children's service in the school. Reading and singing will be similarly affected. Where the Jewish club offers an opportunity for affiliation with an institution, the child will be urged to join and to participate with his fellows in Jewish activities in the club. The act of joining is in itself a Jewish activity. To do so and to be intelligent about it is to function efficiently and to be socialized. This process of socialization leads to the larger community and ultimately to the largest community.

The socialization of the child into the local and larger Jewish communities will require the addition of some other subjects and activities not at present included in the school curriculum.

I. THE LOCAL JEWISH COMMUNITY

It will be desirable to introduce a course of study that will include a description of the institutions of the local community. How did the Jews come there? Why? What are the problems that faced them that

[1] It may also be pointed out that from the point of view of the community the study of Yiddish would put those children in touch with the living Jewish people. It would enable them to read the Yiddish paper and by means of that help to socialize them into the Jewish community of the world.

brought their institutions into existence as a means of coping with the problems? In a city such as New York where the institutions are numbered by the hundreds and where the communities are manifold, such a study would of itself imply considerable socialization. Visits to various institutions of interest and descriptions of these would provide interesting activity to the children. This course would also lead to a study of the larger Jewish community.

II. THE LARGER JEWISH COMMUNITY

This course of study will build on the work done in the previous course and aim to socialize the child into the larger Jewish community—the Jews of America. Why did they come to this country? How did they come? What are some of the problems that faced them and how did they solve them? How are they solving their problems today? Here again visits to some organizations or institutions will be of help and will make learning concrete. The result in both courses should be, in the case of older children, affiliation with some of the institutions visited.

In similar manner the socialization of the child into the largest Jewish community, that of the Jewish people, will require the addition of some subjects and activities to the curriculum.

III. THE TEACHING OF JEWISH CURRENT EVENTS

Jewish current events, at present not taught in many schools, is one of the most effective ways of bringing home to the child the reality of the Jewish people.

Instead of confusing the child's mind with a conglomeration of facts, the aim of the current events lesson should be to impress him with the brotherhood of Israel though scattered throughout the world. The outstanding Jewish problems of the day should serve as pegs upon which to hang all the information gathered in current events. At present it might best be done by dividing current events into four parts; those dealing with the Jews in America, in Eastern Europe, in Palestine, and in the other countries of the world. Accordingly, as an important new problem arises in Jewish life, events will be related which deal with attempts at the solution of that problem. Children can even be organized into separate committees and each committee can give its attention to its problem. Pictures, clippings, school bulletins, and papers can be issued and considerable activity provided for most of the children in the Hebrew school.

IV.   JEWS IN MANY LANDS

This course would include a study of Jews in countries other than America or Palestine. The children would learn how the Jewish people came to these countries and how, without any territorial or political basis, they became an International,[1] tending to bring humanity closer together. The children would then realize how the welfare of their Jewish brothers implies at the same time the welfare of the people in whose midst they live. The problems that face the Jews in these various countries, how they can be solved, and how

[1] For the significance of this Internation, see Berkson, I. B., *Americanization Theories*, pp. 140-142.

they, the children, can help should be included. Pictures, clippings, and personal biography of ancestors will lead to activity on the part of the children.

V. PRESENT-DAY JEWISH PROBLEMS

This would involve the consideration of the outstanding problems that face Jewry today. The rebuilding of Palestine [1] and the reconstruction of Jewry in Eastern Europe may serve as significant examples. These problems would change from time to time, and such changes should affect the curriculum.

VI. READING JUDAICA

If we bear in mind that at present only a small percentage of the children attain the ability to read Hebrew or Yiddish fluently, the practice of reading books in English on Jewish subjects, under guidance, is a good way of training the child for participation in Jewish community life. The presence of such a course might also stimulate the creation of a literature for children as well as adults, of which at present there is but little in existence. It is of great importance that the members of the future Jewish community should be readers of Jewish books as well as general books if they are to help in the solution of Jewish problems.

[1] It is assumed here that in the course of study Palestine would not be a separate subject in the curriculum but would stand out as an important value in relation to the other subjects taught. It would, however, receive special consideration as one of the important problems that face the Jewish people today.

VII.   JEWISH CONTRIBUTIONS TO CIVILIZATION

A study by the highest classes of the Hebrew school of the significance of Jewish idealism and Jewish achievements in the world is of great importance. What the Jews have done as a people as well as what has been done by individual Jews is not merely a matter of cultural value but also of great survival value to the group.

VIII.   JEWISH CULTURAL IDEALS AS REFLECTED IN LITERATURE AND LIFE

This course would come at the end of the elementary school period or in the Jewish secondary school.   Starting with a discussion on the all-inclusive meaning of Jewish culture, this study would serve to analyze the ideals of the Jews as reflected in the literature of various periods.   Present-day Jewish life and literature would be similarly analyzed, and the study would serve as a summary of the entire curriculum of the Jewish elementary school from a new point of view.

The curriculum-maker may be at a loss due to the introduction of these new subjects into the curriculum. But careful selection of what to teach in the traditional subjects by means of adequate criteria will lead to a saving of time for other subjects.[1]   A study of the list of classified values [2] will also show what is worthy of

[1] It might also be advisable for psychological reasons to group some of the courses listed above under Contemporary Jewish History, as the Jews in the Local Community and the Jews in America.

[2] See Appendix.

emphasis in the teaching of the various subjects and what may be just touched upon or omitted altogether.

With the aim of the school centered upon socialization into the Jewish community of the world, all the instruction would gain new meaning. Principals and teachers would all feel engaged in activities large in scope and of great significance, not only to the Jewish group, but to the future of mankind.

C. Practical Applications—A Curriculum for Jewish Extension Education

What are the specific implications of the preceding discussion for the different types of Jewish schools?

It would be best to start with extension education since that represents the lowest minimum of instruction. As has been previously pointed out in the case of New York City, and the facts are no doubt similar in many another city, there is a lack of physical facilities as well as a lack of adequately trained personnel for Jewish education. As a result only a small percentage of Jewish children have access to an intensive Jewish education.[1]

To meet this difficulty attempts have been recently made to introduce Jewish extension education. This usually takes one of three forms: (1) mass education; (2) group education (through the club); (3) classroom education (not intensive, i.e., usually providing for only one or two sessions a week). Of these three forms of extension education the curriculum of the

[1] A Jewish education which provides for classroom attendance after public school hours at least two times a week besides attendance on Sunday.

third will receive separate consideration under the Sunday School.[1]

In the field of mass education the Bureau of Jewish Education of New York City has experimented both with children and with adolescents. While an adequate knowledge of the principles of extension education will be dependent largely upon further experience, some of the basic requirements of the curriculum may now be determined from past experience as well as on the basis of the criteria previously developed.

Jewish extension education must necessarily be so organized as to meet the needs of mass instruction and to meet the needs of the communities presenting differing local conditions.

A second fundamental requirement is that the curriculum be one of essentials, since lack of time will necessarily reduce it to a minimum. In extension education, even more than in the intensive Hebrew school, is a process of adequate selection valuable.

Due to lack of facilities, the method will also differ from that current in classroom practice. The personal contact which the child has with the chairman of a mass gathering or even with the leader of his club is much less than that of a pupil and teacher. For this reason, whatever other means are used to replace the personnel, must be so potent as to bring to the child

[1] As this book goes to press, the commission on Jewish Education of the Union of American Hebrew Congregations and of the Central Conference of American Rabbis, representing the Reform Jews in this country, has publicly declared its desire to introduce at least one additional session into its schools and thus transform the "Sunday School" into a "Jewish Religious School."

at least some of the inspiration that contact with a personality might afford.

Mass instruction and group education should be based on the idea that developing a consciousness of kind is one of the aims of education—is in itself education. To the extent that the child is made a part of the Jewish people by coming together with fellow Jews, a most important step has been taken in his Jewish education. In order that this coming together should result in a consciousness of unity with one's fellows, it is necessary that the masses and groups that meet be organized as distinct "Societies." [1] Once organized into such societies, the very forms of organization may be of content value. Mottoes, greetings, names of clubs, special ceremonies for various ranks of membership can all become of Jewish educational value.

Another important principle is that of inducing Jewish activity on the part of the membership in these organizations. The Jewish festivals have been utilized in the past as the center of correlation, since they still function in Jewish life to a considerable extent and offer opportunity for activity. Members have to pre-

[1] Such organization is actually what has taken place in the extension work of the Bureau of Jewish Education where the "Circle of Jewish Children" and "League of the Jewish Youth" were organized for children and adolescents respectively. See Dushkin, A. M., *Jewish Education in New York City,* pp. 123-126, 352-357; Berkson, I. B., *Americanization Theories,* pp. 205-210; and the archives of the Bureau of Jewish Education in New York City. Young Judæa, Young Israel, and the tendency to organize "Young People's Leagues" in synagogues are also a recognition of the significance of affiliation as a method in Jewish education.

pare for these through dramatics, dancing, singing, making of costumes, and the distribution of tickets to friends. In connection with Jewish festivals the making of ceremonial objects has also been found valuable as a means of inducing activity.[1] Special literature giving the historical background of the festival and its ceremonial aspects has also been prepared for distribution to the members.

One of the fundamental aims of organizations for Jewish extension education should be to induce the kind of activity that will develop a social disposition, a willingness to serve. Thus one of the fundamental ideals of the League of the Jewish Youth is the ideal of service. The young people affiliated with it have already actively participated in relief campaigns, in Federation drives, and in helping to rebuild Palestine.

By means of mass gatherings of various types, holiday celebrations, Jewish moving picture shows, stereopticon slide entertainments, exhibits of Jewish pictures, and song festivals, children may develop a desirable emotional attitude toward the Jewish group.

Bearing in mind that the lack of proper facilities may restrict our methods to mass gatherings, club meetings, literature, and whatever desirable Jewish activity can be stimulated by these, it becomes even more significant to select the content of instruction carefully. Here, if anywhere, content and method are

---

[1] The Bureau of Jewish Education of New York City has prepared a set of such ceremonial objects for some of the Jewish holidays, and the Department of Synagogue and School Extension is now preparing another set.

interwoven. Here, above all, our criteria will have to be carefully applied.

The following is an outline of the content that might be included in such extension education for children and adolescents:

1. Affiliation with a Jewish group
2. Preparation for and celebration of Jewish festivals and the reading of literature related to them
3. Engaging in Jewish activities, e.g.,
   a. Performing Jewish ceremonies
   b. Making ceremonial objects
   c. Helping to rebuild Palestine
   d. Doing acts of charity
   e. Helping in relief work
   f. Attending religious services
   g. Learning to sing Jewish songs
   h. Visiting and helping Jewish institutions
   i. Telling Jewish stories to others
   j. Discussing present Jewish problems on the basis of adequate information
4. Reading on Jewish subjects:
   a. Jewish literature
      (1) Bible (Bible stories for younger children)
      (2) Essay on the Talmud with illustrative readings from English translation (legends from the Talmud, for younger children)
      (3) Selections from medieval Hebrew literature (in translation)
      (4) Selections from modern Hebrew literature (in translation)
      (5) Selections from Yiddish literature (in translation)
   b. Jewish history

c. Jewish biography
d. Jews in many lands
e. Jewish current events

I. THE SUNDAY SCHOOL

The Sunday School also represents a school that is giving a minimum of Jewish instruction. This minimum should serve as a basis of the curriculum for all elements in Jewry. The program of the Sunday School should represent the minimum essentials of a Jewish education. On the basis of this minimum, those who realize the inadequacy of the Sunday School as a means of transmitting a rich social heritage of four thousand years will develop a more intensive curriculum in the week-day school.

Within each subject comparative values can be established only on the application of the criteria as described in the first part of this chapter, but the general program of studies below, proposed for the Sunday School, represents, in the opinion of the writer, the minimum necessary for socializing the child into the Jewish group.[1] It should be remembered in considering this program and the subjects of study in it, as well as the programs of the other types of schools, that they are to be undertaken in a manner to enable the child to function actively as a Jew and as a citizen

[1] Jewish extension education through mass and club-room instruction is even a greater minimum, but it is conceived of merely as an emergency measure due to the present lack of facilities for intensive education. It should be replaced by intensive education as soon as possible and used as an additional means of developing a favorable environment for Jewish educational activity.

in the home, in the local institution, and in the community. This consciousness of the need for actual affiliation with Jewish life during the days of childhood constitutes one of the important differences between current practice and that here proposed.

With these preliminaries in mind, the following elements may be included in the Sunday School curriculum.

1. Study and activities in contemporary Jewish life
   a. Jewish customs and ceremonies
   b. Singing
   c. Jewish current events
   d. The local Jewish community (e.g., Jews in New York or Boston, etc.)
   e. The larger Jewish community (Jews in America)
   f. Jews in many lands
   g. Present Jewish problems
2. Reading and translation of important selections in liturgy, used in the home or synagogue
3. Bible in English (and if conditions permit, other Jewish literature in English)
4. Jewish history

II. THE CURRICULUM OF THE TALMUD TORAH OR CONGREGATIONAL SCHOOL (WEEK-DAY SCHOOL)

Type A [1]

(Five hours a week)

This Hebrew school will pursue the same program of study as outlined for the Sunday School, except that to the minimum there proposed will be added the study

[1] See footnote 1 on p. 170.

of the Hebrew language as a living tongue, and the Pentateuch will be studied in Hebrew instead of in English.

Type B [1]

(Seven and a half hours weekly)

This school will pursue the same course of study outlined for Type A, except that the additional time will permit the inclusion of:

1. Selections from the Aggadah
2. A course in reading Judaica [2]

Type C

(Five or seven and a half hours weekly for special groups)

In case of a group of children who have linguistic difficulty, and are therefore unable to study Hebrew as a living tongue, it might be well to limit the study of Hebrew to preparation for the synagogue (where that institution functions for the group) and to the use of words and phrases in Hebrew which are of peculiar social and religious value. This will allow

---

[1] Where the parents of the children speak Yiddish at home, and where the neighborhood in general is Yiddish-speaking, it would be a mistake to omit Yiddish from the curriculum. In such a case the study of Yiddish for a period of two years at the close of the school course would be an effective means of enabling the child to participate intelligently in the Jewish life about him.

[2] For an explanation of what these studies and activities will include, see pp. 155 ff.

more time for other studies, and it will, therefore, be possible to include in this course:

1. A course in reading Judaica
2. A course in Jewish contributions to civilization
3. Jewish cultural ideals reflected in life and literature.[1]

The value of all these studies and activities will, however, be lost if they are not conducted in a manner to enable the child to be a participator in the actual life of the Jewish home, the Jewish institution, and the Jewish community. The consciousness of the importance of this process on the part of teachers and principals will lead to a gradual transformation of the Jewish curriculum from subjects to values and activities.

D. THE EXTRA-CURRICULAR ACTIVITIES OF THE SCHOOL

Until the curriculum of the Jewish school is completely transformed into a curriculum of values organized into activities in which children can engage, the extra-curricular activities of the school will serve as an excellent means of making the subjects of study real and vital in the lives of the children. The Jewish school should by means of its curriculum, and especially by means of its extra-curricular activities, reflect the life of the Jewish community. "The school must itself be a community life in all which that implies. . . . In place of a school set apart from life as a place for learning lessons, we have a miniature social group in which study and growth are incidents of present shared experience." [2]

---

[1] For an explanation of what these studies and activities will include, see pp. 155 ff.

[2] Dewey, J., *Democracy and Education*, p. 416.

If some of the courses in the school are aiming to enable the children to participate in the synagogue, a children's service should be organized in the school. Liturgy should be based upon this service. If the aim is to enable them to be active members of Jewish institutions like the Federation for Jewish Philanthropic Institutions, the children should during their stay in the Hebrew school organize their own groups for helping the poor and the orphan, the crippled and the aged. If the aim is to enable the children to help in the rebuilding of the ancient Jewish home, they should have their activities in behalf of Palestine in the Hebrew school. The children can contribute small funds, send toys to children in Palestine, prepare an exhibit of life in Palestine, etc. If the Jewish holidays and ceremonies are a subject of instruction with the aim of enabling the children to celebrate these together with their elders, they should have their dramatic groups, their dancing clubs, and their glee clubs, for the purpose of preparing such celebrations in the Hebrew school itself in which they will themselves participate. In preparing for these celebrations the children will not receive education which *prepares* them for Jewish life. They will be *living* Jewish life in the school, and that is the best preparation for further living.

E. Summary

The Jewish school in America is the means of preserving Jewish life and enabling the Jew to adjust himself to his new environment. Unless the curriculum of the Jewish school is so organized as to transmit what is of deep significance to the people, disintegration of Jewish life will follow. Unless the curriculum is so organized as to be in harmony with the present Zeitgeist and with the conditions of American life, the school will fail to appeal to the young. The human ideals of the Jewish people embodied in its language and literature must be transmitted in such an effective manner that they function in the life of the child. This can best be done if present-day Jewish life and present-day Jewish problems will be made the center of correlation of school subjects and activities. Jewish values thus organized and tested by the criteria of democracy and modernism will actually affect the lives of people. It is impossible to go counter to the strong currents of the present Zeitgeist. Only those values which can stand the test of changing conditions will ultimately remain.

The Jewish curriculum that was brought to this country was a transplantation from Eastern Europe. As such, it was suitable to the conditions of life in Russia and Poland but required considerable modification for the American Jewish school. After all, it is vain to fear change, just as it is a meager virtue to welcome it for its own sake. The reconstruction of the curriculum for the sake of a high ideal is not to be feared. Those values of Jewish life which are relatively permanent will continue to function in our lives. They will either be found compatible with the new world outlook or in some cases justly critical of it. In either case, they will improve our lives, enrich our experiences, and, in doing so, enhance the life of others.

APPENDIX

LIST OF CLASSIFIED VALUES

I. The following list of Jewish values is based upon:
1. The Bible;
2. The Shulhan Aruk;
3. The Taryag Mizvot;
4. The Aggadah;
5. A consideration of present-day Jewish life and problems.

II. Those values which no longer function in Jewish life today, such as the laws related to sacrifices, temple, etc., were excluded from the summary of values given below.

III. Detailed values that could be grouped under some general value have been omitted. Thus, "Honesty" includes the Biblical provision concerning just weights and measures, and "Passover" includes the "Seder" and the ceremonies connected with it. It should be noted, however, that the humanistic values are as a rule more inclusive of many specific acts. In comparison with the survival values, they therefore far outnumber them. The original list compiled by the author included about 800 values, and if detailed values had been listed instead of general more inclusive values the list would no doubt have reached into the thousands.

IV. Values which have no humanistic or cultural-æsthetic aspects, but merely survival aspects, were omitted *whenever* they *were not* found to be deeply rooted. As a matter of fact, only three such values

174

were considered deeply rooted, the refusal to intermarry, circumcision, and the Dietary Laws.

V. This list should not be considered all-inclusive, but
the writer believes that it includes practically all
important Jewish values.

VI. The list of values following represents a classification into humanistic and survival values only. The
list has not been subjected to the criteria of universalization, a scientific outlook on life, democracy,
and functionalism.

VII. In subjecting Jewish values to the criterion of functionalism, it may be found in the case of some that
their particular form does not function today and
cannot function today. On the other hand, the
underlying ideas might be made to function if a
new form were created in which to embody them.

A. LIST OF HUMANISTIC VALUES

Anthropocentricity
Chastity
Considerateness
Development of Personality
Duty to Spread Learning
Faith in Better World Order
Freedom
Free Will
God
Health
Honesty
Immortality
Internationalism
Justice
Kaddish
Kindliness

Love
Love of Learning
Love the Stranger
Meekness
Mercy
Modesty
Not to Covet
Not to Entertain Unworthy
    Feelings
Not to Hate in One's Heart
Peace
Prayer
Proper Family Relations
Religious Life
Repentance
Respect for Age

Respect for Law and Authority
Respect for the Learned
Reverence for Holy Places
Sanctity of Human Life and Personality

Self-Control
Self-Reliance
Social Responsibility
Spiritual Interpretation of History
Value of Work

B. Survival Values

HUMANISTIC OR CULTURAL-ÆSTHETIC OR BOTH

1. *Having Essentially Humanistic or Cultural Aspects*

Jews in America
Palestine
Jews in Other Lands
Bible
Talmud
Jewish History
Hebrew Language
Yiddish Language
Modern Hebrew Literature
Medieval Hebrew Literature
Yiddish Literature
Sabbath
Jewish Holidays (in the order of the calendar year)
  Rosh Hashanah
  Fast of Gedaliah
  Yom Kippur
  Sukkot

Hanukkah
10th of Tebet
Hamishah Asar
Purim
Passover
Lag BaOmer
Shabuot
17th of Tammuz
Tisha B'Ab
Jewish Songs
Helping Jewry in Eastern Europe
Jewish Current Events
Jewish Calendar
Sanctification of Life
Chosen People
Bar Mizvah
Jewish Wedding

2. *Essentially Survival but Having Humanistic Aspects*

Mezuzah   Tefillin   Zizit

DEEPLY-ROOTED

(Neither humanistic nor cultural-æsthetic)

Circumcision   Refusal to Intermarry   Dietary Laws

SELECTED BIBLIOGRAPHY

Adler, Cyrus — America. (In *Jewish Encyclopedia*, v. 1, col. 492-506. New York, 1901.)

Ames, Edward S. — *The Psychology of Religious Experience*. Boston, 1910.

Asch, Shalom — *America*. Translated by James Fuchs. New York, 1918.

Ahad, Ha'am — על פרשת דרכים Berlin, 1921.
———— *Selected Essays*. Translated by Leon Simon. Philadelphia, 1912.

Baldwin, James Mark — *Social and Ethical Interpretations*. New York, 1906.

Berkson, Isaac B. — *Americanization Theories*. New York, 1920.

Bernheimer, Charles S. — *The Russian Jew in the United States*. Philadelphia, 1905.

The Bible
Bobbit, Franklin — *The Curriculum*. New York and Boston, 1918.

Bonser, Frederick Gordon — *The Elementary School Curriculum*. New York, 1920.

Bogen, Boris — *Jewish Philanthropy*. New York, 1917.

Bridges, Horace T. — *On Becoming an American*. Boston, 1919.

177

Bryce, James — *Modern Democracies*, 2 v. New York, 1921.

Burgess, Ernest Watson — *The Function of Socialization in Social Evolution.* Chicago, 1916.

Burgin, Herz — *Die Geschichte von der jüdischer Arbeiter Bewegung in America, Russland und England.* New York, 1915.

Coe, George A. — *Education in Religion and Morals.* Chicago, 1904.

Dewey, John — *The Child and the Curriculum.* Chicago, 1918.

——— *Democracy and Education.* New York, 1917.

——— *The Influence of Darwin upon Philosophy.* New York, 1910.

——— *Human Nature and Conduct.* New York, 1922.

——— *Reconstruction in Philosophy.* New York, 1920.

Drachsler, Julius — *Democracy and Assimilation.* New York, 1920.

Dushkin, Alexander M. — *Jewish Education in New York City.* New York, 1918.

Eisenstein, Judah David — United States—Russian Immigration. (In *Jewish Encyclopedia*, v. 12, col. 367-370. New York, 1906.)

Ellwood, Charles A. — *Sociology and Modern Social Problems.* New York, 1919.

——— Social Functions of Religion. (In *American Journal of*

	Sociology, v. 19, pp. 289-307.)
Ethics of the Fathers	
Fishberg, Maurice	*The Jews.* New York, 1911.
Fite, Warner	*Individualism.* New York, 1916.
Frankel, Lee K.	Charity—Effect of Russian persecution. (In *Jewish Encyclopedia*, v. 3, col. 672-676. New York, 1902.)
Friedenberg, Albert M.	Charity—Modern times. (In *Jewish Encyclopedia*, v. 3, col. 671-672. New York, 1902.)
Friedlander, Israel	*The Jews in Russia and Poland.* New York, 1915.
————	*Past and Present.* Cincinnati, 1919.
Friedenwald, Herbert	United States. (In *Jewish Encyclopedia*, v. 12, col. 345-367. New York, 1906.)
Gamoran, Emanuel	*Changing Conception in Jewish Education,* Book One. New York, 1924.
Ginzberg, Louis	*The Jewish Primary School.* Philadelphia, 1907.
Greenstone, Julius H.	Dietary Laws. (In *Jewish Encyclopedia*, v. 4, col. 596-598. New York, 1903.)
————	*The Jewish Religion.* Philadelphia, 1920.
Güdemann, Moritz	*Das jüdische Unterrichtswesen während der spanish-arabischen Periode.* Vienna, 1873.

Güdemann, Moritz

*Geschichte des Erziehungs-
wesens und der Cultur der
abendländischen Juden während des Mittelalters und der
neueren Zeit.*

v. 1: Geschichte des Erziehungswesens und der Cultur
der Juden in Frankreich und
Deutschland, X-XIV Jahr-
hunderts. Vienna, 1880.

v. 2: Geschichte des Erziehungswesens und der Cultur
der Juden in Italien. Vienna,
1884.

v. 3: Geschichte des Erziehungswesens und der cultur
der Juden in Deutschland
während des XIV und
XV Jahrhunderts. Vienna,
1888.

The above three volumes
have been translated into
Hebrew by A. S. Friedberg
under the title of *Ha-torah
we-hahayim.* Warsaw, 1896.
*Quellenschriften zur Geschichte
des Unterrichts und der
Erziehung bei den deutschen
Juden von den ältesten
Zeiten bis auf Mendelssohn.*
Berlin, 1891.

העתיד

Berlin, 1912, v. 5, pp. 87-208.

A symposium on the future
of Judaism.

Heine, Heinrich — Princess Sabbath. (In Friedlaender's *Standard Book of Jewish Verse*, p. 253.)

Hermalin, D. M. — New York—present condition. (In *Jewish Encyclopedia*, v. 9, col. 283-291. New York, 1905.)

Hertz, Joseph H. — *A Book of Jewish Thoughts*. London and New York, 1921.

Honor, Leo L. — The Teaching of Jewish History. (In *Jewish Teacher*, v. 1, no. 2, 3, 4; v. 2, no. 1; edited by Alexander M. Dushkin. New York, 1917-1919.)

Jacobs, Joseph — *The Jewish Race*. London, 1889.

——— United States—statistics. (In *Jewish Encyclopedia*, v. 12, col. 370-378. New York, 1906.)

James, William — *Psychology*, 2 v. New York, 1890.

Joseph, Morris — *Judaism as Creed and Life*. London and New York, 1920.

Joseph, Samuel — *Jewish Immigration to the United States from 1881 to 1910*. New York, 1914.

Kaplan, Mordecai M. — On Affiliation with the Synagogue. (In *Jewish Communal Register*. New York, 1917-18.)

——— What Judaism Is Not. (In *Menorah Journal*, v. 1, no.

4, edited by Henry Hurwitz. New York, 1915.)

Kaplan, Mordecai M.   What Is Judaism. (In *Menorah Journal*, v. 1, no. 5, edited by Henry Hurwitz. New York, 1915.)

The Kehillah, New York City   Jewish communal register of New York City. New York, 1917-18.

Kilpatrick, William Heard   Method and Curriculum. (In the *Journal of Educational Method*, v. 1, no. 8-9. New York, 1922.)

Kohler, Kaufman   Charity and Charitable Institutions. (In *Jewish Encyclopedia*, v. 3, col. 667-671. New York, 1902.)

————   Dietary Laws—from the traditional and critical point of view. (In *Jewish Encyclopedia*, v. 4, col. 598-600. New York, 1903.)

————   The Three Elements of American Judaism. (In *Menorah Monthly*, Nov., 1888.)

Kohler, Max J.   *The German-Jewish Migration to the United States.* New York, 1901.

————   New York. (In *Jewish Encyclopedia*, v. 9, col. 259-283. New York, 1905.)

Landesmann, Alter F.   *A Curriculum for Jewish Religious Schools.* New York, 1922.

Leroy-Beaulieu, Anatole   *Israel among the Nations.* New York, 1904.

Levin, Shmarya   *Out of Bondage.* London, 1919.

Macht, David I.   The Carrier of Life. (In *Menorah Journal*, v. 5, no. 2, edited by Henry Hurwitz. New York, 1919.)

Maciver, R. M.   *Community.* London, 1917.

McMurry, Frank M.   *How to Study.* New York and Boston, 1909.

Norsworthy, Naomi, and Whitley, Mary T.   *The Psychology of Childhood.* New York, 1920.

Pasmanik, D.   לחקר רוח האמה (In השלח v. 20. Odessa, 1909.)

Rabinizki, Israel Haym, and Bialik, Haym Nahmon   ספר האגדה v. 1 and 3, Odessa, 1912; v. 2, Cracow, 1909.

Raisin, Mordecai Zevi   היהודים והיהדות באמריקה (In השלח v. 4-7, edited by Ahad Ha-am. Odessa, 1898-1901.)

Robinson, James Harvey   *The New History.* New York, 1912.

Royce, Josiah   *The Sources of Religious Insight.* New York, 1912.

Ruppin, Arthur   *The Jews of Today.* London, 1913.

Schechter, Solomon   Studies in Judaism. First Series. Especially essay on The Law and Recent Criticism. Philadelphia, 1915.

Slouschz, Nahum   *The Renascence of Hebrew Literature.* Philadelphia, 1909.

Statistics of the Jews of the United States — Compiled by the Board of Delegates of American Israelites and The Union of American Hebrew Congregations. Philadelphia, 1880.

The Two Hundred and Fiftieth Anniversary of the Settlement of the Jews in the United States — New York, 1906.

Thompson, Frank V. — *Schooling of the Immigrant.* New York, 1920.

Thorndike, Edward L. — *The Original Nature of Man.* New York, 1913.

Wallas, Graham — *The Great Society.* New York, 1916.

Webster, Hutton — *Rest Days.* New York, 1916.

Wiernik, Peter — *History of the Jews in America.* New York, 1912.

Woodworth, Robert S. — *Dynamic Psychology.* New York, 1918.

INDEX

Adjustment, meaning of, 76-78; to modernism, 85-88; to America, 89-91.

Affiliation, educational value of, 156ff.

Americanization, 44-46.

Bible, teaching of, 148-150.

Charity, 114-121.

Chosen People, 105.

Community, teaching of local Jewish, 158-159; teaching of larger Jewish, 159.

Congregational schools, developed by Conservatives, 5-6; curriculum of, 169-171.

Criteria, in general education, 69-70; in Jewish education, 71-92; arising from modernism, 85-88; arising from adjustment to American environment, 89-92; conflicts between, 94-95; applicable to all Jewish groups, 96-99; applicable to other groups, 99-100.

Current events, teaching of, 159-160.

Curriculum, nature of, 55-56; steps in making a, 56-57; unchanged in Jewish school, 57-60; need for adjusting, 61-63; and permanent values, 65.

Customs and Ceremonies, 141.

Democracy, aims of, 25ff.; conception of progress in, 25; place of individual in, 26-27; criteria of an educational aim in, 27-28; as a criterion of Jewish values, 89-90.

Dietary laws, observance of, 20; as a Jewish survival value, 134-139; and the criteria of values, 138-139.

Dynamism, 71-75.

Extension education, need for, 66-68; curriculum for, 163-168.

Extra-curricular activities, 171-172.

Functionalism, as a criterion, 90-92.

Group preservation, meaning of, 78-79; means of, 82.

Hebrew, teaching of, 142-145; aims in teaching, 142-144.

History, teaching of, 145-147; failure of present methods in, 147.

Immigration of Jews, Spanish-Portuguese, 1-2; German, 2-3; Eastern European, 3-4.

Individual, the, 28-30; growth of, 32-33.

Industrialism, evils of, 10-11.

Intermarriage, 20-21; reasons for opposition to, 79-81.

Jews in America, historical background, 1ff.; political status, 7-8; economic conditions, 9-11; educational conditions, 11-13; social life, 13ff.; effect on immigrants of changed environment, 12-13, 16-17ff.

Jews, in many lands, teaching of, 160-161.

98225